Simple Elegance

A Culinary Collection of Simple to Elegant Recipes

D1552286

Our Lady of Perpetual Help Women's Guild
Germantown, Tennessee

Copies of **Simple Elegance** may be obtained by sending a check for $16.95 plus $2.50 mailing cost to:

Our Lady of Perpetual Help Women's Guild
8151 Poplar Avenue
Germantown, Tennessee 38138

First Printing 4,000 copies

Library of Congress Catalog Card Number 92-60860

ISBN 0-9633165-0-8

Copyright©1992 by
Our Lady of Perpetual Help Women's Guild

This book contains favorite recipes of members of Our Lady of Perpetual Help Women's Guild and their friends. We do not claim that they are original, only that they are our favorites. We do regret that we were unable to include many recipes which were submitted due to similarity or lack of space.

Printed in the USA by
WIMMER BROTHERS
A Wimmer Company
Memphis • Dallas

Introduction

Simple Elegance represents new, exciting, and treasured recipes from our parish community. In today's complex world, sharing a meal with family is a simple delight and the essence of life. Sharing a meal with good friends becomes a time-treasured event that will long be remembered and savored.

It is with joy that we bring you a culinary collection of simple to elegant recipes...new and exciting recipes to represent the '90's. With the emphasis toward lighter eating, we have created a Light and Luscious category that is brimming with flavor. For those times when you want to entertain with just a touch of indulgence, we have an array of tantalizing and delectable recipes. Whether it be one of our fast and easy beat-the-clock recipes to impress your family or when entertaining becomes a question of what to serve, any one of our many fine kitchen tested recipes will bring **Simple Elegance** to your every meal.

Purpose Of The Women's Guild

Our Lady of Perpetual Help Women's Guild is a non-profit organization founded in 1951 which endeavors to unite all women of the parish in religious, educational, community, and social activities. The purpose of the Guild is the care and maintenance of the altar area, to assist the Pastor financially with altar expenses, and to cooperate with the Parish Council in meeting the needs of our ever growing parish.

It is with heartfelt appreciation that we acknowledge everyone involved with this cookbook. Our sincere thanks to our diligent and dedicated committee, our recipe testers, and recipe donors who have made **Simple Elegance** a reality. Your generous contribution of time and talent is immeasurable.

A special thank you to Father Michael L. Stewart, Father Milton J. Guthrie, and the parish office staff for their loyal and ongoing support of this project.

The proceeds realized from the sale of this book will fund ongoing projects in our parish and various community charities. .

Cookbook Patrons

Mr. & Mrs. Walter F. Chandler

Kent & Sherry Clothier

Mr. & Mrs. Ken Dick

Sue Chris & Dickie Gauthreaux

Germantown Knights of Columbus

Dick & Marilyn Guilliams

Joan & Bill Leathers

Jim & Rita C. Leonard

John & Gretchen Mattingly

Roxanne & Hayden Morris

Our Lady of Perpetual Help Moms & Tots Group

Our Lady of Perpetual Help Merry Makers

The Terminex International Company

Mr. & Mrs. Ron Wade

Mary Anne Wehrum

Les & Nancy R. Willingham

We sincerely thank these individuals for their generous contributions.

About Our Artist

Pamela M. Richert currently resides in Germantown, Tennessee and is a member of the Tennessee Watercolor Society. She has attained star artist membership in the Memphis/Germantown Art League. An award winning artist, her works are displayed in private collections, galleries, and art exhibitions in California, Wisconsin, Texas, Tennessee, Arkansas, and Mississippi.

A special thank you to Pamela for her exquisite artwork on our cover and category pages.

Chairman:	**Co-Chairman:**
Rita C. Leonard	Nancy R. Willingham

Editor: Rita C. Leonard

Section Editors:

Appetizers & Beverages:	**Soups:**
Gretchen Mattingly	Nancy R. Willingham
Breads:	**Brunch:**
Mary Fehse	S. Kay Clifton
Pasta:	**Entrées:**
Agnes Zodda	Diane O'Shea
	Rochelle Mistretta
Vegetables:	
Helen Bertelsen	**Light & Luscious:**
	Nancy Barnwell
Salads:	
Aline Tatro	**Desserts:**
	Jane Reynolds
Celebrity Favorites:	
Sue Chris Gauthreaux	

Committees:

Artist:	**Proofreading:**
Pamela M. Richert	Chairman, Nancy R. Willingham
	Helen Bertelsen
Typists:	Theresa Ellison
Rita C. Leonard	Mary Fehse
Nancy Barnwell	Sue Chris Gauthreaux
Gretchen Mattingly	Rita C. Leonard
	Diane O'Shea
Marketing:	Lisa Parker
Nancy R. Willingham	Jane Reynolds
Diana Wade	Aline Tatro
Fran Costa	Patti Trethaway
	Agnes Zodda
Publicity:	
Janet Hinrichs	**Finance:**
	Roxanne Morris
Wine Consultant:	Sue Chris Gauthreaux
Mac Edwards	

Table Of Contents

CASUAL TO ELEGANT MENUS 9

APPETIZERS AND BEVERAGES 37

SOUPS 73

SALADS AND DRESSINGS 87

BREADS AND MUFFINS 109

ENTRÉES

    Meats 128

    Poultry 143

    Seafood 165

    Pasta 171

    Brunch 186

VEGETABLES 203

LIGHT AND LUSCIOUS 229

CELEBRITY FAVORITES 249

DESSERTS

    Cakes 270

    Pies 281

    Cookies 286

    Desserts 291

    Candies 302

INDEX 309

Testers

Sharon Amos
Gloria Arnold
Fran Batt
Barbara Becker
Helen Bertelsen
Nancy Barnwell
Mildred Blacksmith
Loretta Bronson
S. Kay Clifton
Sherry Clothier
Joe Costa
Terry Curp
Pauline Cychowski
Sarah W. D'Addabbo
Nancy Dick
Anne Dorn
Karen DouBrava
Nancy Ehrman
Theresa Ellison
Mary Fehse
Joan Foote
Eileen Fusakio
Liz Gano
Sue Chris Gauthreaux
Rhonda Green
Marilyn Guilliams
Lynn Grunthaner
Mary Beth Harja
Janet Hinrichs
Joyce Hirschman
Temple Hughes
Nancy Jackson
Rosalie Johnson

Judith W. Jones
Virginia Kilgore
Margaret Kluthe
Rita C. Leonard
Pat Marr
Gretchen Mattingly
Rochelle Mistretta
Florence Moisan
Roxanne Morris
Pat O'Brien
Cyndy Ortwein
Diane O'Shea
Carol Panasuk
Lisa Parker
Beverly Pica
Rae P. Podgorski
Nancy Quinn
Jane Reynolds
Nancy Rich
Virginia Schoenster
Phyllis Schwarzmann
Johnnie B. Smith
Lucille Stock
Beth Sturman
Aline Tatro
Patti Trethaway
Diana Wade
Sharon Waits
Dorothy B. Watkins
Helen Westerman
Nancy R. Willingham
Rhonda Yakopec
Agnes Zodda

Casual to Elegant
Menus

LOUISIANA BAYOU GATHERING

By Sue Chris and Dickie Gauthreaux

Capture the taste of Louisiana bayou country with this casual, colorful, and easy menu. Gather family and friends to share these traditional robust and rich tasting dishes...don't forget the chicory laced coffee. Just roll up your sleeves and enjoy. This is a bayou-style dinner with lots of spicy satisfaction.

Serves 6

Blue-Crab Stuffed Mushrooms

Olive Salad

Peppered Shrimp

Sweet Potato-Pecan Pie

Wine Suggestion:

Dry Chenin Blanc or one of the new California cuvées (blends).
Fruitiness to quench your thirst and crisp acidity
to cleanse the palate between bites.

Blue-Crab Stuffed Mushrooms

40	medium *or* large mushrooms	¼	cup minced fresh parsley
1	pound backfin lump blue-crabmeat *or* other crabmeat	1	teaspoon salt
		1	teaspoon cayenne pepper
		1½	cups shredded Monterey Jack cheese
¾	cup dry bread crumbs	1	cup unsalted butter *or*
6	thinly sliced green onions		margarine

Preheat oven to 350°. Remove stems from mushrooms and discard. Place mushroom caps in a colander; quickly rinse under running water. Drain mushroom caps upside down on paper towels. Gently pat dry with paper towels; set aside. Pick over crabmeat; remove and discard any small pieces of shell or cartilage. Place crabmeat in a large bowl; add bread crumbs, green onions, parsley, salt, cayenne pepper and cheese. In a saucepan, melt ¾ cup butter, pour butter over crabmeat mixture. Toss gently to combine. Melt remaining ¼ cup butter in a shallow baking pan large enough to hold mushrooms in a single layer. Tilt pan to coat with melted butter. Fill each mushroom cap with stuffing; round off stuffing about ½-inch above cap. Place stuffed mushrooms in pan. Bake until mushrooms are dark and juicy and stuffing is slightly browned, about 10-15 minutes. Serve on platter with toothpicks.

Olive Salad

1	(32-ounce) jar broken green olives (unstuffed)	2	tablespoons chopped capers, drained
6	garlic cloves, minced	1	tablespoon dried leaf oregano
2	(3¼-ounce) jars marinated cocktail onions, drained	1	teaspoon finely ground pepper
4	celery stalks, halved lengthwise and thinly sliced	3	tablespoons red wine vinegar
1	(4-ounce) jar chopped pimientos, drained	⅓	cup olive oil

Drain olives; reserve 3 tablespoons brine. In a medium bowl, combine olives, garlic, onions, celery, pimientos and capers. In a small bowl, whisk reserved olive brine, oregano, pepper and vinegar until combined. Add olive oil in a slow, steady stream, whisking constantly. Pour dressing over salad; toss. Spoon into a jar with a tight fitting lid. Refrigerate until served or up to 3 weeks. Serve at room temperature.

Peppered Shrimp

3	cups unsalted margarine	1	teaspoon grated nutmeg
1	(8-ounce) bottle clam juice	1	tablespoon Hungarian paprika
5	garlic cloves, minced		
4	bay leaves	½	cup very finely ground black pepper
4	teaspoons dried rosemary		
1	teaspoon dried basil	¼	cup fresh lemon juice
1	teaspoon dried oregano	6	pounds shrimp, unpeeled and uncooked
1	teaspoon salt several dashes Tabasco® sauce		French bread

In a heavy 10-quart Dutch oven, melt margarine over medium heat. Add all remaining ingredients except shrimp. Cook uncovered, stirring occasionally, until margarine is a rich hazelnut brown, about 20 minutes. Add shrimp to sauce; stir gently to coat well. Cook over medium heat just until all shrimp are coral pink, 10-12 minutes. Ladle shrimp into soup plates; spoon a liberal amount of buttery sauce over each portion. *Note:* Remove bay leaves before serving. Serve with plenty of French bread for the sauce and lots of napkins!!

Sweet Potato-Pecan Pie

1	(9-inch) deep dish pie shell, baked	½	teaspoon ginger
2	tablespoons unsalted margarine, melted	½	teaspoon cinnamon
		½	teaspoon nutmeg
		1	teaspoon vanilla
1	cup cooked and mashed sweet potato (1 large sweet potato)	½	teaspoon salt
		½	cup dark corn syrup
		1	cup evaporated milk
2	eggs, slightly beaten	1½	cups coarsely chopped pecans
¾	cup firmly packed light brown sugar		

Preheat oven to 375°. In large bowl, stir butter into sweet potatoes. Add remaining ingredients except pecans. Blend well. Pour filling into cooled crust. Sprinkle pecans evenly over top. Bake until filling is set and a knife inserted into center comes out clean, 40-45 minutes. Cool in pan on wire rack to room temperature before slicing.

Topping:

2	cups whipping cream	¼	cup praline liqueur *or* Frangelico
3	tablespoons powdered sugar		pecan halves

Combine first 3 ingredients in large bowl. Beat with mixer until large soft peaks form. Cover and refrigerate until ready to serve. Just before serving, spoon whipped cream on pie and top with pecan halves.

SOUTHWEST FIESTA

By Nancy Barnwell

You won't even have to hear a mariachis band to put you in the mood. Get the margaritas ready and sample an array of classic Mexican dishes. With this authentic and easy menu, you may even have time for an afternoon siesta. Casual entertaining served buffet style. Olé!

Serves 6

Chicken Fajitas

Refried Beans

Mexican Rice

Guacamole

Salsa Fresca

Churros

Wine Suggestion:

For fun, try Spanish wines. The reds are hardy and spicy; the whites crisp, clean, and well balanced, just like the food.

Chicken Fajitas

3	fresh long green chilies *or* 1 (4-ounce) can green chilies, cut in strips	1	red bell pepper, thinly sliced
¼	teaspoon ground cumin	1	tablespoon fresh lime juice
¼	teaspoon paprika	½	teaspoon salt
½	teaspoon chili powder	1	garlic clove, minced
2	tablespoons vegetable oil	1	tablespoon minced fresh cilantro
1	onion, sliced	2	pounds chicken breasts, boned, skinned and cut in strips
1	yellow bell pepper, thinly sliced		steamed tortillas

Condiments:

shredded Cheddar cheese   salsa fresca
shredded lettuce   guacamole
sour cream

If you are using fresh green chilies, they must be roasted before being added to the recipe. Place chilies on a broiling pan and broil about 2 inches from heat until skins are blackened, turning frequently. This will take approximately 15 minutes. Transfer to a plastic bag. Seal tightly and let cool before handling. Wash, peel, seed and slice. Combine cumin, paprika and chili powder in a small bowl. Set aside. In a 12-inch skillet, heat oil over low heat. Add onions, bell peppers, chilies, lime juice and salt to pan. Sauté for about 10 minutes or until vegetables are tender. Add garlic and cilantro to skillet and continue cooking for 2 minutes. Increase to high heat. Add chicken and spice mixture to pan and sauté until chicken is slightly browned. Season to taste. Serve on steamed tortilla. Add assorted condiments.

Refried Beans

1	pound dried pinto	1	teaspoon pepper
	or pink beans	½	cup grated Cheddar
1	onion, diced		cheese *or* Monterey
1	garlic clove, minced		Jack
1	teaspoon salt		

Soak beans in 5 cups cold water overnight in a large saucepan. The next day add the onion, garlic, salt and pepper to the beans and water. Bring to a boil. Reduce heat to low and simmer until beans are tender, about 3 hours. Mash beans with a potato masher. Continue cooking, stirring occasionally, until beans are thickened. Taste and add more salt and pepper if needed. Spread beans in a shallow baking dish and sprinkle cheese on top. Bake at 350° for 15 minutes. *Note:* Prior to final baking of beans, the dish can be refrigerated covered for 1-2 days.

Mexican Rice

3	tablespoons oil	3	cups beef consommé
	(preferably olive)	1	cup boiling water
1	large onion, chopped	1½	teaspoons cumin
2	garlic cloves, minced	⅛	teaspoon cayenne pepper
2	cups long grain rice		salt to taste
1½	cups peeled and finely chopped tomatoes		

Heat oil in a large skillet and cook onion until tender, but not browned, 3-5 minutes. Add garlic and rice; cook another 3-5 minutes, stirring often, until rice is opaque. Add tomatoes, consommé, water, cumin, cayenne and salt. Bring mixture to a boil over high heat. Cover and simmer over very low heat until the liquid is absorbed and rice is tender, approximately 20 minutes.

Guacamole

2	medium avocados, peeled and pitted (reserve one pit)	⅓	cup thinly sliced green onions
2	tablespoons fresh lime juice	⅛	teaspoon ground cumin
1	garlic clove, minced	1	medium tomato, peeled and chopped
			salt and pepper to taste

In a small mixing bowl, using a fork, mash avocados with lime juice and garlic until smooth and creamy. Add remaining ingredients and combine well. Place the reserved pit in the center of guacamole and cover to prevent darkening. Remove pit before serving. This is best if served within 2 hours.

Salsa Fresca

4	to 6 ripe tomatoes, chopped	2	fresh jalapeño peppers, seeded and chopped
1	garlic clove, minced		
5	green onions, chopped	1	teaspoon fresh lime juice
2	tablespoons minced fresh cilantro		salt

Combine all ingredients in a small bowl. Season to taste with salt. Allow to stand 1 hour and serve at room temperature.

Churros

1¼	cups water	1	cup all-purpose flour
2	tablespoons unsalted butter	2	eggs
			oil
1	tablespoon sugar		powdered sugar
¼	teaspoon salt		

In a saucepan, combine water, butter, sugar and salt. Bring to a boil. Remove from heat and add flour, all at once. Beat with a wooden spoon until mixture pulls away from the sides of the pan and is smooth. Stir in eggs, one at a time, beating well after each addition. Pour oil into a large skillet to a depth of 2-inches; heat to about 400°. Spoon batter into a pastry tube or cookie press. Pipe batter into the hot oil in 3-inch strips. Fry until golden brown, turning once, about 3-4 minutes. Drain on paper towels. Sprinkle with powdered sugar. Serve warm.

CAJUN COUNTRY CUISINE

By S. Kay and Otto Clifton, Jr.

The appeal of this menu reflects down home country cuisine. From zesty seasonings in the gumbo to the traditional specialties of grillades and sweet potatoes, you will sample old fashioned goodness in every bite.

Serves 6

Seafood Gumbo

Grillades (Gree Yods)

Sweet Potato Croquettes

Pop Rouge (Strawberry Ice Cream)

Wine Suggestion:

A fruity (not sweet) Riesling or Gewürztraminer will complement these dishes. Spicy foods and fruity wines blend well on the palate.

Seafood Gumbo

1	cup oil	½	cup chopped fresh parsley
1	cup all-purpose flour	2	pounds shrimp
2	large onions, chopped	1	pound crabmeat
1	cup chopped celery	1	pint raw oysters
1	bunch green onions, chopped	¼	teaspoon cayenne pepper
			salt and pepper to taste
1	gallon water		cooked rice

In a large gumbo pot, mix oil and flour to make a roux. See **Roux** recipe for instructions. Add onions and celery, sauté until tender. Stir in green onions. Add water, cover and boil gently over low heat for 1 hour. Add parsley and shrimp, cook for 20 minutes on low heat. Add crabmeat and oysters. Add cayenne pepper, salt and pepper to taste. Serve over rice. *Note:* If okra gumbo is desired, cook down cut-up okra (about ½ to 1 cup) until okra is not slimy. Add to gumbo during boiling period. The secret to making the roux is browning the flour but not burning it and stirring constantly.

Grillades (Gree yods)

2	pounds beef *or* pork	1	garlic clove, finely
	salt and pepper		chopped
2	tablespoons all-purpose	½	tablespoon chopped fresh
	flour		parsley
2	tablespoons cooking oil	¾	cup water
1	medium onion, chopped		salt and cayenne pepper
1	medium green bell pepper,		to taste
	chopped		hot grits *or* rice

Cut meat into 1-inch strips. Season strips with salt and pepper; dust with flour. In an iron skillet, brown strips in heated oil and remove. Make a brown roux (see **Roux** recipe for instructions). Add remaining ingredients. On medium heat, cook for 15 minutes, stirring constantly until mixture gets thick. Add meat strips, cover and simmer until meat is tender, about 1 hour. Serve over hot grits or rice.

Sweet Potato Croquettes

5	medium sweet potatoes	6	to 8 large marshmallows
2	tablespoons sugar	2	egg whites, slightly beaten
2	tablespoons butter	2	cups crushed corn flakes
1	teaspoon lemon juice		

Cook sweet potatoes in jackets. Peel and mash. Season with sugar, butter and lemon juice. Mix well. Shape potato mixture around marshmallows. Place in refrigerator to chill for 1 hour. Dip croquettes in egg white, roll in corn flake crumbs and deep fry in hot oil, heated to 375°, until brown. Drain on absorbent paper.

Pop Rouge (Strawberry Ice Cream)

3	(10-ounce) bottles	2	(14-ounce) cans sweetened
	strawberry pop		condensed milk
2	(12-ounce) cans evaporated		
	milk		

Pour into a gallon freezer bucket by alternating first with 1 bottle pop, 1 can evaporated milk and 1 can condensed milk. Repeat in order given, ending with the third bottle of pop. Freeze in hand or electric freezer. Allow to stand for ½ hour before serving. You can substitute orange pop for the strawberry.

WOMEN'S GUILD ENTERTAINS

By Jane Reynolds

Every year, Our Lady of Perpetual Help Women's Guild hosts a social event for the ladies of the parish and their friends, a Card Party/Luncheon/Fashion Show. Early reservations are a must at this annual tradition where fellowship abounds, excellent food is the norm, and the latest fashions are modeled. We feature one of the many fine menus served at these luncheons.

Serves 8

Secret Caesar Salad

Italian Stuffed Shells

Spinach Soufflé

Mocha Nut Torte

Wine Suggestion:

A Merlot or red Zinfandel served at cellar temperature, 60-65°.

Secret Caesar Salad

Dressing:

6	tablespoons olive oil	2	garlic cloves, crushed
2	tablespoons red wine vinegar	¼	teaspoon pepper
1	tablespoon lemon juice	½	cup freshly grated Parmesan cheese
1	teaspoon Worcestershire sauce	1	teaspoon capers, mashed
		1	teaspoon Dijon mustard

Salad:

1	large head romaine lettuce	8	slices bacon, cooked crisp and crumbled
1	cup croutons		
½	cup Parmesan cheese		

Combine all dressing ingredients in a bowl and set aside. Tear lettuce into bite-size pieces in salad bowl. Add croutons, cheese and bacon. Toss with dressing and serve.

19

Italian Stuffed Shells

1	(12-ounce) package jumbo shells	¾	cup chopped onion
1	pound ground beef	¾	teaspoon oregano
½	pound ground pork	½	teaspoon salt
½	pound Italian sausage (remove casing and crumble)	⅛	teaspoon pepper
		4½	cups spaghetti sauce (commercial or your own)
4	eggs, slightly beaten		grated Parmesan cheese
1	cup Italian bread crumbs		grated Romano cheese
1	cup mozzarella cheese		

Preheat oven to 350°. Cook shells according to package directions and drain. In a large skillet, brown beef, pork and sausage. Drain well. In a large bowl, combine cooked meats, sausage, eggs, bread crumbs, cheese, onion, oregano, salt and pepper. Blend well. Fill each shell with meat filling. Spread thin layer of sauce on bottom of a 9x13 inch baking pan. Place stuffed shells open side down in a single layer and cover with remaining sauce. Sprinkle with Parmesan, then Romano cheese. Cover with aluminum foil. Bake for 45 minutes or until bubbly.

Spinach Soufflé

2	(10-ounce) packages frozen chopped spinach	½	teaspoon garlic salt
		2	cups fresh white bread crumbs
1	cup sour cream	3	tablespoons margarine, melted
⅓	cup grated Parmesan cheese		

Preheat oven to 350°. Cook spinach according to package directions. Drain well. Mix spinach, sour cream, cheese and garlic salt. Pour into buttered baking dish and top with bread crumbs. Drizzle margarine over top. Bake for 20 minutes or until lightly browned.

Mocha Nut Torte

½	cup all-purpose flour	3	egg yolks
2	teaspoons baking powder	1	cup strong cold coffee
2	cups crushed graham crackers	1	teaspoon vanilla
		¾	cup chopped nuts
½	cup shortening	3	egg whites, stiffly beaten
1	cup sugar		

Preheat oven to 375°. Line bottom of 2 (8-inch) round pans with waxed paper. Stir together flour, baking powder and cracker crumbs. In a mixing bowl, cream shortening and sugar. Add egg yolks and beat. Add flour mixture, alternately with coffee, beating until smooth. Stir in vanilla and nuts. Fold in beaten egg whites. Divide batter in 2 pans. Bake for 30-35 minutes. Cool in pan. When cool, remove cake from pan and split each layer crossways, (4 layers). Fill each layer and frost with **Filling**.

Filling:

1	(5¼-ounce) package instant vanilla pudding	1	(8-ounce) container frozen whipped topping, thawed
1¾	cups milk		chocolate curls
1¼	teaspoons instant coffee		

Prepare pudding with milk, add coffee, chill until pudding is thickened. Fold in whipped topping mix. Spread filling between each layer and over top. Sprinkle with chocolate curls.

AN ENCHANTED SUMMER EVENING

By Lois Poper

Summer is here and the living is easy. Perfect for dining alfresco on your patio. Set an intimate table with casual but elegant dinnerware and with this menu, you'll have the right elements for an enchanted evening. The preparation for this dinner can all be done ahead. Just grill the hens and cook the pasta before serving. So, pour yourself a cool drink, fire up the grill, relax, and enjoy.

Serves 6

Sensational Spinach Dip

Spaghetti Vinaigrette

Cornish Hens Mont Ventoux

Grilled Vegetables

Peaches And Cream Pie

Wine Suggestion:

Fumé Blanc (dry Sauvignon Blanc). Nice to sip and enjoy while the food is cooking and perfect with this dinner.

Sensational Spinach Dip

2	(10-ounce) packages frozen chopped spinach, thawed	¼	teaspoon ground nutmeg
		12	slices bacon, cooked crisp and crumbled
2	(8-ounce) packages cream cheese, cubed	2	tablespoons lemon juice
			large tortilla chips for dipping
6	tablespoons milk		
4	tablespoons butter		

Cook spinach and drain well. In a saucepan over low heat, cook and stir together cheese, milk, butter and nutmeg until cheese melts. Add spinach and half the crumbled bacon. Turn into a serving dish and top with remaining bacon. Serve with tortilla chips. *Note:* Can be made ahead and heated at 350° for about 30 minutes or warm in microwave.

Spaghetti Vinaigrette

1	cup olive oil	12	ripe plum tomatoes, chopped
1	cup red wine vinegar		
1	tablespoon minced garlic cloves	1½	cups diced red onions
		1	bunch fresh basil, chopped
1½	teaspoons salt		green onions, chopped
1	(16-ounce) package thin spaghetti		

Combine the first 4 dressing ingredients in a lidded container and shake well to blend. Cook spaghetti al dente and drain. Mix half the dressing with pasta and blend in tomatoes, red onions and basil. Add remaining dressing as needed and garnish with green onions. Serve warm.

Cornish Hens Mont Ventoux

4	(1-pound) Cornish hens, halved, washed and dried	4	tablespoons minced fresh herb (choose basil, oregano, thyme or mint)
⅓	cup kosher salt		
10	garlic cloves	¼	cup olive oil
		1½	cups feta cheese

Place hens in a non-aluminum pan. Combine kosher salt with garlic cloves in blender. Add water up to the quart measurement and blend until puréed. Pour mixture over hens and marinate 8-24 hours. Drain. Rub hens with oil and grill skin side down, turning occasionally, until juices run clear. Sprinkle hens and **Grilled Vegetables** with herb of your choice and feta cheese. Place under broiler and broil just until cheese melts. Arrange on serving platter and serve.

Grilled Vegetables

3	small zucchini, halved lengthwise	3	small Japanese eggplants, halved
3	red bell peppers, quartered	¼	cup olive oil
3	leeks, halved (white part only)	4	tablespoons minced fresh herb (choose basil, oregano, thyme *or* mint)

Marinate all vegetables in oil and your choice of herb for 1 hour. Grill about 6 minutes per side or until tender. Set aside and refer to **Cornish Hens Mont Ventoux** for further directions. *Note:* Can be grilled ahead and reheated with Cornish hens just before serving.

Peaches And Cream Pie

1¼	cups crushed vanilla wafers	1	tablespoon lemon juice
⅓	cup butter, melted	1	cup whipping cream
3	cups miniature marshmallows	2	to 3 cups sliced and peeled fresh peaches
2	tablespoons orange juice		

Combine vanilla wafers and butter together and press into a 9-inch pie pan. Do not bake. In a non-stick skillet over low heat, combine marshmallows, orange juice and lemon juice; stir until marshmallows melt. Cool. Whip cream and fold in sliced peaches. Fold whipped cream mixture into the cooled marshmallow mixture. Pour into pie pan and chill several hours or overnight.

AUTUMN HARVEST CELEBRATION

By Roxanne Morris

The leaves are changing and aglow with color, vegetables are plentiful, there's a chill in the air, and the evenings are crisp and cool. Before Jack Frost nibbles at your squash, celebrate the occasion with this menu offering a variety of Fall flavors and textures.

Serves 4

Pumpkin Soup In A Pumpkin

Pork Tenderloin With Mustard Sauce

Braised Red Cabbage With Cranberries

Green Beans With Almonds

Purchased Cracked Wheat Rolls With Herb Butter

Autumn Harvest Cheesecake

Wine Suggestion:

*Sample one of California's newest wines,
Pinot Gris, one of the "Rhone Rangers".*

Pumpkin Soup

¼	cup butter *or* margarine	3	cups chicken broth (can use canned chicken broth)
1	cup chopped onion		
1	garlic clove, crushed		
1	teaspoon curry powder	1¾	cups cooked pumpkin *or* 2 (16-ounce) cans pumpkin
½	teaspoon salt		
⅛	to ¼ teaspoon ground coriander	1	cup half-and-half
⅛	teaspoon crushed red pepper		sour cream
			fresh chives

In large saucepan, melt butter and sauté onion and garlic until soft. Add curry powder, salt, coriander and red pepper; cook 1 minute. Add broth; boil gently, uncovered, for 15-20 minutes. Stir in pumpkin and half-and-half; cook 5 minutes but do not boil. Pour into blender and blend until creamy. Serve warm. This can be made a day ahead and reheated. Garnish with a dollop of sour cream and chopped chives. *Note:* For a beautiful presentation, serve this soup in a pumpkin or in small individual pumpkins. After cleaning the pumpkin, warm it in a 350° oven for 20 minutes.

Pork Tenderloin With Mustard Sauce

1	(1-pound) pork tenderloin	3	green onions, sliced
1/3	cup all-purpose flour		(white and green
1/2	teaspoon salt		parts separated)
1/4	teaspoon pepper	1/3	cup dry white wine
3	tablespoons butter *or*	1	cup whipping cream
	margarine	1/4	cup Dijon mustard
			brown *or* white cooked
			rice

Cut tenderloin crosswise into 1/2-inch thick pieces. Using a meat mallet, pound tenderloin between sheets of waxed paper to 1/4-inch thickness. Combine flour, salt and pepper in a shallow bowl. Melt butter in a large heavy skillet over medium heat. Dredge pork slices in flour mixture and shake off excess. Add pork to skillet and cook about 2 minutes per side or until nicely browned. Remove and keep warm. Add more butter as needed if cooking pork in batches is necessary. Add white parts of chopped green onions to skillet. Sauté until just tender, about 1 minute. Stir in white wine and boil until liquid is reduced to about 2 tablespoons, about 3 minutes. Add whipping cream and simmer until thick, about 5 minutes. Whisk in Dijon mustard. Place pork slices over bed of prepared rice, top with mustard sauce and garnish with chopped green onions.

Braised Red Cabbage With Cranberries

1	tablespoon olive oil	2	pounds red cabbage,
7	tablespoons brown sugar		cored and shredded
4	tablespoons minced garlic		(10 cups)
	(about 10 cloves)	1/8	to 1/4 teaspoon cayenne
3	cups fresh *or* frozen		pepper
	cranberries		salt
1/2	cup red wine vinegar		

In a large non-aluminum pot, heat oil and 3 tablespoons brown sugar over medium heat. Add garlic and sauté for 2 minutes. Add 2 cups cranberries and vinegar. Cover and cook until berries burst, about 4-6 minutes. Add red wine vinegar and cabbage. Cover and cook, stirring occasionally until the cabbage is tender, about 15 minutes. Add remaining 4 tablespoons of brown sugar and cayenne pepper and mix well. Stir in the remaining 1 cup cranberries. Remove from heat. Cover and let sit 5 minutes. Season with salt to taste. *Note:* This can be served hot or cold and can be made 1 day ahead and warmed 10-12 minutes. Goes well with pork and veal.

Green Beans With Almonds

1	pound fresh green beans	3	tablespoons butter *or*
3	tablespoons slivered		margarine
	almonds	1½	teaspoons fresh lemon
			juice

Snap and clean green beans, rinse and steam for 10-12 minutes. In a small skillet, lightly toast almonds, turning until a light golden brown. Place steamed green beans in serving dish. Melt butter and mix with lemon juice. Pour over green beans then sprinkle with almonds.

Herb Butter

2	cups butter *or* margarine, softened	2	tablespoons chopped fresh chervil *or*
4	tablespoons chopped fresh parsley		tarragon

Combine all ingredients together and serve in a hollowed out cabbage or winter squash. Will keep in the refrigerator 2 days or may be frozen 2 months.

Autumn Harvest Cheesecake

Crust:

1	cup graham cracker crumbs	3	tablespoons sugar
½	cup finely chopped pecans	¼	cup margarine, melted
		½	teaspoon cinnamon

Preheat oven to 350°. Combine all ingredients together and press into a greased 9-inch springform pan. Bake for 10 minutes.

Filling:

2	(8-ounce) packages cream cheese, softened	4	cups peeled and thinly sliced Granny Smith apples (other cooking apples can be used)
½	cup sugar		
2	eggs		
½	teaspoon vanilla	⅓	cup sugar
		½	teaspoon cinnamon
		¼	cup chopped pecans

Combine cream cheese and sugar. Beat at medium speed until blended. Add eggs, one at a time, mixing well after each addition. Blend in vanilla and pour over crust. Toss apples with combined sugar and cinnamon. Spoon this apple mixture over the cream cheese filling. Sprinkle top with pecans. Bake at 350° for 1 hour and 10 minutes. After cheesecake is removed from oven, loosen sides of the springform pan and allow to cool completely.

SPECIAL EVENING WITH FRIENDS

By Rita C. Leonard

Whenever the mood strikes you for tantalizing food and good conversation, invite your friends to a special evening. Start your party with panache by serving a tempting appetizer of delicate pesto and cheese pastries. For dessert, who can resist a luscious creation of chocolate, laced with amaretto liqueur and served with a dazzling raspberry sauce. With good friends, good food, and good atmosphere, success is yours for a special evening.

Serves 8

Pesto And Cheese In Phyllo

Tossed Salad With Apples And Cheese

Chicken Marsala

Mushroom Wild Rice

Crumb-Topped Broccoli

Carrots With Tarragon

Raspberry Chocolate Truffle Pie

Wine Suggestion:

Choose one of the lighter Italian reds, Montepulciano d'Abruzzo, Valpolicella or Bardolino.

Pesto And Cheese In Phyllo

12	sheets frozen phyllo dough, thawed	6	(7x3½-inch) Swiss cheese slices
½	cup unsalted butter, melted	6	tablespoons grated Parmesan
¾	cup purchased pesto		fresh basil sprigs (optional)

Preheat oven to 375°. Place 1 phyllo sheet on work surface, keep remaining phyllo covered with damp towel. Brush phyllo lightly with butter. Top with second phyllo sheet. Brush lightly with butter. Spread 2 tablespoons pesto in 4x8-inch rectangle along short side of phyllo sheet, 1-inch from edge. Place cheese slice on top of pesto. Sprinkle with 1 tablespoon Parmesan. Fold in long sides, then beginning at cheese end, roll up phyllo jelly roll style. Place seam side down on cookie sheet. Lightly brush top with butter. Repeat with remaining phyllo and ingredients. Bake for 25 minutes or until golden brown. Slice rolls into 1-inch lengths. Arrange decoratively on platter. Garnish rolls with fresh basil sprigs if desired and serve immediately. *Note:* To cut down on calories, coat second phyllo sheet with butter-flavored cooking spray.

Tossed Salad With Apples And Cheese

Red Wine Vinegar Dressing:

¼	cup red wine vinegar	½	teaspoon salt
⅓	cup salad oil	¼	teaspoon oregano
1	teaspoon Worcestershire sauce	1	tablespoon sugar dash of pepper
1	garlic clove, crushed		

Combine all ingredients in a lidded container and shake well to mix. Refrigerate until ready to use. Add dressing to taste.

Salad:

2	golden delicious apples, chopped	½	cup crumbled blue cheese (optional)
2	tablespoons lemon juice	6	slices bacon, cooked crisp and crumbled
4	cups torn fresh spinach		
4	cups torn red leaf lettuce	½	cup fresh sliced mushrooms
½	cup coarsely chopped cashews		

In a ziploc bag, toss chopped apples with lemon juice and refrigerate until ready to serve. Prepare spinach and lettuce. When ready to serve, lightly toss together all salad ingredients. Add dressing to taste. *Suggestion:* Pass blue cheese on the side to allow guest to add this to their taste. Increase salad ingredients slightly in order to serve 8. Double dressing recipe but add gradually to salad. Do not oversaturate salad with dressing.

Chicken Marsala

12	chicken breast halves, boned and skinned	1	cup Marsala wine
½	cup all-purpose flour	1	cup chicken broth
½	teaspoon salt	1	teaspoon garlic powder
¼	teaspoon pepper	1	teaspoon lemon juice
2	tablespoons olive oil	1	cup chopped green onions
1	tablespoon butter	3	tablespoons chopped fresh parsley
12	ounces fresh mushrooms, sliced		

Preheat oven to 350°. Cut each breast in 2 to 3 pieces. Combine flour, salt and pepper; dredge chicken pieces in flour. In a large non-stick skillet, brown chicken in oil until light golden, transfer chicken pieces onto a paper towel as they are done and add more oil to skillet as needed. Repeat until all chicken is browned. Add butter to skillet and sauté sliced mushrooms until juices start to flow. Add remaining ingredients and simmer 2-3 minutes. Place chicken in a 9x9-inch baking dish, pour sauce over chicken and bake for 25-30 minutes. Can be prepared ahead of time, refrigerate and bake just prior to serving.

Mushroom Wild Rice

2	(6¼-ounce) boxes long grain and wild rice (original fast cooking recipe)	8	ounces fresh mushrooms, sliced
2	tablespoons butter or margarine	1	(8-ounce) can water chestnuts, chopped
1	large onion, chopped	½	pound mild or hot bulk sausage (optional)

Cook rice according to package directions. In a large pan, melt butter and sauté onions and mushrooms until tender. Mix cooked rice with onion and mushroom mixture. Stir in chestnuts and turn into a 9x9-inch glass dish. Cook sausage, drain well, place sausage on paper towel to absorb more grease; then add to rice mixture, stirring gently to combine. Serve immediately or refrigerate and reheat in microwave just prior to serving.

Crumb-Topped Broccoli

4	slices white bread	6	tablespoons butter *or* margarine
1	bunch broccoli *or* 2 (10-ounce) packages frozen broccoli spears	½	teaspoon lemon juice
1½	teaspoons chicken flavored instant bouillon	¼	cup grated Parmesan cheese

Preheat oven to 350°. Process bread slices in blender or food processor just until coarse crumbs are formed. Spread crumbs in shallow baking pan. Bake in 350° oven for 15 minutes or until toasted. Meanwhile, prepare and cook broccoli in 2-inches water, add chicken bouillon and cook covered until crisp-tender, about 8-10 minutes. Drain well. Toss with 2 tablespoons of the butter. Place broccoli on serving platter and keep warm. Melt remaining 4 tablespoons butter, stir in lemon juice, Parmesan cheese and toasted bread crumbs. Spoon crumb mixture around broccoli on serving platter and return to oven for 2-3 minutes to recrisp crumbs.

Carrots With Tarragon

12	to 14 carrots, sliced diagonally	1	teaspoon butter *or* margarine
1	teaspoon chicken flavor instant bouillon	½	teaspoon tarragon

In a medium saucepan, combine carrots in about 1-inch water and add bouillon. Cook covered until crisp tender. Drain liquid; add butter and tarragon. Cover. When butter has melted, stir carrots gently to distribute seasoning.

Raspberry Chocolate Truffle Pie

10-12 servings

Sauce:

2	(10-ounce) packages frozen raspberries in lite syrup, thawed	¾	cup sugar
		¼	teaspoon cream of tartar

To prepare sauce, process raspberries in blender for 4-5 seconds, then press raspberries through a strainer to make 1 cup purée. Discard seeds. In a small saucepan, combine sugar and cream of tartar; blend well. Stir in purée. Over medium heat, bring mixture to a boil, boil 3 minutes, stirring constantly. Cover and refrigerate.

Filling:

1	(9-inch) pastry shell, baked	4	ounces (4 squares) unsweetened chocolate, melted
½	cup sweetened condensed milk		
⅔	cup whipping cream	2	egg yolks
5	ounces (5 squares) semi-sweet chocolate, melted	2	tablespoons raspberry-flavored liqueur
		2	tablespoons amaretto

In medium heavy saucepan, combine condensed milk and whipping cream, blend well. Over medium heat, bring mixture to a boil. Remove from heat, cool 5 minutes. In food processor bowl with metal blade, combine milk mixture and melted chocolates, process 5-10 seconds. Add egg yolks, process 5 seconds. Add raspberry flavored liqueur and amaretto, process 5 seconds. Pour blended mixture into a large bowl, set over ice. Stir for 5-7 minutes or until mixture is cool. Beat mixture on highest speed of mixer for 2-3 minutes or until soft peaks form. Pour into cooled, baked crust. Refrigerate about 1 hour or until firm. *Note:* Electric mixer can be used for filling. In a large bowl, combine milk mixture and melted chocolate, beat on medium speed for 30 seconds. Add egg yolks, beat 15 seconds, add raspberry- flavored liqueur and amaretto and beat 30 seconds or until smooth. Continue as above.

Topping:

1⅓	cups whipping cream	chocolate curls (optional)
2	tablespoons powdered sugar	whole raspberries (optional)
½	teaspoon vanilla	

In a small bowl, beat whipping cream until soft peaks form. Add powdered sugar and vanilla, beat until stiff peaks form. Spread over cooled filling. Garnish with chocolate curls and whole raspberries. Refrigerate until serving time. Remove from refrigerator 1 hour before serving. Serve with raspberry sauce.

FESTIVE HOLIDAY DINING

By Trudy S. and Bill Eissler

When the occasion calls for crystal, silver, and candlelight, entertain with style and elegance with this splendid dinner. It will delight the palate and excite the eye. A menu that sparkles with holiday spirit and is worthy of any festive occasion.

Serves 8

Baked Brie

Splendid Raspberry Spinach

Tarragon-Rum Shrimp

Saffron Rice

Green Beans In Mustard Marinade

Date-Nut Cake Roll

Wine Suggestion:
A fine California Chardonnay will be the perfect match for this meal.

Baked Brie

1	(4-ounce) wheel of Brie	2	sheets frozen phyllo dough, thawed
2	tablespoons chopped walnuts	2	tablespoons butter, melted
2	tablespoons crumbled blue cheese		

Preheat oven to 425°. Cut Brie in half horizontally. Press 1 tablespoon walnuts into lower half. Sprinkle with blue cheese. Return top half of Brie over blue cheese. Cut both sheets of phyllo in half and brush 1 halved sheet with butter, keeping remaining 3 halves covered with a damp cloth. Place Brie in center of buttered phyllo sheet and wrap. Butter next sheet, place Brie upside down on sheet and wrap again. Repeat with remaining 2 sheets. Press remaining walnuts on top. Bake for 10 minutes until dough is golden brown and Brie has started to melt. *Note:* If using 1 pound of Brie, double ingredients but do not halve phyllo sheets.

Splendid Raspberry Spinach

2	tablespoons raspberry vinegar	¾	cup coarsely chopped macadamia nuts
2	tablespoons raspberry jam	1	cup fresh raspberries
⅓	cup vegetable oil	3	kiwi fruits, peeled and sliced
8	cups spinach, rinsed, stemmed and torn into pieces		

To prepare dressing, combine vinegar and jam in blender or small bowl. Add oil in a thin stream, blending well. Toss spinach, ½ of nuts, ½ of raspberries and ½ of kiwi fruits with the dressing. Top individual salad servings with remaining nuts, raspberries and kiwi fruit. Serve immediately. *Note:* Strawberry vinegar, strawberry jam and fresh strawberries can be substituted and is as equally splendid.

Tarragon-Rum Shrimp

3½	pounds shrimp	1	cup chopped green onions, (tops and bottom)
½	cup butter		
½	teaspoon salt	2	teaspoons dried tarragon
½	teaspoon coarsely ground black pepper	6	tablespoons light rum

Peel and devein shrimp; set aside. In skillet large enough to hold the shrimp, melt 4 tablespoons butter over medium heat. Add shrimp, salt and pepper. Sauté for 2 minutes, tossing gently until shrimp turn bright pink. Remove with a slotted spoon to a plate and set aside. Melt remaining 4 tablespoons butter in skillet, add green onions and tarragon; sauté over medium heat for 3 minutes. Add rum, stirring constantly to deglaze and cook for 30 seconds. Return shrimp and any liquid in plate to skillet and sauté for another minute or until shrimp are thoroughly heated.

Saffron Rice

2	tablespoons butter	2	cups long grain rice (not instant)
1	teaspoon loosely packed saffron	3	cups water
		½	teaspoon salt

Melt butter in a saucepan over medium heat. Add saffron; stir. Add rice and stir well. Add water and salt. Bring to a boil. Cover and cook over low heat for approximately 18 minutes or until rice is tender and all liquid is absorbed.

Green Beans In Mustard Marinade

1	tablespoon dried rosemary	1½	teaspoons red wine vinegar
2	pounds fresh green beans, washed and trimmed	4½	tablespoons extra virgin olive oil
1	teaspoon coarse grain mustard		salt and freshly ground black pepper

Fill 1½-quart saucepan with water. Bring to a boil. Add rosemary and boil for about 2 minutes. Add beans and continue to boil for about 10 minutes or until beans are crisp without being tough. Drain beans and rinse with cold water to stop the cooking process. Drain and set aside. To make the marinade, combine the mustard, vinegar and oil in a small bowl. Whisk together; add salt and pepper to taste. Dry the beans and toss them with the marinade. Refrigerate until ready to serve. May be made a day ahead.

Date-Nut Cake Roll

1	cup pitted whole dates, snipped	½	cup sugar
1	cup water	1	cup all-purpose flour
¼	cup sugar	1	teaspoon baking powder
⅛	teaspoon salt	½	teaspoon salt
3	eggs	½	teaspoon allspice
		¾	cup chopped walnuts

In small saucepan, combine dates, water, sugar and salt. Bring to a boil; cook and stir over low heat until thick, about 4 minutes. Remove from heat and cool to room temperature. In mixer bowl, beat eggs at high speed for 5 minutes. Gradually beat in sugar. Stir together flour, baking powder, salt and allspice. Fold into egg mixture. Spread in greased and floured 10x15-inch jelly roll pan. Top with walnuts. Bake for 12-15 minutes. Turn out onto towel sprinkled with a little powdered sugar. Starting at narrow end, roll up cake and towel together; cool. Unroll and spread with **Cream Cheese Filling.** Reroll and chill.

Cream Cheese Filling:

2	(3-ounce) packages cream cheese, softened	½	teaspoon vanilla
4	tablespoons butter *or* margarine	1	cup sifted powdered sugar

Beat together cream cheese, butter and vanilla. Add powdered sugar and beat well.

Appetizers and Beverages

Kahlua-Pecan Brie

12-16 appetizer servings

¾ cup finely chopped pecans
¼ cup Kahlua
3 tablespoons brown sugar

1 (14 to 16-ounce) whole mini Brie

Spread pecans in a 9-inch pie plate; microwave on high 4-6 minutes, stirring every 2 minutes until toasted. Add Kahlua and brown sugar, stirring well. Remove rind from top of Brie and discard. Place Brie on a microwave-safe serving plate. Spoon pecan-Kahlua mixture evenly over top of Brie. Microwave, uncovered, on high 1-1½ minutes or until Brie softens to desired consistency, giving dish a half-turn after 45 seconds. Serve with melba toast or assorted crackers.

Variation: Mix together chopped pecans, Kahlua and ¾ cup brown sugar. Spoon mixture over Brie and bake in a preheated 350° oven for approximately 20 minutes.

A delicious and unusual appetizer.

Gretchen Mattingly
Rita C. Leonard

Brie En Croute

12-15 servings

3 (3-ounce) packages cream cheese
½ cup butter, cold
1½ cups all-purpose flour
pinch of salt

1 (1-pound) whole baby Brie
1 egg, beaten
1 teaspoon water
apple slices, pear slices
lemon juice

Slice cream cheese and butter in pieces and blend in flour and salt with a pastry blender, mixer or food processor. Chill several hours. Roll out pastry on floured surface to ⅛-inch thickness. Cut a circle large enough to place under and overlap top of baby Brie by about 1-inch. Fold pastry over top rim of Brie and place on lightly greased cookie sheet. Mix egg with water and brush pastry with egg wash. Cut another circle of pastry and cover top of folded area. Brush with egg wash. Chill about 1 hour. About 1 hour before serving time, preheat oven to 425°. Bake for 20 minutes. Cool 30 minutes before moving or cutting baked Brie. Serve with sliced apples and pears which have been dipped in lemon juice. *Note:* For a special decorative touch, cut a design from the remaining pastry dough and place on top of dough. Brush with egg wash. Can be made ahead and frozen. Bake frozen Brie an additional 5-10 minutes.

A wonderfully delicious appetizer. A bottle of wine and a frozen "Brie en Croute" make a wonderful gift.

Gretchen Mattingly

Canapé Pie

about 30 servings

¼ pound Braunschweiger
2 tablespoons mayonnaise
pinch oregano
Worcestershire sauce
to taste
6 ounces cream cheese,
softened *or* chive
cream cheese
½ cup chopped chives
1 to 2 teaspoons milk *or*
cream
chopped pecans (optional)
about 1 pound ham salad
(commercially
prepared or homemade)

4 hard-cooked egg yolks
2 tablespoons butter
2 teaspoons lemon juice
1 teaspoon sugar
salt and pepper to taste
mayonnaise to thin, if
necessary
1 round loaf rye bread,
unsliced
⅓ cup butter, softened
(approximately)
1 (10-ounce) jar stuffed
olives, drained and
sliced

Prepare Braunschweiger filling by combining the first 4 ingredients together, blending until mixture is of spreading consistency; set aside. In a separate bowl, prepare cream cheese filling. Beat softened cream cheese until fluffy, add chives and enough milk or cream to thin to spreading consistency. Set aside. (If using chive cream cheese, do not add chopped chives. Chopped pecans can be added to this filling.) Keep ham salad in a separate bowl. To prepare egg yolk filling, combine egg yolks, butter, lemon juice, sugar, salt and pepper to taste, adding mayonnaise to thin, if necessary. Set aside. Slice bread crosswise into 5 slices, remove all crusts and spread each slice with butter.

To assemble canapé, arrange filling on each slice of bread in the following order. First, spread Braunschweiger filling in a circle at the center of each slice. Next, spread cream cheese filling around Braunschweiger filling, followed by the ham salad for the outer circle. Using a pastry bag, flute egg mixture between each filling and arrange sliced olives on the outer edge of each bread slice. Cut each slice into small wedges and arrange on serving tray by placing a complete slice in the center of tray with sliced wedges around it. *Note:* It is best to chill each prepared canapé approximately 30 minutes before slicing.

A beautiful presentation!

Karen DouBrava

Caviar Pie

26-30 servings

8	hard-cooked eggs, chopped	⅔	cup sour cream
⅓	cup mayonnaise		dash white pepper
	salt to taste		dash hot pepper sauce
4	green onions, finely chopped (drain 20 minutes on paper towels)	1	(4-ounce) jar red caviar
		1	(4-ounce) jar black caviar
		¼	cup chopped fresh parsley
10	ounces cream cheese, softened		crackers

Combine eggs with mayonnaise, add salt to taste and spread mixture evenly in a buttered 9-inch springform pan. Sprinkle top of eggs with onions. Blend cream cheese with sour cream, add dash of pepper and hot sauce. Carefully spread cream cheese mixture over onions. (Place heaping tablespoonsful of mixture and spread together so as not to mess up other layers.) Cover and chill well, preferably overnight. Just before serving, remove springform rim. Section pie into eights using 1-inch deep pieces of cardboard pressed just slightly into top of pie. Alternate sections of red and black caviar and spread in thin layers on top of pie. Remove cardboard dividers, sprinkle parsley on dividing lines. Serve with small plain crackers. Keeps well for several days. *Note:* For a 10-inch pan, use 12 ounces cream cheese and ¾ cup sour cream.

A favorite for caviar lovers. Use leftovers, if any, on baked potatoes.

Geri Cuoghi

 When cooking in glass pans, reduce oven temperature by 25°.

Easy But Elegant Liver Pâté

12 or more servings

¾ cup margarine, reserve
½ cup
1 pound chicken livers
8 ounces fresh mushrooms, chopped
⅓ cup sliced green onions with tops
1 teaspoon salt
⅔ cup white wine
1 garlic clove, minced

½ teaspoon dry mustard
⅛ teaspoon rosemary
⅛ teaspoon dill weed
8 ounces Neufchâtel cream cheese, softened
1 teaspoon parsley flakes
melba toast rounds, cocktail bread *or* crackers

Melt ¼ cup margarine in skillet. Add chicken livers, mushrooms, onions and salt. Sauté over medium heat for 5 minutes. Add wine, garlic, mustard, rosemary and dill. Cook 5-10 minutes, until liver is cooked and no longer pink and liquid is almost gone. Cool slightly and remove any membrane from chicken livers; discard. Scrape chicken liver and pan liquid into a blender or food processor. Process until smooth. Add reserved ½ cup softened butter; process until smooth.

Line a 5x9-inch loaf pan or 2 to 3 (3x5-inch) loaf pans with plastic wrap, leaving wrap extended outside of pan. Pack liver mixture into pan. Wrap and chill 4-5 hours until firm. Remove from pan and transfer onto a serving plate and frost with softened Neufchâtel cheese. Decorate frosting by using a fork to make a zigzag pattern on pâté and put a sprinkle of parsley down the center. Serve with melba toast rounds, cocktail bread or crackers.

An elegant looking pâté that tastes wonderful!

Pamela M. Richert

Tuna Pâté

12-16 servings

1	(3-ounce) package lemon gelatin	1	cup chopped celery
½	cup boiling water	3	tablespoons minced onion
2	tablespoons vinegar	1	cup tuna, drained
½	teaspoon salt	¾	cup mayonnaise *or* light mayonnaise
1	(2-ounce) jar pimiento, drained and chopped		leaf lettuce
			crackers

Dissolve gelatin in boiling water and set aside. Mix remaining ingredients together. Add to gelatin mixture and mix well. Turn into a gelatin mold and refrigerate until set. Overnight is best. To serve, unmold on lettuce lined plate and serve with crackers.

Irresistibly delicious! The best tuna dish you've ever tasted.

Pat Marr

Spicy Crab Bites

36 crab bites

3	(6½-ounce) cans crabmeat, drained	1½	teaspoons Old Bay seasoning
1	egg, beaten	1	teaspoon Worcestershire sauce
1	cup plain dry bread crumbs		
½	cup finely chopped red bell pepper	¼	teaspoon dry mustard
		1⅛	teaspoons cayenne pepper
⅓	cup finely chopped parsley	½	cup plain bread crumbs
4	tablespoons mayonnaise	4	tablespoons vegetable oil
4	to 5 green onions, chopped	4	tablespoons butter
½	teaspoon salt		

Combine first 12 ingredients in a bowl; mix well. Shape into patties, using a tablespoon as a measure. Roll each in ½ cup bread crumbs. Combine half of the oil and half of butter in a large skillet. Over medium-high heat, cook half the patties in oil mixture until golden brown on both sides. Drain on paper towels. Discard oil mixture and use remaining butter and oil for remainder of patties. Arrange crab bites on a tray and if desired, garnish with green and red grapes, strawberries and fresh parsley. *Note:* May be prepared and fried 30 minutes ahead and reheated at 350° for 5-10 minutes.

An excellent appetizer that will delight your palate and please your guests.

Cyndy Ortwein

Shrimp Diablo

28 appetizers

1	pound cooked shrimp, cleaned and chopped	1	tablespoon coarse grain mustard
½	cup chopped onion		juice of ½ lemon
2	hard-cooked eggs, chopped		dash of hot pepper sauce
¼	cup mayonnaise	2	(14 ounce) cans artichoke hearts, drained

Mix all ingredients together except artichoke hearts. Cut artichoke hearts in half. Fill hearts with one tablespoon of the shrimp salad mixture. Chill.

May be served as an appetizer or served on lettuce as the first course.

Maureen Kolb

Sesame Seed Chicken

16-20 servings

5	pounds chicken wings *or* small thighs	½	cup sugar
2	cups all-purpose flour	½	teaspoon garlic powder
	vegetable oil	⅓	cup sesame seeds, untoasted
½	cup soy sauce		

Coat chicken with flour and shake off excess. In large frying pan, fry chicken in ¾ to 1-inch vegetable oil. Fry until golden brown, approximately 7 minutes on each side. Drain chicken on paper towels. To prepare sauce, combine soy sauce, sugar and garlic powder in a small saucepan. Heat sauce to boiling point, stirring constantly, remove from heat. Using tongs, dip each chicken piece in sauce, be sure to cover completely. Drain on paper towel. When all chicken has been dipped and drained, sprinkle chicken with sesame seeds.

Finger-lickin good! These will disappear quickly.

Marcy Holladay

 Never put a cover on anything that is cooked in milk because it will boil over.

Christine's Coquille St. Jacques

8-10 servings

1½	pounds scallops	7	tablespoons butter
1½	cups dry white wine	½	pound mushrooms, chopped
1	teaspoon salt	¼	cup all-purpose flour
6	peppercorns	¾	cup milk
3	sprigs parsley	3	egg yolks
1	small bay leaf	½	cup heavy cream
¼	teaspoon thyme	1	teaspoon lemon juice
4	tablespoons chopped green onions		cayenne pepper
½	cup water	½	cup grated Swiss cheese

Combine first 9 ingredients in saucepan. Bring to boil, cover and simmer 5 minutes. Strain off liquid; there should be about 2 cups. Place liquid back on heat, boil for 10 minutes or until reduced to 1 cup. Pick scallops out from among herbs, cut into small pieces and set aside. Heat 2 tablespoons butter in skillet, add mushrooms and sauté. Drain and set aside.

To make sauce, melt 3 tablespoons butter in saucepan. Blend in flour. Gradually add milk, stirring constantly, until mixture is thick and smooth. Add reduced cooking liquid and cook, stirring for 1 minute. In a bowl, beat egg yolks with cream. Beat in the hot sauce a little at a time. Put sauce back in pan and cook, stirring for about 2 minutes, until slightly thickened. Remove from heat; add lemon juice and dash of cayenne. Refrigerate sauce, scallops and mushrooms separately. Before serving, let scallops and mushrooms come to room temperature. Heat the sauce in top of double boiler. Remove 1 cup of sauce and set it aside. Add scallops and mushrooms to remaining sauce in double boiler and heat. Spoon the scallop mixture into buttered scallop shells or individual casseroles. Spoon 2 tablespoons of the reserved sauce into each shell. Sprinkle with Swiss cheese. Dot with remaining butter. Broil 6-8 inches from heat for about 3 minutes or until just lightly browned and bubbly.

Agnes Zodda

Daddy's Tasty Chicken

8 servings

15 chicken legs and/or wings	1 teaspoon chicken spice
1 teaspoon tenderizer	1 teaspoon Greek seasoning
1 teaspoon garlic salt	¼ cup dried onion flakes
2 cups white wine	

Preheat oven to 225°. Line a 9x13-inch baking dish with aluminum foil. Wash chicken and remove wing tips. Sprinkle chicken with tenderizer and garlic salt. Place in baking dish and cover with white wine. Bake for 2 hours. Turn chicken over. Sprinkle with chicken spice, Greek seasoning and dried onions. Pour some liquid out. Increase oven temperature to 450° and bake for 20-30 minutes. Season to individual taste, adding more spice if necessary.

Spicy party pleaser that makes an excellent hors d'ouevre.

Lyn Crowley

Bacon Crisps

as many as you wish

grated Parmesan cheese	bacon, cut in half
Waverly crackers	

Preheat oven to 200°. Put about 1 teaspoon of cheese on top of each cracker. Wrap a half strip of bacon around cracker and cheese. Place on broiler pan rack. Bake for about 2 hours. You do not need to turn the bacon crisps. Remove from oven. Leave bacon crisps on the broiler pan to cool about 1 hour before serving.

This is great as an appetizer or for brunch and men love it! A broiler pan is most necessary.

Sharon Amos

Always chill juices or sodas before adding to recipe.

45

Cheese Crispies

about 60 crispies

2 cups all-purpose flour	2 cups grated sharp
¼ teaspoon red pepper	Cheddar cheese
1 cup margarine, softened	2 cups Rice Krispies
	paprika

Preheat oven to 375°. In a large bowl, combine flour with red pepper and stir to blend. Add margarine and cheese to flour and stir to blend, until mixture is crumbly. Stir in krispies and mix well. Form into ½-inch balls, place on ungreased cookie sheet and flatten balls with a fork. Sprinkle top with paprika and bake for 10-12 minutes or just until lightly brown on top.

A snap to make and quite addictive.

Nancy R. Willingham

Water Chestnuts

approximately 25 appetizers

1 (8-ounce) can whole water chestnuts, drained	¼ cup mayonnaise
¾ pound bacon, cut in half or thirds	½ cup ketchup
	½ cup packed brown sugar

Preheat oven to 350°. Wrap bacon piece around water chestnut and secure with a toothpick. Combine remaining ingredients in a small saucepan. Heat to dissolve brown sugar. Dip bacon-wrapped water chestnuts into sauce and then place in greased 9x13-inch baking dish. Bake for about 45 minutes.

Virginia Heffernan

Mushroom Turnovers

about 50 turnovers

1 (8-ounce) package cream cheese, softened
1 cup margarine, softened
⅛ teaspoon salt
2 cups sifted all-purpose flour
¾ pound fresh mushrooms, chopped very fine
1 small onion, minced
3 tablespoons butter
½ teaspoon salt
pepper to taste
2 teaspoons all-purpose flour
½ cup sour cream
1 teaspoon dill weed
1 egg yolk
2 teaspoons milk

In a mixing bowl, combine cheese and margarine, beat until smooth. Add salt and work in flour until smooth. Wrap dough and chill for about 1 hour. To make filling, sauté chopped mushrooms and onion in butter. Add salt and pepper. Add flour and cook 1-2 minutes. Remove from heat. Add sour cream and dill; set aside. Roll pastry ⅛-inch thick on floured board. Cut with a 2¾-inch biscuit cutter. Place ½ teaspoon of filling on each round. Fold pastry over and press edges firmly with a fork. Mix egg yolk with milk. Brush tops and edges of turnovers with this glaze. Place on ungreased cookie sheet. Cover and chill. About 25 minutes before serving, preheat oven to 450° and bake turnovers for 12 minutes or until golden. *Note:* Can be prepared ahead and frozen. Bake frozen turnovers in a preheated 375° oven for 15-20 minutes.

Well worth the effort.

Gretchen Mattingly

Burgundy Mushrooms

4 pounds mushrooms

4	pounds mushrooms	1	teaspoon black pepper
1½	cups butter	2	teaspoons MSG (optional)
4	cups inexpensive Burgundy wine	2	teaspoons garlic powder
		2	cups boiling water
2	tablespoons Worcestershire sauce	4	beef bouillon cubes
		4	chicken bouillon cubes
1	teaspoon dill weed		salt to taste (optional)

Wash mushrooms and cut stems off. Put all ingredients in a large pot. Bring to a boil, reduce heat and simmer covered for 5-6 hours. Remove cover and simmer for an additional 3-5 hours or until liquid is barely covering top of mushrooms. Serve warm in chafing dish with toothpicks or over grilled steaks. *Note:* Make ahead or you can cook this in 2 different stages if you need to. Freezes great, can be frozen in smaller quantities in ziploc bags.

This is an extraordinary dish!

Rosalie A. Johnson

Madeira Mushrooms

8 servings

18	large mushrooms, stems removed and reserved	½	cup Madeira wine
		4½	tablespoons dry bread crumbs
4	to 5 tablespoons butter, melted	½	cup grated Swiss cheese
9	tablespoons minced green onions, tops included	¾	teaspoon tarragon
		4	to 5 tablespoons heavy cream
3	tablespoons butter		salt and pepper to taste
1½	tablespoons vegetable oil		

Preheat oven to 375°. Place mushroom caps in a buttered 9x13-inch baking pan and brush mushrooms with melted butter. Chop mushroom stems and sauté with onions in butter and oil. Add Madeira and boil rapidly until reduced slightly. Remove from heat, stir in remaining ingredients. Spoon into mushroom caps. Bake 15-20 minutes.

The blending of Madeira wine and tarragon make these mushrooms totally exquisite!

Trudy S. Eissler

Stuffed Mushrooms

12 appetizers

1	(3-ounce) package cream cheese, softened	½	teaspoon garlic powder
1	(7-ounce) can minced clams, drained	12	large mushrooms, stemmed
1	tablespoon minced parsley	¼	cup French fried onions, chopped

Whip cream cheese until smooth. Add the next 3 ingredients and blend well. Stuff mushroom caps with cream cheese-clam mixture. Put mushrooms on microwave-safe plate and sprinkle with French fried onions. Cook in microwave 3½ - 4½ minutes. Rotate plate and microwave for 2 more minutes.

Virginia Heffernan

Stuffed Mushrooms Parmigiana

12 stuffed mushrooms

12	large fresh mushrooms	½	cup finely crushed Ritz crackers
2	tablespoons butter *or* margarine	1	tablespoon snipped fresh parsley
1	medium onion, finely chopped	3	tablespoons grated Parmesan cheese
2	ounces pepperoni, diced	½	teaspoon oregano
¼	cup finely chopped green bell pepper	½	teaspoon seasoned salt
1	garlic clove, chopped		dash pepper
		⅓	cup chicken broth

Preheat oven to 325°. Wash mushrooms and remove stems. Finely chop stems and reserve. Drain mushroom caps on paper towels. Melt butter in skillet, add onion, pepperoni, green pepper, garlic and reserved mushroom stems. Sauté several minutes. Add cracker crumbs, parsley, cheese, oregano, seasoned salt, and pepper. Mix well. Stir in chicken broth. Spoon stuffing into mushroom caps; rounding tops. Place stuffed mushrooms in shallow baking pan with about ¼-inch water covering bottom of pan. Bake uncovered for about 25 minutes or until heated through.

Everyone will love these pepperoni stuffed mushrooms.

Sheila Van Auken

49

Susie's Onions

6 cups

½ cup vinegar
1 cup sugar
2 cups water

6 medium sweet onions,
   thinly sliced
½ cup mayonnaise
1 teaspoon celery salt

Combine vinegar, sugar and water. Soak sliced onions in this mixture for 2 to 4 hours. Drain onions well. For dressing, combine mayonnaise and celery salt. Toss drained onions with dressing. Serve with saltine crackers, if desired.

Simple and good for an unusual addition to a selection of finger foods.

Janet Hinrichs

Vegetable Pizza

24 appetizers

1 (8-ounce) can refrigerated
   crescent rolls
1 (8-ounce) package cream
   cheese, softened
1 teaspoon dill weed
1 teaspoon minced onion
⅓ cup mayonnaise
½ teaspoon garlic powder
2 tablespoons bottled ranch
   dressing

½ cup chopped raw broccoli
½ cup chopped raw carrots
½ cup chopped fresh
   mushrooms
¼ cup chopped black olives
½ cup diced green bell
   pepper
½ cup Parmesan cheese

Preheat oven to 350°. Unroll crescent rolls on ungreased cookie sheet. Pat seams together. Bake for 10 minutes. Cool. Mix next 6 ingredients; frost crust with mixture. Finely chop all vegetables, food processor can be used. Top cheese mixture with chopped vegetables and gently press into crust. Sprinkle with Parmesan cheese. Cover and refrigerate. Slice when chilled.

Different and so good! You'll often be asked for the recipe.

Paula Schweinfest

Terry's Tortilla Pinwheels

100 servings

1 (16-ounce) carton sour cream

1 (8-ounce) package cream cheese, softened

2 (2.5-ounce) packages corned beef, diced

1 bunch green onions with tops, diced

1 (1-pound 2-ounce) package flour tortillas (10 count) picante sauce *or* salsa

Blend sour cream and cream cheese together. Add corned beef and green onions to sour cream mixture. Spread each tortilla with one rounded tablespoon of mixture and roll up tortillas. Place rolled tortillas in an airtight plastic bag and chill for 2 hours. Remove from refrigerator and slice each rolled tortilla into 1-inch slices. Serve with picante sauce or salsa.

Always the first appetizer to disappear.

Terry Curp

Tea Sandwiches

about 2 dozen servings

1 pound bacon, cooked crisp and crumbled

1 large *or* 2 small green bell peppers, diced

1¼ cups mayonnaise *or* salad dressing

1 loaf very thinly sliced white bread

Combine bacon, peppers and mayonnaise. Trim crusts from bread, if desired. Spread mayonnaise mixture on one slice of bread; top with another slice. Cut into fourths.

These sandwiches are a hit at parties, especially with men! Everyone is so curious about the ingredients.

Rosalie A. Johnson

51

Three Pepper Quesadillas

24-32 appetizers

1 cup thinly sliced green bell pepper
1 cup thinly sliced yellow bell pepper
1 cup thinly sliced red bell pepper
1 cup thinly sliced onions
¼ cup margarine
¼ teaspoon ground cumin
1 (4-ounce) can chopped green chilies, undrained
1 (8-ounce) package cream cheese, softened
8 ounces grated Cheddar cheese
1 (18-ounce) package home-style flour tortillas
margarine
cumin *or* chili powder to taste
8 ounces sour cream
¼ cup salsa

Sauté peppers and onions in margarine in a large skillet. Stir in cumin. Spoon out any liquid in the skillet. Set pepper mixture aside. In a small bowl, combine green chilies, cream cheese and Cheddar cheese. (The recipe may be prepared one day in advance up to this point.) Two to three hours in advance, assemble quesadillas as follows: Spread about 3-4 tablespoons of cheese mixture on ½ of a flour tortilla. Top with sautéed peppers and onions. Fold over. Very lightly spread margarine on the top of the folded tortilla and sprinkle with cumin or chili powder. Place on cookie sheet and bake in preheated 400° oven for 10-15 minutes or until bubbly and lightly browned. Cut into thirds or fourths. Mix sour cream and salsa together and serve as a dip with the cut quesadillas.

A wonderful appetizer to use when ready for rave reviews!!

Rosalie A. Johnson

Swiss And Rye Appetizers

20-25 servings

1 cup mayonnaise
1½ tablespoons grated onion
1½ tablespoons parsley flakes
salt and pepper to taste
1 teaspoon Worcestershire sauce
1 loaf sliced party rye bread
8 ounces sliced Swiss cheese

Mix first five ingredients well. Spread 1 teaspoon of this mixture on each piece of party rye bread. Cut Swiss cheese slices to size of the rye bread. Top each slice of bread with Swiss cheese. Place on ungreased cookie sheet. Place under broiler just until cheese melts.

Beverly Jordan

Holiday Appetizer Quiche

45-50 appetizers

Crust:

1½	cups unsifted all-purpose flour	⅔	cup butter flavored shortening
1½	cups finely crushed Ritz crackers	¼	to ½ cup water

Combine flour and cracker crumbs. Cut in shortening until mixture resembles coarse cornmeal. Sprinkle with ½ cup water, a tablespoon at a time, tossing with a fork until crumb mixture is completely moistened. Press mixture into bottom of ungreased 10x15-inch jelly roll pan. Prick crust with a fork.

Filling:

2	cups shredded Swiss cheese	1	(4-ounce) jar diced pimiento, well drained
⅔	cup chopped ham, crumbled cooked sausage, diced pepperoni *or* crumbled cooked bacon	5	eggs
		1	cup whipping cream
		1	cup half-and-half
¾	cup thinly sliced green onions and tops	1	teaspoon salt
¼	cup snipped fresh parsley	¼	teaspoon pepper

Preheat oven to 400°. Sprinkle first 5 ingredients evenly over unbaked crust. Beat eggs, cream, half-and-half, salt and pepper together. Pour over filled crust. Bake for 25-30 minutes or until set. Cool 10 minutes and cut in ½-inch to 2-inch pieces. Serve.

A colorful presentation your whole family will enjoy.

Mary Jo Kelly

53

Surprise Sandwiches

6-8 servings

1	cup cooked diced chicken	¼	cup cooked crisp and
½	cup chopped dates		crumbled bacon
¼	cup chopped hazelnuts	½	cup mayonnaise
		12	slices bread

In a mixing bowl, mix together the first 5 ingredients. Trim crusts from bread and spread mixture on 6 slices bread. Top with remaining 6 slices. Cut in 2 triangles for lunch, 4 triangles for tea time or 6-8 pieces for canapés. Garnish serving plate with fresh fruit and parsley sprigs.

A flavorful and tasty sandwich, perfect for a ladies luncheon.

Lois Poper

Crab Sandwich

6 servings

2	(6-ounce) cans crabmeat	2	teaspoons basil
1	(8-ounce) package cream cheese, softened	2	teaspoons seasoned salt
3	tablespoons mayonnaise	1	package English muffins, split
2	green onions, chopped	2	cups shredded pasteurized process cheese
2	teaspoons garlic powder		
2	teaspoons pepper		

Preheat oven to 350°. Put crabmeat in colander and drain. Cream together cheese and mayonnaise; add chopped onions, seasonings and crabmeat. Spread mixture on English muffin half, sprinkle cheese on top and brown for 15-20 minutes.

Great appetizer for casual summer get togethers.

Mary Frances Newcomer

Bread Roll

6-8 servings

1	loaf frozen bread dough	2	tomatoes, sliced
¼	pound sliced ham	1	onion, sliced
¼	pound sliced salami	¼	pound sliced Swiss cheese

Let bread dough thaw. Preheat oven to 350°. Spread dough on a greased, rectangular shaped cookie sheet. In the middle of the dough and placed one on top of another, layer a row of ham, salami, tomatoes, onion and Swiss cheese. Pull the long sides of the dough up over the mixture and pinch together, then pinch short sides together making a long loaf. Bake for 30 minutes and then slice. *Note:* The amount of ham, salami, tomato, onion and Swiss cheese is approximate. More or less can be used according to individual taste.

This is delicious with homemade soup or chili.

Maureen Kolb

Stuffed Bread

12-18 servings

1	large loaf round bread	1	cup sour cream
1	(8-ounce) package lite cream cheese, softened	3	teaspoons Worcestershire sauce
1	(2.5-ounce) jar dried beef, diced	1	bunch green onions, diced
2	cups grated sharp Cheddar cheese	1	loaf French bread, cut in cubes

Preheat oven to 350°. Slice top off the loaf of round bread. Scoop out center of bread and reserve top. Beat cream cheese until fluffy and add remaining ingredients, except French bread. Mix well. Fill hollowed round bread with this mixture and place top back on the round loaf. Wrap in foil. Bake 1½ hours. Bake bread cubes the last 20 minutes or until crisp. Remove foil and arrange toasted bread cubes around the stuffed bread.

This is a favorite with men!!

Sue Chris Gauthreaux

Cheese Ball

1 cheese ball

5	ounces blue cheese, softened	4	(3-ounce) packages cream cheese, softened
2	(5-ounce) jars sharp pasteurized process cheese spread, softened	1	teaspoon Worcestershire sauce
		¼	cup snipped fresh parsley
		½	cup chopped pecans

Blend all ingredients together except parsley and pecans. Shape into ball and place in bowl that has been double-lined with wax paper. Refrigerate overnight. One hour before serving, roll cheese ball in nuts and snipped parsley or roll in nuts only and place on parsley lined plate.

Nancy Ehrman
Peg Kottke

Dried Beef Cheese Ball

1 cheese ball

1	(8-ounce) package cream cheese, softened	⅓	cup chopped green stuffed olives
¼	cup grated Parmesan cheese	1	(2.5-ounce) jar dried beef, chopped
1	tablespoon horseradish		

Mix first 4 ingredients together and shape into ball. Chill and then roll into chopped beef.

An easy and tasty cheese ball that can be made ahead and frozen.

Agnes Woodward

Italian Cheese Ball

12 servings

4	(3-ounce) packages cream cheese, softened	¼	cup mayonnaise
⅓	cup grated Parmesan cheese	½	teaspoon oregano
		⅛	teaspoon garlic powder
			parsley flakes

Combine all ingredients, chill slightly and form into a ball. Before serving, roll ball in parsley flakes or garnish of your choice. Serve with bread sticks or crackers.

Bridgette A. Correale

Cheese Ring

30-40 appetizers

16 ounces grated sharp
Cheddar cheese
½ medium onion, finely
grated
⅔ cup mayonnaise
¼ teaspoon garlic powder
¼ teaspoon white pepper

dash of cayenne pepper
1 cup coarsely chopped pecans
1 (16-ounce) jar strawberry
preserves *or* pepper
jelly
assorted crackers

Mix first 6 ingredients well. Add pecans and stir well. Form mixture into a ring on serving plate. Chill overnight. Before serving, fill center of ring with strawberry preserves or pepper jelly. Serve with assorted crackers.

Variation: Use 1 onion, ¾ cup mayonnaise, 1 garlic clove, pressed and ½ teaspoon hot pepper sauce. Omit garlic powder and white pepper.

Paula Schweinfest
Virginia Heffernan
Jane Reynolds

Chutney Cheese Spread

3 cups

2 (8-ounce) packages cream
cheese, softened
1 (9-ounce) bottle Major
Grey's Chutney

2 teaspoons curry powder
½ teaspoon dry mustard
½ cup sliced almonds

Beat cream cheese until creamy and smooth. Add remaining ingredients and stir until evenly blended. Store mixture in a tightly covered container in refrigerator. Serve with your favorite crackers. *Note:* Mixture may be stored up to 2 months in tightly covered container in the refrigerator.

Great and different spread to have on hand when guests drop in unexpectedly.

Nancy Dick

Hot Cheese Dip

3 cups

8	ounces sharp Cheddar cheese, grated	1	cup mayonnaise
		1	small onion, grated

Preheat oven to 400°. Combine all ingredients and pour into 1-quart casserole. Bake for about 20 minutes. Serve with crackers.

Sheila Van Auken

Artichoke Dip

3 cups dip

1	(14-ounce) can artichoke hearts, drained and finely chopped	2	teaspoons lemon juice few drops Worcestershire sauce
1	cup mayonnaise *or* light mayonnaise	2	green onions, finely chopped (white part only)
1	cup grated Parmesan cheese	¼	teaspoon garlic powder

Preheat oven to 350°. Combine all ingredients together and turn into a 1½-quart glass dish. Bake for 20-30 minutes or until mixture just begins to brown lightly on top. Serve with wheat crackers.

Variation: use ½ cup Parmesan cheese, omit lemon juice, Worcestershire sauce, green onions and garlic powder.

A heavenly dip that's always a favorite. Pretty with a dash of paprika on top.

Rita C. Leonard
Amy Dahler

Cheese Soufflé Spread

12 or more servings

¾ cup mayonnaise
1 teaspoon prepared mustard
1 to 2 dashes Worcestershire sauce
½ onion, finely chopped

1 cup shredded sharp Cheddar cheese
1 large egg white, stiffly beaten
2 teaspoons paprika

Preheat oven to 350°. Combine first 5 ingredients in a mixing bowl and fold in beaten egg white and paprika. Place in an ungreased 1 quart soufflé dish. Place dish in larger pan containing ½ inch water and bake uncovered for 30 minutes. Serve warm to spread on crackers, toasted bread pieces or use as a dip.

Melba Fristick

California Artichoke Spread

4-6 servings

1 (15-ounce) can water packed artichoke hearts, drained and finely chopped
1 (6½-ounce) jar marinated artichoke hearts, drained and finely chopped
1 (4-ounce) can diced green chilies, drained

2 garlic cloves, pressed
¼ cup shredded Cheddar cheese
¼ cup mayonnaise
¼ cup light sour cream
¾ cup grated Parmesan cheese, reserving ¼ cup for topping

Preheat oven to 350°. Combine all ingredients except cheese for topping and blend well. Spread into a small ungreased ovenproof serving dish. Sprinkle top with ¼ cup Parmesan cheese. Bake for 15 minutes or until golden and bubbly. Serve with crackers.

Nancy Barnwell

Addictive Avocado Dip

about 3 cups

1 (14-ounce) can Mexican tomatoes, well drained
2 (7¾-ounce) cans frozen avocado dip, thawed
3 green onions, sliced
juice of ½ lemon
½ teaspoon garlic salt

¾ cup sour cream
1 (4-ounce) can chopped green chilies, undrained
1 pound bacon, cooked crisp and crumbled
tortilla chips

Chop tomatoes. Combine first 7 ingredients and chill. Sprinkle ½ of the bacon on top of the dip and reserve the remaining bacon to replenish as needed. Serve with tortilla chips.

This dip keeps well and doesn't turn brown. It is really a treat and is always attacked by guests!

Rosalie A. Johnson

Crabmeat Appetizer

12-16 servings

12 ounces cream cheese, softened
1 tablespoon lemon juice
¼ teaspoon minced onion
2 tablespoons Worcestershire sauce
2 tablespoons mayonnaise
dash garlic salt

½ (12-ounce) bottle chili sauce
1 (12-ounce) can crabmeat, drained and cartilage removed
finely chopped fresh parsley

Mix first 6 ingredients together and blend well. Spoon into bottom of a greased 9-inch pie plate and spread evenly. Top with chili sauce. Layer crabmeat over sauce and sprinkle generously with chopped parsley. Pat down and refrigerate overnight. Leave in pie plate and serve with crackers.

Looking for an appetizer that is special yet easy to make? This is it.

Dorothy B. Watkins

Camille's Clam And Swiss Spread

2	(6-ounce) cans minced clams, undrained	2	tablespoons parsley flakes
6	ounces Swiss cheese, shredded	1	teaspoon dried oregano
2	teaspoons lemon juice	⅓	cup butter, melted
1	medium onion, minced	¾	cup Italian flavored bread crumbs
			pepper to taste

Preheat oven to 350°. In a bowl, combine all ingredients. Mix well. Place in a greased 8x8-inch baking dish and bake for 20 minutes. Serve immediately with party rye bread or crackers.

Always a hit at parties!

Agnes Zodda

Hot Clam Dip

12-15 servings

12	ounces cream cheese, softened	2	(7-ounce) cans minced clams, drained
1	(5-ounce) jar sharp pasteurized process cheese spread		dash Tabasco® sauce
½	large onion, chopped		white pepper to taste
			Worcestershire sauce

Heat all ingredients together in a pan until cheeses are melted. Serve warm with crackers.

Virginia Heffernan

Hot Crab Dip

2	(8-ounce) packages cream cheese, softened	½	cup half-and-half *or* milk
2	(5-ounce) jars sharp pasteurized process cheese spread	1	tablespoon Worcestershire sauce
		1	(7-ounce) can crabmeat *or* fresh lump crabmeat

Combine first 4 ingredients in top of double boiler and cook over low heat until cheeses are melted. Stir to blend ingredients; add crabmeat. Serve warm with crackers, miniature pita bread, cold vegetables or breadsticks.

Louise M. Van de Vuurst

Crab Dip

10-16 servings

3   (8-ounce) packages cream
    cheese
½   cup mayonnaise
½   cup white wine
2   teaspoons powdered sugar
1   teaspoon dry mustard

1   teaspoon prepared
    mustard
½   teaspoon salt
1   pound lump crabmeat,
    picked for shells

In top of double boiler, combine together cheese, mayonnaise, wine, sugar, mustard and salt. Stir until cheese is melted and add crabmeat. Serve warm with crackers.

Jane Reynolds

Crustacean Dip

12 to 15 servings

2   (4¼ ounce) cans shrimp,
    drained and chopped
1   (6-ounce) can crabmeat,
    drained and chopped
1   cup sour cream
1   (8-ounce) package cream
    cheese, softened

1   (0.7-ounce) package dry
    Italian dressing mix
2   teaspoons lemon juice
2   tablespoons chopped
    onions
3   tablespoons mayonnaise

Combine all ingredients and chill. Serve cold with corn chips or wheat crackers. This can also be spread on crackers and broiled for a hot appetizer.

Wonderful party pleaser.

Jane Reynolds

Smoked Salmon Spread

2 cups

1 (8-ounce) package cream
   cheese, softened
¼ cup whipping cream
1 green onion, thinly sliced
1 teaspoon fresh lemon juice

dash Tabasco® sauce
4 ounces smoked salmon,
   gently shredded
2 tablespoons red salmon
   caviar

Gently mix cream cheese and cream in a mixing bowl. Stir in green onion, lemon juice and Tabasco® sauce. Gently fold in the smoked salmon and caviar until well combined, but do not over mix. The shreds of salmon and the caviar should remain whole.

This spread is perfect brunch fare on black bread or bagels. Or, hollow out a thick loaf of French bread, fill it with mixture and slice for an hors d'oeuvre.

Vicki Sherrard

Mock Oysters Rockefeller

12 servings

2 (10-ounce) packages
   frozen chopped
   broccoli
1 medium onion, grated
½ cup margarine

1 (10¾-ounce) can cream of
   mushroom soup
1 (4.5-ounce) jar chopped
   mushrooms, drained
1 (6-ounce) roll garlic cheese

Cook broccoli according to package directions and drain well. Combine all ingredients in a saucepan and heat until cheese and margarine are melted. Serve in a chafing dish with corn chips, melba toast or crackers.

Variation: Use 1 package chopped broccoli, omit onion and mushrooms and use 2 rolls garlic cheese.

Virginia Heffernan
Carol Panasuk

63

Ripe Olive Spread

12 servings

1 (8-ounce) package cream
   cheese, softened
2 (4.5-ounce) cans chopped
   ripe olives, drained
2 teaspoons grated onion
   dash garlic powder

dash salt
2 drops hot pepper sauce
   juice from ½ lemon
1 cup mayonnaise
½ cup chopped pecans

Beat cream cheese until fluffy. Combine all ingredients and blend well.
Serve with crackers.

An unusual dip which may also be used as a sandwich spread.

Virginia Heffernan

Sharp Dip For Veggies

about 4 cups

2 beef bouillon cubes
¼ cup water
2 (5-ounce) jars sharp
   pasteurized process
   cheese spread

1 (8-ounce) package cream
   cheese, softened
2 cups mayonnaise
1 small onion, chopped

Dissolve bouillon in water. Melt the cheeses together. Add mayonnaise,
chopped onion and dissolved bouillon. Blend together until mixed. Serve
warm or cold with raw vegetables. *Note:* Do not use electric mixer. Use
food processor to blend ingredients.

Quick and easy dip for ball games, parties, etc.

Rose Kull

Vegetable Dip

16-20 servings

2	envelopes unflavored gelatin	1	cup chopped celery
¾	cup boiling water	1	small onion, chopped
¾	cup cold water	1	cucumber, chopped
2	tomatoes, chopped	2	cups mayonnaise
1	medium green bell pepper, chopped	1	teaspoon salt

Dissolve gelatin in boiling water. Add cold water, stir and set aside to cool. When cool, add chopped vegetables, mayonnaise and salt. Refrigerate until ready to serve. Serve with crackers or use as a sandwich spread.

Variation: Use 1 envelope unflavored gelatin and 3 tablespoons water. Add ¼ teaspoon pepper. Let vegetables sit for 2 hours in a bowl and pour off accumulated water.

Virginia Heffernan
Gretchen Mattingly

Pizza Dip

15-20 servings

1	(8-ounce) package cream cheese, softened	½	cup green bell pepper, chopped
3	(4-ounce) jars shrimp cocktail	6	green onions, chopped
½	cup black olives, chopped	1	large tomato, chopped
		8	ounces shredded mozzarella cheese

Spread cream cheese on large serving plate. Layer remaining ingredients in order listed as you would when making pizza. Serve with crackers.

A great appetizer for a large gathering.

Pauline Cychowski

Reuben Dip

4-5 cups

2 cups diced Swiss cheese	1 (2.5-ounce) package sliced
2 cups mayonnaise	corned beef, diced
½ cup finely chopped onion	cocktail rye bread rounds
⅔ cup sauerkraut, well	
drained and minced	

Preheat oven to 325°. Combine all ingredients (except bread rounds) and place in ungreased 1-quart baking dish. Bake uncovered for 20 minutes, or until hot and cheese is melted. Serve with cocktail rye bread rounds. *Note:* This can be prepared ahead, covered and refrigerated until ready to bake. Bake until heated through and cheese is melted. A food processor is helpful to prepare this dish.

Jill Gasperini

Spicy Beef Dip

10 servings

1 (10-ounce) can Rotel	1½ teaspoons garlic salt
tomatoes, diced	2 drops Tabasco® sauce
1 pound ground round,	1 (16-ounce) can refried
cooked and drained	beans (optional)
1 pound pasteurized process	
cheese, cubed	

Combine all ingredients in a crockpot and heat on low temperature for 2 hours. Or you can heat all ingredients in a saucepan until cheese melts and use a crockpot or chafing dish to serve so dip will stay warm. Serve with corn chips or tortilla chips.

Excellent!

Theresa Ellison

Fiery Bean Dip

1½ cups

1	medium onion, chopped	1	to 2 (4-ounce) cans
1	garlic clove, minced		jalapeño peppers,
2	tablespoons bacon		minced
	drippings	¾	cup shredded Longhorn
1	(16-ounce) can red kidney		cheese
	beans, undrained		
	and mashed		

Sauté onion and garlic in bacon drippings in a medium skillet for 1 minute. Add beans and cook, stirring constantly until thickened. Add peppers and ½ cup cheese. Stir until cheese melts. Spoon into a serving dish; sprinkle remaining cheese on top. Serve with chips. *Note:* Use 1 can peppers for moderately hot dip and 2 cans for super hot dip.

Delicious! Everyone will come back for more.

Jane Reynolds

Taco Dip

10-12 servings

2	(10½-ounce) cans jalapeño	1	package taco seasoning
	bean dip		mix
3	avocados, peeled and	1	(4.5-ounce) can black
	mashed		olives, drained and sliced
2	tablespoons lemon juice	2	chopped tomatoes
¼	teaspoon pepper	¾	cup sliced green onions
½	teaspoon salt	1	cup shredded Cheddar
1	cup sour cream		cheese
½	cup mayonnaise		

Spread bean dip evenly on a large serving platter. Mix together avocados, lemon juice, pepper and salt. Spread over bean dip. Combine sour cream, mayonnaise and taco seasoning. Spread this mixture over the avocado mixture. Layer remaining ingredients in order given. Serve with tortilla chips.

Virginia Heffernan

Seafood Cocktail Sauce

1 cup

⅓ cup finely chopped dill   2 teaspoons prepared
    pickle   horseradish
¾ cup chili sauce   dash liquid hot pepper
¼ teaspoon Worcestershire   seasoning
    sauce   dash lemon juice

Combine all ingredients in a small bowl, stirring to mix well. Cover and refrigerate until chilled. Serve with shrimp, crab or lobster cocktail.

Nicki Knight

Coffee Cordial

makes approximately 9 cups

¼ pound finely ground coffee   1 pint 190-proof vodka
1 quart boiling water   1 pint distilled water
2 pounds fine sugar   2 ounces vanilla extract
5 cups water

Put coffee into a large crock container (do not use metal). Pour 1 quart boiling water over the coffee. Let stand for 24 hours. Then strain through 2 large coffee filters which have been placed in a colander. Combine 2 pounds fine sugar and 5 cups of water in a saucepan and heat just until sugar dissolves to make a light syrup. Add syrup to coffee and add remaining ingredients. Mix thoroughly, then bottle in individual bottles and let stand 6 weeks. This is even better after 6 months!

This recipe comes from an old Mexican woman who lives in the desert of New Mexico.

Margie Brennan

Baking powder will remove tea or coffee stains from china.

Fireside Coffee Mix

6 cups mix

2	cups non-dairy coffee creamer	1½	cups sugar
1½	cups hot cocoa mix	1	teaspoon cinnamon
1½	cups instant coffee granules	1	teaspoon ground nutmeg

Combine all ingredients, mixing well. Store in a closed container. To make 1 cup, spoon 3 tablespoons mix into mug or cup. Add boiling water and stir until well blended.

In a container with a bow, this mix makes a great gift for any occasion.

Lynne Grunthaner

Eva's Cranberry Tea

25 servings

1	quart fresh cranberries	1	quart orange juice (made from frozen concentrate)
2	quarts water		
2	cups sugar		
2	cups water	1½	cups fresh *or* frozen lemon juice, thawed (not lemonade)
4	cinnamon sticks		

In large stewpot, cook cranberries in 2-quarts water until mushy. Drain through colander, reserving liquid. Discard mushy berries. Combine sugar with 2 cups water and cinnamon sticks and cook 10-15 minutes. Add orange and lemon juices. Combine this with reserved cranberry juice. Serve hot. *Note:* For juices, use only fresh or frozen as indicated in ingredients. This can be made ahead as it will keep up to 2 weeks in the refrigerator. Reheat in its entirety or as needed.

A wonderful drink at Christmas time, lunch, brunch, carolers, PTA, bridge, etc. Always a hit with your guests.

S. Kay Clifton

69

Raspberry Champagne Punch

3 quarts

2 (10-ounce) cans frozen red raspberries in syrup, thawed
⅓ cup lemon juice from concentrate
½ cup sugar

1 (750-milliliter) bottle red rosé wine, chilled
1 quart raspberry sherbet
1 (750-milliliter) bottle Asti Spumanti *or* champagne, chilled

In blender container, purée raspberries. In large punch bowl, combine puréed raspberries, lemon juice, sugar and wine; stir until sugar dissolves. Just before serving, scoop sherbet into punch bowl and add Asti Spumanti. Stir gently.

Delicious, easy and pretty!

Jean M. Morton

Champagne Punch

20 (4-ounce) servings

1 (750-milliliter) bottle of champagne
½ cup vodka
1 cup apricot brandy

3 (12-ounce) cans ginger ale whole strawberries, frozen in ice ring

Mix all ingredients in a punch bowl. Float strawberry ring in punch for a festive touch.

Great for a special occasion!

Pauline Cychowski

Red Robbins

20 servings

1 quart cranberry juice
1 quart lemonade
1 quart orange juice

1 quart vodka
1 quart gingerale *or* 7-Up

Freeze first 4 ingredients in large bowl. Vodka will keep mixture from freezing completely. Let thaw 2 hours before serving and add soda.

Has the appearance and taste of a daiquiri.

Jane Reynolds

Slush

20 servings

1	cup bourbon whiskey	1	(6-ounce) can frozen
1	cup sugar		orange juice
1	(12-ounce) can frozen	2	cups strong tea
	lemonade	6	cups water

Mix ingredients together; freeze overnight. Serve in glasses.

Delicious slushy drink for parties with a limited amount of alcohol.

Jane Reynolds

Sangria

Sugar Syrup:

2 cups water   1 cup sugar

In a saucepan, combine water and sugar and bring to a boil. Cook over moderate heat, undisturbed, for 5 minutes. Let cool. *Note:* Makes 2½ cups syrup and keeps indefinitely in a sealed jar in the refrigerator.

Sangria:

1	cup Sugar Syrup	⅓	cup orange-flavored
2	(750-milliliter) bottles dry		liqueur
	red wine	½	orange, ½ lemon, ½ lime, all
¾	cup orange juice		sliced thinly
		1½	cups chilled soda water

Combine all ingredients except soda and chill for at least 4 hours. Add chilled soda just before serving. *Note:* Sugar Syrup may be increased to taste.

Beverly Pica

Amaretto Liqueur

2	cups water	1	tablespoon chocolate
3	cups sugar		extract
	peel from 1 lemon	½	cup bourbon
6	ounces almond extract	3	cups vodka
1	tablespoon vanilla extract		

Bring water, sugar and lemon peel to a boil in a large stainless steel stew pot. Reduce heat and simmer 20 minutes. Remove from heat and cool. Add extracts and stir well. Remove lemon peel and add bourbon and vodka. Cool and store in tightly closed bottles.

I use Grolesch beer bottles to store amaretto. This makes a nice Christmas gift too.

S. Kay Clifton

Irish Creme Liqueur

makes about 3½ cups

1	cup Irish whiskey	4	ounces milk
1	(14-ounce) can sweetened	1	tablespoon chocolate syrup
	condensed milk	1	tablespoon powdered
1	cup heavy cream		instant coffee

Shake or stir all ingredients together. Store in the refrigerator.

Best Irish creme you've ever tasted! Much better than store bought and less expensive, too.

Florence Powell

Never boil coffee, it brings out the acid and causes a bitter taste.

Soups

Gazpacho

6 servings

4	tomatoes, peeled, cored and chopped	¼	cup chopped fresh parsley *or* a hefty sprinkle of dry
1	small onion, chopped		
½	green *or* red bell pepper, chopped	¼	cup chopped fresh basil *or* a hefty sprinkle of dry
1	cucumber, peeled and chopped		a light sprinkle of tarragon and chervil (optional)
2	tablespoons olive oil	½	cup beef broth *or*
3	tablespoons wine vinegar		consommé, undiluted
1	garlic clove, pressed		juice of ½ lemon *or* lime

Mix all ingredients in a bowl. In a blender, blend ingredients in batches on high speed in short bursts (1 to 2 seconds) so that ingredients are still slightly chunky. Return ingredients to bowl and refrigerate. Serve chilled. *Note:* This soup keeps well in refrigerator for 3-4 days. Parboil tomatoes for 30-60 seconds for easy peeling.

Best made in summer when tomatoes are at their peak. This tangy, refreshing soup is most appealing.

Judith W. Jones

Paul's Gazpacho

8-12 servings

1	garlic clove	1	cup finely chopped cucumber
2	teaspoons salt	2	teaspoons chopped fresh chives
⅓	cup chopped fresh mushrooms		
3	tablespoons olive oil	1	teaspoon chopped fresh parsley
1	cup finely chopped onions	1	teaspoon freshly ground black pepper
2	cups finely chopped fresh tomatoes		
1¼	cups finely chopped green bell pepper	¼	to ½ teaspoon Tabasco® sauce
1	cup finely chopped celery	½	cup tarragon wine vinegar
		3	cups tomato juice

Crush garlic in 1 teaspoon of salt. Sauté mushrooms in olive oil until lightly browned. Combine garlic and mushrooms with the remaining ingredients in a glass bowl. Cover and chill overnight for best flavor.

The longer this soup chills, the stronger the flavor becomes.

Florence Moisan

Ecuadorian Shrimp Cebiché

6-8 servings

3 medium onions, thinly sliced and cut in half
juice of 5 medium lemons
3 tablespoons olive oil
½ teaspoon salt
1 tablespoon red wine vinegar
2 pounds medium or large shrimp, shelled, cooked, and cut into ½-inch pieces

2 cups ketchup
2 cups club soda
4 tablespoons fresh or 1 tablespoon dried cilantro
¼ teaspoon Tabasco® sauce
⅛ teaspoon pepper

Marinate onions overnight in lemon juice, olive oil, salt and wine vinegar. In a large bowl, combine shrimp and onions from marinade and ½ of the marinade liquid. Reserve remaining half of liquid. Add ketchup and mix well. Add club soda, cilantro, Tabasco® and pepper. Stir and taste for tartness. Cebiché should have a lot of juice and be a bit tart. Add more of the reserved marinade to taste. Serve cold and keep refrigerated.

Serve in small bowls with a twist of lemon as a cold soup or appetizer. "Buen Porvecho!" An absolute must for your next special occasion.

Pamela M. Richert

Elegant Pimiento Soup

6-8 servings

1 (16-ounce) jar pimientos, drained and chopped
5 cups chicken broth
5 tablespoons butter
¼ cup all-purpose flour
3 cups half-and-half

salt and freshly ground pepper to taste
sour cream
sprigs of watercress, fresh dill, minced fresh parsley or minced fresh chives

In a medium saucepan, heat pimiento and 2 cups chicken broth until simmering. Pureé mixture in blender and set aside. In medium saucepan, melt butter. Stir in flour and cook until bubbly. Gradually add half-and-half, stirring constantly. Simmer for 3 minutes or until thickened. Stir in puréed pimiento mixture and the remaining 3 cups of chicken broth. Simmer for 3 minutes or until heated through. Season with salt and pepper. Chill if desired. Serve with a dollop of sour cream topped with herb of choice.

This unique soup may be served hot or cold and is an excellent first course for a special dinner party.

Toni Kennedy

75

Asparagus Soup

4 servings

1 pound fresh asparagus	½ cup heavy cream
½ cup thinly sliced scallions	fresh lemon juice
¼ cup butter	salt and white pepper to
2 tablespoons all-purpose	taste
flour	snipped chives (optional)
4 cups full bodied chicken	sieved hard-cooked eggs
broth, hot	(optional)
2 large egg yolks	

Break off and discard tough ends from asparagus. Peel stalks and cut into 1-inch pieces, reserving tips. In a large saucepan, sauté scallions in butter over medium heat until softened. Add asparagus pieces, (not tips) sprinkle mixture with flour and cook for 3 minutes, stirring constantly. Pour in hot broth in a stream, whisking to blend. Bring mixture to a boil, reduce heat and simmer for 15 minutes or until asparagus are tender. In a blender, purée mixture in batches to avoid spilling. Pour into a large strainer and force purée mixture back into the saucepan. *Note:* At this point, the purée may be covered and refrigerated or frozen for later use. If refrigerated or frozen, thaw and slowly heat purée.

Add the reserved tips to purée mixture and simmer for about 5 minutes or until tips are tender. Beat together egg yolks and cream. Add 1 cup of the hot soup in a stream, whisking to blend, to the yolk and cream mixture. Whisk the yolk mixture back into the remaining soup and simmer, stirring for about 3 minutes. DO NOT BOIL! Season with lemon juice, salt and pepper. Ladle into heated bowls and garnish with fresh snipped chives or sieved hard-cooked eggs if desired.

An excellent first course for a special dinner party.

Beverly Pica

 If soup tastes too salty, a piece of raw potato placed in a pot will absorb the salt.

Bean And Bacon Soup

6-8 servings

1	pound dried navy beans	2	medium onions, finely chopped
6	cups water		
2	teaspoons salt *or* to taste	1	small green bell pepper, finely chopped
¼	teaspoon pepper *or* to taste		
2	garlic cloves, minced	½	cup finely chopped carrots
1	bay leaf	1	(8-ounce) can tomato sauce
4	slices bacon	1	teaspoon minced fresh parsley

Sort and wash beans; place in a large Dutch oven. Cover with 2-inches water above beans; soak overnight. Drain beans and add 6 cups water. Add salt, pepper, garlic and bay leaf. Cook bacon until crisp; remove bacon, reserve drippings. Crumble bacon and set aside. Add onion and green pepper to drippings; sauté until tender. Drain to remove excess fat. Add onions, green pepper and carrots to beans. Bring to a boil. Reduce heat, cover and simmer 1 hour. Add tomato sauce and parsley to soup. Cover and simmer an additional 30 minutes or until tender. Ladle into serving bowls and garnish with crumbled bacon.

Easy and delicious!

Regina O. Scruggs

Broccoli Cheese Soup

10-12 servings

¾	cup chopped onion	2	(10-ounce) packages frozen chopped broccoli
1	tablespoon butter *or* margarine		
		¼	teaspoon garlic powder
6	cups water	6	cups milk
6	chicken bouillon cubes	1	pound pasteurized process cheese, cubed
1	(8-ounce) package fine egg noodles		pepper to taste
1	teaspoon salt		

In a Dutch oven, sauté onion in butter. Add water and bouillon cubes. Bring to a boil and gradually add noodles and salt. Cook uncovered for 3 minutes. Stir in broccoli and garlic powder. Cook for an additional 3 minutes and stir in milk. Add cheese and pepper and stir until cheese is melted.

Variation: Use 2 tablespoons salad oil instead of butter, ⅛ teaspoon garlic powder; add ⅛ teaspoon seasoned salt.

A hearty and nourishing soup that is made in minutes.

Rochelle Mistretta
Beverly Jordan

Janey's Cheese Soup

6-8 servings

¼	cup butter	4	cups chicken broth
½	cup finely chopped celery	2	cups pasteurized processed
¼	cup finely chopped onions		cheese, cubed *or*
½	cup chopped carrots		American cheese,
½	cup diced potatoes		cubed
¼	cup all-purpose flour		salt and pepper to taste

In a Dutch oven, melt butter and sauté celery, onions and carrots. Add potatoes and cook until tender. Add flour and stir until smooth. Gradually add broth, then cheese and stir until well blended and cheese is melted. Salt and pepper to taste.

A rich and delicious soup that is made in minutes.

Jane Reynolds

Corn And Crabmeat Soup

4-6 servings

1	cup fresh yellow corn (canned or frozen corn can be used)	2	cups half-and-half
		1	pound lump crabmeat
			salt and pepper to taste
¼	cup butter	⅛	teaspoon garlic powder *or*
¼	cup all-purpose flour		to taste
2	cups chicken stock		

Cut fresh corn from cob; saving scrapings and milk. Set aside. Melt butter in saucepan. Add flour and blend well. Add chicken stock, stirring constantly. Cook until thick and smooth. Stir in cream, crabmeat, corn, corn scrapings and seasonings. Cook over low heat until corn is tender.

Very rich and elegant tasting. Great for special occasions.

Angela Collins

The secret of good cooking is in the seasoning.

Exquisite French Onion Soup

8 servings

5	cups thinly sliced yellow onions (1½ pounds)	3	(10¾-ounce) cans condensed beef bouillon
3	tablespoons butter *or* margarine	3	cups boiling water
1	tablespoon vegetable oil	½	cup dry white wine
1	teaspoon salt		salt and pepper to taste
¼	teaspoon sugar	3	ounces Swiss *or* mozzarella cheese, cut in thin slivers
3	tablespoons all-purpose flour	1	cup croutons

Cook onions slowly with butter and oil in heavy, covered 4-quart saucepan for 15 minutes. Stir in salt and sugar; raise heat to medium, cook uncovered 35-40 minutes, stirring often, until onions are a deep golden brown. Sprinkle with flour; stir 3 minutes. Remove from heat; add bouillon and boiling water. Blend well. Add wine, season to taste. Simmer partly covered, about 35 minutes longer. Pour soup into individual bowls. Sprinkle cheese and croutons on top. Freezes well.

Though the preparation takes time and care, the hearty aroma and wonderful flavor of this soup make it worth the effort.

Sue Burnett

Mushroom Cream Soup

4 servings

½	pound fresh mushrooms, sliced	1	tablespoon all-purpose flour
1	cup chopped fresh parsley	1¾	cups beef broth
1	medium onion, chopped	1	cup sour cream
¼	cup butter, melted		parsley sprigs

Sauté mushrooms, parsley and onion in butter, stirring until tender. Stir in flour. Remove from heat and blend in broth. Bring to a boil, stirring constantly. Blend mixture, in portions, in a blender or food processor with sour cream until smooth. Reheat gently. Garnish with parsley sprigs.

Nancy Barnwell

Easy Vegetable Soup

6-8 servings

1	pound ground beef *or* ground turkey	1	(20-ounce) package frozen mixed vegetables
3	(14½-ounce) cans chicken broth	1	(14½-ounce) can stewed tomatoes
4	cups water	1	teaspoon Worcestershire sauce
1	envelope dry onion soup mix		salt and pepper to taste
2	celery stalks, chopped	½	cup dry macaroni
			Parmesan cheese (optional)

In a Dutch oven, brown ground beef and drain well. Add chicken broth, water, onion soup and celery. Bring to a boil, lower heat and simmer for 20 minutes. Add frozen vegetables, stewed tomatoes, Worcestershire sauce, salt and pepper. Cook for 15 minutes. Add macaroni and boil for 10 minutes. Serve immediately. If desired, sprinkle with Parmesan cheese.

Maurine Vihlen

Beef And Vegetable Soup

10-12 servings

4	pounds soup bones	4	celery stalks, chopped
1	pound stew beef	¼	cup rice *or* barley
1	gallon water	6	medium potatoes, peeled and cut in 1-inch cubes
4	cups tomato juice		
2	(16-ounce) cans tomatoes, undrained	1	to 2 tablespoons salt
2	(16-ounce) cans mixed vegetables *or* frozen packages	1	tablespoon pepper
		1	to 2 tablespoons chili pepper
2	large onions, chopped	2	to 4 cups shredded cabbage (optional)
5	carrots, sliced		

In large soup pot, cook soup bones and stew beef for 3 hours in 1 gallon of water. Remove meat; cut in bite-size pieces and discard bones. Strain and degrease broth. Return meat to broth and add all other ingredients, except potatoes. Simmer on low heat for 2 hours. Add potatoes and simmer another hour.

Pauline Cychowski

K. C. Steak Soup

10-12 servings

¾ cup margarine *or* butter
1 cup all-purpose flour
2 cups water
2 pounds lean ground chuck
   or round
1 cup diced onions
1 cup diced carrots
1 cup diced celery
1½ cups water
1 (10-ounce) package frozen
   mixed vegetables

1 (10-ounce) package frozen
   corn
2 quarts chopped tomatoes
   or 3 (14½-ounce)
   cans stewed tomatoes
2 teaspoons garlic powder
2 plus tablespoons Kitchen
   Bouquet *or* bovril
   salt and pepper to taste

In large stockpot, melt butter and add flour to make a paste. Gradually stir in 2 cups water. In a skillet, brown meat and drain well. Add meat to stockpot. In saucepan, add onions, carrots and celery with 1½ cups water. Bring to a boil and boil 10 minutes. Add boiled vegetables and remaining water to stockpot. Add frozen vegetables and tomatoes; stir to mix and break up tomato chunks. Add garlic powder and enough of the Kitchen Bouquet or bovril to make soup rich brown in color. Salt and pepper to taste. Simmer covered for 2-3 hours. Freezes well.

This recipe has been tried and changed until it has become a favorite of family and friends. Great served with cornbread.

Rosalie A. Johnson

Cream Of Potato Leek Soup

12-16 servings

2 large leeks, chopped (white
   part only)
½ cup minced onion
½ cup butter
2 teaspoons all-purpose flour

8 cups chicken broth
4 cups peeled, diced potatoes
1 cup heavy cream
   salt and pepper to taste ·
   chopped chives

Sauté leeks and onion in butter until translucent, do not brown. Gradually stir in flour to make a roux. Stir in chicken broth and add potatoes. Boil until potatoes are tender. Cool mixture and then process in blender until smooth. Add cream and heat through, do not boil. Salt and pepper to taste. Add chopped chives for garnish.

Delicious and elegant. Best if made the day before.

Judith W. Jones

Soups

Easy Tortilla Soup

10-12 servings

1½	pounds ground chuck	1	(10¾-ounce) can cream of potato soup
1	small onion, chopped	1	(1¼-ounce) package taco seasoning mix
1	(15-ounce) can red kidney beans	2	(16-ounce) cans Mexican tomatoes, chopped
1	(10¾-ounce) can cream of celery soup	1	(8-ounce) can tomato sauce

Toppings:
shredded Cheddar cheese   salsa *or* sour cream
crushed corn chips

In a large Dutch oven, brown meat with onion. Drain well. Add remaining ingredients and blend. Simmer 1 hour and serve with your choice of toppings. *Note:* For a spicier flavored soup, use hot red kidney beans and hot taco seasoning mix.

A very tasty and fun dish.

Rosalie A. Johnson

Wonton Soup

4 servings

7½	cups chicken broth	2	cups cubed cooked chicken *or* turkey
4	ounces extra wide egg noodles	⅛	teaspoon salt
1	tablespoon soy sauce		pepper to taste
1	tablespoon sesame oil	5	ounces fresh spinach, stemmed and torn into pieces (about 2½ cups packed)
1	(8-ounce) can sliced bamboo shoots, drained	4	green onions, sliced

In a Dutch oven, bring broth to a boil. Add noodles and boil 6 minutes or just until tender. Add soy sauce, sesame oil, bamboo shoots and chicken. Salt and pepper to taste. Cook over medium heat until heated through, about 2 minutes. Add spinach and green onions and serve immediately.

A quick and easy meal that is also light and luscious! Your kids will love it and guests will be impressed!

Geneva Guerrette
Madawaska, Maine

Italian Sausage Soup With Tortellini

8-10 servings

1	pound hot *or* mild Italian sausage	1	tablespoon chopped fresh fennel *or* 1 teaspoon fennel seeds
1	garlic clove, minced	½	teaspoon salt
1	large onion, chopped	½	teaspoon ground black pepper
4	(14½-ounce) cans tomatoes, undrained and chopped	1	(9-ounce) package tortellini
2	cups water		

Remove sausage casing; crumble in large Dutch oven. Add garlic and onion; cook until meat is browned. Drain well. Add tomatoes and next 4 ingredients. Cover and simmer 15 minutes. Cook tortellini in boiling water until slightly less than done or ten minutes less than package directions. Drain and add to soup. Cover and simmer 10-15 minutes. *Note:* For added color, use half package spinach tortellini with half package regular.

Very tasty, a real hit!

Nicki Knight

Wild Rice Soup

10-12 servings

1½	to 2 cups wild rice	2	teaspoons garlic salt
¼	cup butter	2	bay leaves
4	large celery stalks, diced	½	teaspoon crushed thyme leaves
2	large carrots, diced	8	cups chicken broth
1	small onion, diced	3	to 4 cups cooked and diced chicken breasts *or* stir-fried
1	small red onion, diced		
½	cup sliced green onions		
1	(2-ounce) jar diced pimiento, drained	3	to 4 cups sliced fresh mushrooms
1	to 1½ teaspoons dill weed		toasted almonds
½	to ¾ teaspoon pepper		
½	teaspoon salt		

Soak wild rice overnight in water. Drain. In large skillet, melt butter; add celery, carrots, onions and pimiento. Cook until slightly softened, about 5 minutes. Add seasonings to vegetables. In a large Dutch oven, bring broth and rice to a boil; reduce heat and add cooked vegetables. Simmer 45-60 minutes. Meanwhile, stir-fry chicken in small amount of vegetable oil, about 10 minutes. Remove from pan. Stir-fry mushrooms about 5 minutes. Add chicken and mushrooms to soup, heat gently, do not boil. Discard bay leaves and serve immediately. Garnish individual soup bowls with toasted almonds.

A Michigan favorite!

Peg Kottke

Hearty Wild Rice Chowder

6-8 servings

¾ cup wild rice, rinsed
1½ cups water
½ cup chopped onion
2 garlic cloves, minced
2 tablespoons margarine
4 cups water
4 chicken bouillon cubes
2 (10¾-ounce) cans cream of potato soup
1 large potato, cubed
1 cup sliced carrots
½ teaspoon thyme leaves
½ teaspoon nutmeg
⅛ teaspoon pepper
1 bay leaf
1 (15-ounce) can whole corn, undrained
3 cups cubed ham
2 cups half-and-half
2 tablespoons parsley sprigs

In medium saucepan, combine wild rice and water. Bring to a boil. Reduce heat and simmer 45 minutes. Do not drain. In a Dutch oven, sauté onion and garlic in margarine. Gradually add 4 cups water and bouillon cubes, stirring until cubes are dissolved. Add rice, cans of soup, potato, carrots, thyme, nutmeg, pepper and bay leaf. Cover and simmer 30 minutes. Add corn, ham, half-and-half and simmer for a few minutes to heat through. Remove bay leaf and garnish with parsley sprigs.

A wonderfully flavored chowder. The nutmeg makes it unique.

Kathy Larson

Easy Clam Chowder

8-10 servings

3 (10¾-ounce) cans cream of potato soup
2 (10¾-ounce) cans New England style clam chowder soup
2 (6½-ounce) cans minced clams, drained
3 tablespoons margarine
½ cup chopped onion
2 cups half-and-half
2 cups milk
¼ teaspoon minced garlic
¼ teaspoon white pepper
bacon, cooked crisp and crumbled (optional)

Put all the ingredients in a 5-quart crockpot and mix well. Set temperature on low and allow to simmer 4-5 hours. Garnish individual servings with crumbled bacon.

Excellent served with a salad and crusty bread.

Nicki Knight

Mobile Bay Gumbo

10-12 servings

1⅓	cups all-purpose flour	1	cup ketchup
⅔	cup bacon fat	2	pounds okra, chopped
4	celery stalks, chopped	1	dozen raw crabs, cleaned
1	garlic clove, minced	1	pound lump crabmeat (use
2	large onions, chopped		crab body or claws if
3	quarts boiling water		available)
2	(16-ounce) cans tomatoes,	2	pounds shrimp, shelled
	chopped		and deveined
	salt to taste	1	tablespoon gumbo filé
	Worcestershire to taste		cooked rice
	Tabasco® sauce to taste		

Make a roux by browning flour in fat very slowly until it is dark brown. Do not burn or allow to stick. Stir constantly and cook slowly. (Refer to **Roux** recipe for instructions.) Add celery, garlic and onions. Simmer for 30 minutes. Add roux to boiling water. Stir until smooth. Add tomatoes and seasonings to taste. Add ketchup. Cook slowly for 3 hours. Add okra. Cook 15 minutes. Add crabs, crabmeat and shrimp. Cook for 30 minutes. Remove from heat and stir in filé. Serve over hot rice.

Takes time to make but very well worth the effort.

Shona Moore

Roux

oil	chopped onions (if called
flour	for in your recipe)

Use equal amounts of flour and oil unless your recipe specifies different quantities. In a heavy pan add oil, keeping heat low to medium, and stir in flour. Stir, stir, stir, constantly stirring flour and oil to prevent burning until mixture becomes golden, medium golden or deep brown; whatever your recipe calls for. A good roux takes 15-30 minutes to make. If your recipe calls for onions, now is when they are added, cooking them until they are clear. Continue with your recipe. ***Note:*** If you burn your roux or if there is the slightest indication of over-browning, throw it away and start over. Otherwise, your recipe will be ruined. Remember, you must make Roux slowly.

Roux is needed for many French and Cajun recipes. Go slow and stir constantly. Master these two steps and success is yours. Bon Appetit!

S. Kay Clifton

Wild Rice and Mushroom Soup

4-6 servings

1	medium carrot, grated	1	cup half-and-half
1	teaspoon minced onion	1	pound fresh mushrooms,
1	celery stalk, minced		sliced
6	tablespoons butter, melted	1	cup chopped cooked
½	cup all-purpose flour		chicken, turkey *or*
3	cups chicken broth		shrimp
2	cups cooked wild rice		

In a skillet, sauté carrot, onion and celery in butter. Blend in flour, stirring constantly. Gradually stir in broth to avoid lumps. Slowly bring to a boil, stirring often. Boil 1 minute. Stir in cooked rice, half-and-half and mushrooms, reserving some mushroom slices for garnish. Simmer for 5 minutes. Add choice of poultry or seafood. Garnish with reserved mushroom slices arranged in a flower petal fashion and add fresh parsley sprigs.

Wonderful cold weather supper.

Sarah W. D'Addabbo

Hamburg-Vegetable Soup

6-8 servings

1	pound ground beef	¼	teaspoon pepper
1	large onion, chopped	1	(16-ounce) can French-
2	garlic cloves, minced		style green beans,
5	cups water		drained
3	carrots, chopped	2	(14½-ounce) cans stewed
½	cup long grain rice		tomatoes
3	tablespoons instant		
	chicken bouillon		

In a Dutch oven, cook ground beef, onion and garlic until beef is cooked through; stirring often to break up meat. Drain well. Add 5 cups water, carrots, rice, chicken bouillon and pepper. Bring to a boil, cover and simmer for 20-25 minutes or until carrots and rice are tender. Add green beans and stewed tomatoes, breaking up tomatoes with a spoon. If desired, process tomatoes in blender before adding to soup. Heat through and serve.

A hearty and totally satisfying soup. You will want to make this quick and easy soup often.

Angela McBriairty
Fort Kent, Maine

Salads and Dressings

Blueberry Salad

8 servings

2	(3-ounce) packages grape gelatin	1	(20-ounce) can crushed pineapple, undrained
2	cups boiling water	1	(21-ounce) can blueberry pie filling

Topping:

1	(8-ounce) package cream cheese, softened	½	cup sugar
1	(8-ounce) carton sour cream	4	teaspoons vanilla chopped pecans

Dissolve gelatin in boiling water. Add pineapple and pie filling. Pour into a 9x13-inch glass pan and chill until firm. For topping, combine together cream cheese, sour cream, sugar and vanilla. Beat until smooth. Spread over firm gelatin and sprinkle with chopped pecans.

The visual appeal and taste of blueberries makes this salad unique.

Mary Frances Newcomer

Frozen Cranberry Salad

12 servings

1	(16-ounce) can whole cranberry sauce	1	(8-ounce) container frozen whipped topping, thawed
1	(14-ounce) can sweetened condensed milk	1	(8-ounce) can crushed pineapple, drained
		1	cup chopped pecans

Line muffin pan with 12 paper cups. Combine all ingredients in a bowl and mix well. Spoon mixture into muffin cups and freeze. Cover with foil. Remove as needed.

Great for surprise company, snacks for kids, buffet table, etc.

Eva M. Edwards

Cranberry Salad Mold

12-14 servings

2 (3-ounce) packages cherry gelatin	2 medium oranges
2½ cups boiling water	2 cups sugar
2 cups fresh cranberries	1 cup finely chopped celery
3 medium apples	1 cup finely chopped nuts (optional)

Dissolve gelatin in boiling water. In food processor, grind cranberries, unpeeled apples, one unpeeled orange and one peeled orange. Add ground fruits, sugar, celery and nuts to gelatin. Mix well and pour into gelatin mold. Refrigerate until set.

Peg Kottke

Loretta's Pear Salad

8-10 servings

1 (16-ounce) can pears	1 (8-ounce) package cream
1 (3-ounce) package lime	cheese, softened
gelatin	4½ ounces frozen whipped
	topping, thawed

Drain pears and add water to juice to make 1¼ cups liquid. Boil liquid, add gelatin and stir until dissolved. Blend together cream cheese, whipped topping and pears in blender. Add liquid gelatin to blender and process until mixture is well blended. Pour into a 2-quart mold. Refrigerate until firm.

A delicious salad you will want to serve again and again. Also delicious substituting a 16-ounce can of peaches and a 3-ounce package of strawberry gelatin for pears and lime gelatin.

Phyllis Schwarzmann

Buy a bunch of parsley and wash, chop and freeze for future use.

Strawberry Gelatin Salad

8-10 servings

2	(3-ounce) packages strawberry gelatin	1	(8-ounce) can crushed pineapple, undrained
2	cups boiling water	2	large ripe bananas, sliced
1	(10-ounce) package frozen sliced strawberries	1½	to 2 cups sour cream

Dissolve gelatin in boiling water. Add berries, stirring occasionally until thawed. Add pineapple with juice and bananas. Pour half of mixture (about 2½ cups) into a 7x11-inch dish. Chill until firm. Spoon sour cream evenly over chilled gelatin. Pour remaining gelatin over sour cream. Chill until firm. To serve, cut into squares.

Variation: Use 1 (15½-ounce) can crushed pineapple, 1 banana, 1 cup sour cream and 9x9-inch dish.

Mary Fehse
Liz Gano

Favorite Fruit Salad

12-14 servings

3	tablespoons lemon juice	1	(11-ounce) can mandarin oranges, drained
2	(20-ounce) cans unsweetened pineapple chunks, drain and reserve juice	1	cup halved seedless white *or* red grapes
1	(3.4-ounce) vanilla pudding (not instant)	4	bananas, sliced ¼-inch thick
		¼	cup quartered maraschino cherries, drained (optional)

Pour lemon juice in a 2-cup measure and add reserved pineapple juice to make 1½ cups. Combine juice and pudding and cook according to package directions. Cool to room temperature. Combine all fruit in a large bowl, pour pudding over fruit and refrigerate. *Note:* Sugar-free pudding can be substituted.

This colorful salad keeps well for 2-3 days and bananas do not darken.

Betty Curp

Lemon-Lime Salad

6-8 servings

1	(3-ounce) package lemon gelatin	1	teaspoon sugar
1	cup boiling water	1	teaspoon vanilla
1	(8-ounce) package cream cheese, softened	½	cup chopped walnuts
1	(8-ounce) can crushed pineapple, undrained	2	to 3 drops green food coloring
		1	(8-ounce) can lemon-lime carbonated drink

Dissolve gelatin in boiling water. With mixer, beat cream cheese with dissolved gelatin until smooth. Stir in pineapple, sugar, vanilla and walnuts to mixture. Add green food coloring and then the lemon-lime carbonated drink. This must be the last ingredient added. Pour into a 4-cup gelatin mold. Chill until firm, about 5 hours.

Tip On Unmolding Gelatin:

Before unmolding gelatin, turn knife tip around top edge of mold to loosen. Working quickly, dip mold just to rim in warm water for about 10 seconds. Do not use hot water as it will melt the gelatin. Lift from water, hold upright, and shake gently to loosen gelatin. Place a cold moistened serving plate on top of mold and invert mold and plate together, gently removing mold. If gelatin does not release easily, dip the mold in warm water again.

Mary Fehse

Asparagus With Vinaigrette

4-6 servings

2	pounds asparagus	1½	teaspoons fresh lemon juice
1	teaspoon minced garlic		
½	teaspoon salt	4	tablespoons sesame oil
½	teaspoon white pepper	1	tablespoon sesame seeds, toasted
2	teaspoons Dijon mustard		

Cut off tough lower ends of asparagus spears and discard. Steam asparagus until tender. Drain and run under cold water. Dry thoroughly. Set aside. Blend next 6 ingredients in a blender. Pour over asparagus. Sprinkle with toasted sesame seeds. Can be served at room temperature or cold.

Nancy Barnwell

Broccoli Salad

6-8 servings

1	bunch broccoli, cut in small pieces	¼	cup sugar
6	green onions, chopped	2	tablespoons vinegar
½	cup white raisins	8	to 10 slices bacon, cooked crisp and crumbled
1	cup mayonnaise		

In a large bowl, combine broccoli, onions and raisins together. Mix mayonnaise, sugar and vinegar together and add to salad ingredients. Chill several hours. Add bacon when ready to serve.

Variation 1: Use ½ red onion, chopped, 1 cup raisins, ⅓ cup sugar, 3-4 tablespoons vinegar, omit bacon and add 1 cup dry roasted peanuts.

Variation 2: Use 2 bunches broccoli, flowerets only, ½ red onion, chopped, 1 cup raisins, ⅓ cup sugar, 12 slices bacon and add 1 cup sunflower seeds.

Variation 3: Use flowerets only, omit raisins, use ½ cup mayonnaise, ⅓ cup sugar, 1 teaspoon vinegar, 4-5 slices bacon, add 8 ounces fresh sliced mushrooms and 2 cups shredded Cheddar cheese.

Lyn Edler
Charlotte Sharpe
D. J. Kopriva
Florence Powell

Broccoli And Cauliflower Salad

6-8 servings

1	cup mayonnaise	1	head cauliflower
¼	to ½ cup chopped onion	½	cup yellow raisins
¼	cup sugar		imitation bacon pieces to taste
2	tablespoons cider vinegar		
1	bunch broccoli		

Combine first 4 dressing ingredients together and refrigerate 6-12 hours. Cut broccoli and cauliflower into flowerets. Pour dressing over vegetables 1 hour before serving. Add raisins and bacon just before serving.

Variation: Use 1 tablespoon minced dry onion, ½ cup sugar, 1 cup raisins; add 1 (8-ounce) can sliced water chestnuts, drained; omit bacon pieces. Mix dressing ingredients and toss with vegetables. Refrigerate 4 hours before serving.

Agatha LaPaglia
Karen Breunig

North African Carrot Salad

8-10 servings

2	garlic cloves, unpeeled	2	tablespoons fresh lemon juice
1	pound carrots, peeled and julienned	1	tablespoon oil
1	scallion, minced	½	teaspoon ground cumin
2	tablespoons fresh dill *or* 2 teaspoons dried	¼	teaspoon paprika
2	tablespoons minced fresh parsley		pinch cinnamon
			pinch cayenne pepper

In a steamer, boil 1-inch water and add garlic to water. Steam carrots until crisp tender. Remove garlic. Put carrots in a large bowl with scallion, dill and parsley. Peel and mash garlic into a paste. Combine with lemon juice, oil and remaining seasonings. Pour over hot carrots. Refrigerate overnight.

Great side dish for any entrée.

Sarah W. D'Addabbo

Corn Salad

6-8 servings

1	(17-ounce) can whole kernel corn, drained	¼	cup finely chopped green *or* red bell pepper
1	cup finely chopped celery		mayonnaise to bind
¼	cup finely chopped onion		salt and pepper to taste

Combine all ingredients. Chill and serve. *Note:* Do not use more than ¼ cup onions as it will overpower this salad.

A quick, easy, colorful and delicious salad!

Judith W. Jones

Cottage cheese will keep twice as long if stored upside down.

Red & Green Christmas Salad
With Warm Champagne Vinegar Dressing

8 servings

10	cups torn spinach leaves	seeds of 1 pomegranate
1	medium avocado, thinly sliced	

Place spinach leaves in a large salad bowl and arrange avocado slices in a circle around the edge of salad. Place pomegranate seeds in the center. Pour 1 cup of the warm dressing over salad. At the table, toss and serve.

Dressing:

1	cup champagne vinegar	1	egg, beaten
2	tablespoons sugar	3	tablespoons whipping cream
1½	tablespoons all-purpose flour	2	cups olive oil
2	teaspoons dry vermouth		salt and pepper
1	teaspoon Dijon mustard		

Combine vinegar, sugar, flour, vermouth and mustard in saucepan. Heat over medium heat until thickened. Gradually whisk in egg and cream over low heat. Do not boil. Whisk in the oil in a thin stream. Season with salt and pepper to taste.

A festive holiday salad with eye appeal.

Vicki Sherrard

Alice B's Strawberry Salad

8 servings

1	head romaine lettuce (no substitute)	½	red onion, thinly sliced
		2	cups sliced strawberries

Dressing:

1	cup mayonnaise (no substitute)	2	tablespoons lemon juice
1	tablespoon poppy seeds	4	tablespoons sugar

Tear lettuce into pieces. Add sliced onion and strawberries. Toss. Combine all dressing ingredients, mix well and refrigerate. Just before serving, pour over salad and toss to mix. You can add more strawberries, if desired.

The combination of luscious strawberries and sweet onion add pizzazz to this wonderful salad.

Virginia Schoenster

Warm Spinach Salad

4-6 servings

1 package fresh spinach
or 2 large bunches,
stemmed

2 hard-cooked eggs,
chopped

1 bunch green onions, thinly
sliced

8 ounces mushrooms, sliced

6 ounces bacon, cooked crisp
and crumbled

Dressing:

1 cup vegetable oil
¾ cup sugar
⅓ cup ketchup
¼ cup vinegar

2 tablespoons
Worcestershire sauce
salt to taste

Tear spinach leaves in bite-size pieces. Place in salad bowl. Top with eggs, onions, mushrooms and crumbled bacon. Combine all dressing ingredients in a medium saucepan and cook until just starting to boil. Spoon over salad, toss and serve immediately.

This warm salad is wonderful served as the main luncheon entrée with a loaf of French bread.

Barbara Morphy

Spinach Salad
With White Wine Vinegar Dressing

10-12 servings

Dressing:

¼ cup white wine vinegar
¼ cup lemon juice
1 cup salad oil
2 teaspoons salt

½ teaspoon pepper
2 teaspoons sugar
1 teaspoon dry mustard
2 garlic cloves, whole

Mix all ingredients together and refrigerate overnight. Remove garlic before serving.

Salad:

2 bunches fresh young
spinach (8 cups)

1 pound bacon, cooked crisp
and crumbled

2 hard-cooked eggs, chopped
1 cup sliced fresh
mushrooms

Remove stems from spinach and tear into pieces. Add remaining ingredients to salad. Before serving, pour dressing and toss lightly. *Note:* Sliced red onions, mandarin orange sections or sliced water chestnuts can be added.

Anne Dorn

95

Spinach Strawberry Salad With Nuts And Mushrooms

6-8 servings

Dressing:

⅓	cup red wine vinegar	1	teaspoon dry mustard
½	cup sugar	2	tablespoons water
1	cup salad oil	¼	cup chopped onion
1	teaspoon salt		

Put all dressing ingredients in blender and blend until smooth. Refrigerate until well chilled.

Salad:

1	bunch spinach, stemmed and torn in bite-size pieces	1	pint fresh strawberries, hulled and sliced*
½	cup coarsely chopped pecans *or* walnuts	12	fresh mushrooms, sliced

Prepare spinach and chill. When ready to serve, add nuts, strawberries and mushrooms. Toss with dressing and serve. *Drained mandarin oranges can be substituted for strawberries.

Only one word to describe this salad, "sensational"!

Patricia Freeman

Pea Pod Salad

4-6 servings

2	(10-ounce) boxes frozen pea pods, thawed	1	red onion, sliced
8	ounces fresh mushrooms, sliced	1	envelope Italian dressing, mixed according to package directions
2	(1-pint) containers cherry tomatoes, halved		Parmesan cheese

Mix first four ingredients in a large glass bowl. Add Italian dressing to taste. Sprinkle with Parmesan cheese.

A very colorful and tasty salad.

Jane Reynolds

Strawberry-Spinach Salad

8-10 servings

2	pounds fresh spinach, stemmed and torn in bite-size pieces	2	teaspoons sesame seeds, toasted
2	tablespoons fresh dill *or* 1 teaspoon dried dill weed	2	pints strawberries, hulled

Dressing:

1	cup salad oil (not olive oil)	½	teaspoon onion powder
½	cup red wine vinegar	½	teaspoon salt
½	cup sugar (scant)	½	teaspoon pepper
½	teaspoon garlic powder	½	teaspoon dry mustard

Place spinach in large bowl. Sprinkle with dill and sesame seeds. If strawberries are large, cut in half. Add to spinach. Combine all dressing ingredients in a jar with cover, shaking to blend. Pour over salad and toss. Refrigerate salad with dressing for 30-60 minutes before serving.

Absolutely wonderful both in taste and color.

Pat Marr

Mandarin Salad

4-6 servings

¼	cup sliced almonds	1	cup chopped celery
4	teaspoons sugar	2	green onions, sliced
¼	head iceberg lettuce	1	(11-ounce) can mandarin oranges, drained
¼	head romaine lettuce		

Cook almonds and sugar over low heat, stirring constantly, until sugar is melted and almonds are coated. Spoon onto wax paper and let cool. Once cooled, break almonds apart and set aside. Tear lettuce into bite-size pieces. Place in salad bowl with celery, onions and orange segments. When ready to serve, toss with dressing and top with almonds.

Dressing:

¼	cup salad oil	½	teaspoon salt
2	tablespoons vinegar		dash pepper
2	tablespoons sugar		dash hot pepper sauce
1	tablespoon snipped parsley		

Combine all dressing ingredients in a lidded jar and shake to mix. Pour dressing over greens, toss to coat.

Excellent salad and wonderful with poultry.

Mary Beth Harja

Overnight Layered Green Salad

8-12 servings

1	large head iceberg lettuce, shredded	1	cup thinly sliced celery
½	cup thinly sliced green onions	2	cups mayonnaise
		2	tablespoons sugar
1	(8-ounce) can sliced water chestnuts, drained	1	teaspoon seasoned salt
		1	cup grated Cheddar cheese
1	(10-ounce) package frozen green peas, thawed	1	cup cooked crisp and crumbled bacon
		3	hard-cooked eggs, chopped

Layer the first 9 ingredients, in the order given, into a 9x13-inch glass dish. Cover tightly with plastic wrap and chill overnight. Just before serving, sprinkle bacon and eggs on top.

Variation: Layer shredded lettuce in bottom of large bowl, add dash salt to lettuce. Use 1¾ cups mayonnaise and mix with 2 tablespoons prepared mustard; spread over layered vegetables and sprinkle top with 1 tablespoon sugar. Omit seasoned salt, Cheddar cheese, bacon and eggs. Toss before serving.

Great for buffets. Salad will keep 2 to 3 days in refrigerator.

Anita Leathers
Mary Fehse

Fresh Mushroom Salad

6-8 servings

½	cup salad oil	1	tablespoon finely chopped green bell pepper (optional)
¼	cup vinegar		
¼	cup sliced green onions		
1	teaspoon salt	½	pound fresh mushrooms, trimmed and sliced
¼	cup snipped parsley		
1	teaspoon sugar	1	head romaine lettuce, washed and chilled
1	teaspoon dry mustard		
⅛	teaspoon red pepper	1	head iceberg lettuce, washed and chilled

Shake first 9 ingredients for dressing in a tightly covered jar and refrigerate until well chilled. Shake again before using. About 40 minutes before serving, add mushrooms to dressing. Line large salad bowl with romaine leaves. Tear remaining romaine and iceberg lettuce into bite-size pieces. Pour dressing with mushrooms over greens and toss.

An attractive salad and just as good as it looks.

Patricia Freeman

Marinated Vegetable Salad

16 servings

1½	cups red wine vinegar	¼	pound fresh green beans
1½	cups water	2	green bell peppers
½	cup vegetable oil	1½	bunches green onions
2	tablespoons sugar	2	(4-ounce) cans pitted ripe
4	garlic cloves, minced		olives, drained
1	large head cauliflower	2	(8¾-ounce) cans garbanzo
4	celery stalks		beans, drained
4	large carrots		

Combine first 5 ingredients for dressing and set aside. Separate cauliflower into small flowerets. Cut celery, carrots and green beans into 1-inch diagonal pieces. Cut green peppers into 1-inch pieces. Place cauliflower, celery, carrots, green beans and green peppers in a 6-quart saucepan. Pour prepared dressing over vegetables and stir. Cover and simmer over moderate heat 5-6 minutes. Cut green onions into 1-inch diagonal pieces. Stir green onions, olives and garbanzo beans into vegetables. Simmer 3 minutes longer. Place in a large bowl. Cover and refrigerate overnight. Can be refrigerated up to 2 weeks.

Include this zesty and colorful salad for your next cookout or block party.

Pat O'Brien

Creamy Vegetable Salad

10-12 servings

1	head cauliflower, chopped	1	cucumber, peeled and
1	head broccoli, chopped		chopped
1	green bell pepper,	1	medium zucchini, chopped
	chopped	5	ounces frozen peas
1	bunch green onions,		
	chopped		

Marinade:

1	cup mayonnaise-type	1	teaspoon salt
	salad dressing	1	tablespoon sugar
½	cup sour cream	1	tablespoon vinegar

Chop all vegetables except peas into bite-size pieces. In a large bowl, combine all vegetables and set aside. Combine all marinade ingredients and pour over vegetables. Mix well and refrigerate. Will keep up to one week.

Peg Kottke

Fire And Ice Tomatoes

6	ripe tomatoes, peeled and quartered	¼	cup cold water
1	large green bell pepper, thinly sliced	1½	teaspoons celery seed
		1½	teaspoons mustard seed
1	large onion, thinly sliced and separated	4	teaspoons sugar
		1	teaspoon salt
¾	cup vinegar	¼	to ½ teaspoon pepper

Prepare vegetables and arrange in a large, but not deep, bowl. Combine remaining ingredients in a saucepan. Heat and boil for 1 minute. Pour boiling liquid over vegetables. Cover and chill overnight. *Note:* Should be prepared a day in advance for flavors to marry. Keeps well for a week.

Great with fresh crusty bread.

Sarah W. D'Addabbo

Tomato Aspic

10-12 servings

1	(12-ounce) can tomato juice	2	dashes Tabasco® sauce
		2	celery stalks with tops
1	(10½-ounce) can beef bouillon	1	medium onion, chopped
		2	envelopes unflavored gelatin
1	tablespoon Worcestershire sauce		
		½	cup cold water
1	tablespoon salt		juice of 1 lemon

Simmer tomato juice, bouillon, Worcestershire, salt, Tabasco®, celery and onion for 5 minutes. Strain and reserve hot tomato juice. Dissolve gelatin in water for 5 minutes. Add gelatin and lemon juice to hot tomato juice and stir well. Pour into mold or ring. Refrigerate to congeal. *Note:* Chopped raw vegetable, olives, almonds, shrimp, etc. can be added.

This is one of the OLPH choir's favorite treats after the Easter Vigil.

Sue Ciucki

Wild Rice and Orange Salad

8-10 servings

1½ cups wild rice
4½ cups boiling water
3 green onions *or* scallions, sliced with green tops
1 small red onion, thinly sliced

1 (11-ounce) can mandarin oranges, drained
salt and freshly ground pepper to taste

Place wild rice in a sieve and wash under cold running water for 2 minutes. In a heavy saucepan, bring 4½ cups water to a boil. Add rice. Cover and simmer over low heat until rice is cracked and puffy, about 50 to 55 minutes. Drain rice and chill. Place chilled rice in bowl. Add onions, oranges and **Vinaigrette Dressing**. Add salt and pepper to taste. Toss gently and refrigerate until ready to serve.

Vinaigrette Dressing: 2 cups
½ cup red wine vinegar
2 teaspoons Dijon mustard
1½ cups oil

1 teaspoon sugar (optional)
salt and freshly ground pepper to taste

Mix vinegar and mustard in a bowl. Whisk in the oil. Taste for seasoning and add sugar, salt and pepper to taste. If kept in an airtight container, Vinaigrette will stay fresh almost indefinitely in refrigerator.

This unique and attractive salad can be prepared earlier in the day and combined just before serving.

Julie Angle

To ripen green pears, just place 2 or 3 in a brown bag, loosely closed, and store at room temperature out of direct sunlight.

Rice Salad

6 servings

1 (6.8-ounce) package chicken Rice-a-Roni	1 cup mayonnaise
1 teaspoon curry powder	3 green onions, chopped
1 (6-ounce) jar marinated artichokes, drain and reserve marinade	½ green bell pepper, chopped

Cook Rice-a-Roni according to package directions, adding curry. Chop artichokes and set aside. Mix artichoke marinade with mayonnaise, onions and green pepper. In a mixing bowl, stir together Rice-a-Roni, mayonnaise mixture and artichokes. Chill and serve cold.

A good and different summer salad or side dish.

Nancy Dick

Better Than Ever Potato Salad

9 servings

3 to 4 pounds red potatoes, unpeeled	¼ cup sweet pickle relish
½ cup diced onion	1 (2-ounce) jar diced pimiento, drained
½ cup diced celery	¼ cup plain nonfat yogurt
¼ cup chopped sweet red bell pepper	¼ cup reduced calorie mayonnaise
¼ cup chopped green bell pepper	2 tablespoons spicy brown mustard
¼ cup grated carrot	⅛ teaspoon pepper
¼ cup diced dill pickle	⅛ teaspoon red pepper

Wash potatoes and cut into ½-inch cubes; cook in boiling water for 8-10 minutes. Drain and let cool. Combine potatoes and next 8 ingredients; toss gently. Set aside. Combine yogurt and next 4 ingredients. Stir well and pour over potato mixture. Toss gently, cover and chill.

Pat O'Brien

Coleslaw

4 servings

½	cup mayonnaise	½ teaspoon salt
⅓	cup chopped onion	½ teaspoon celery seed
1	tablespoon sugar	3 cups coleslaw
1	tablespoon vinegar	

Mix all ingredients together except coleslaw. Blend well. Stir in coleslaw. Chill 2-3 hours.

Creamy with wonderful flavor. For added color, you may want to add chopped carrots, red bell pepper or radishes.

Maureen Kolb

Italian Coleslaw

12-15 servings

1	head cabbage	¾ cup oil
1	large onion	2 tablespoons celery seed
1	cup sugar	1 tablespoon dry mustard
1	cup vinegar	2 teaspoons salt

Shred cabbage and cut onion into rings. Alternate layers of cabbage and onion rings. Pour 1 cup sugar over top of layers. Put remaining ingredients in pan and bring to a boil. Pour while hot over sugar layer. Refrigerate for 24 hours before serving.

Gerry Darr

When recipe calls for adding raw eggs to hot mixture, begin by adding a small amount of hot mixture to the beaten eggs slowly to avoid curdling.

Crabmeat Salad

1½ cups

½	cup mayonnaise	1	teaspoon horseradish
1	tablespoon minced fresh parsley	1	tablespoon chopped pimiento
1	tablespoon finely chopped capers	1	hard-cooked egg, chopped
		½	teaspoon lemon juice
1	teaspoon dry mustard	1	cup lump crabmeat, cleaned

Mix first 5 ingredients in a medium bowl. Add pimiento, egg and lemon juice; mix gently. Gently mix in crabmeat. Refrigerate at least 1 hour prior to serving. To serve, spoon crabmeat salad on a medium serving plate; arrange hard-cooked egg wedges, ripe olives and tomato wedges around crab salad. Serve with crackers.

A delicious salad to serve on a hot summer day.

Gretchen Mattingly

Chicken Taco Salad

4-6 servings

Dressing:

1	medium ripe avocado, peeled and sliced	1	garlic clove, minced
		½	teaspoon sugar
1	tablespoon lemon juice	½	teaspoon chili powder
½	cup sour cream	¼	teaspoon salt
¼	cup vegetable oil	¼	teaspoon hot pepper sauce

Salad:

½	large head iceberg lettuce, shredded	½	cup sliced black olives
		¼	cup sliced green onions
2	cups cooked cubed chicken	8	slices bacon, cooked crisp and crumbled
1	tomato, seeded and chopped	¾	cup grated Cheddar cheese
		1	cup crushed tortilla chips

Combine all dressing ingredients in a blender and blend until smooth. In a glass bowl, layer the salad ingredients beginning with lettuce and ending with chips. If making in advance, wait until serving time to add chips and dressing. *Note:* The beauty is in the layering so use a glass bowl.

Great served with **3 Pepper Quesadillas**. *This is a yummy salad. All dieters will gladly surrender.*

Rosalie A. Johnson

Luscious Chicken Salad

6-8 servings

2	large golden delicious or York apples, cubed	1/4	cup cream *or* evaporated milk
1	ripe avocado, cubed	1	teaspoon minced onion
2	tablespoons lemon juice	1/4	cup blue cheese, crumbled
1/2	cup mayonnaise	2	cups cubed cooked chicken lettuce leaves

Sprinkle apples and avocado with lemon juice. For dressing, combine mayonnaise with cream and add minced onion. Toss together apples, avocado, cheese and chicken with cream dressing. Serve on lettuce leaves.

A luscious main dish salad to enjoy for a special luncheon.

Fran Batt

Chicken And Pasta Salad

4-6 servings

1/2	pound vermicelli, cooked per package directions and drained	1	cup mayonnaise
1/2	cup Italian dressing salt and pepper to taste	4	teaspoons chopped fresh parsley
3	cups cooked shredded chicken	1/2	cup chopped green onions
1	(6-ounce) jar marinated artichoke hearts, drained and chopped	1	teaspoon oregano
		1	teaspoon basil lemon pepper to taste

Combine cooked vermicelli, Italian dressing, salt and pepper in a container and marinate overnight. Combine remaining ingredients and mix with vermicelli mixture. Chill for a few hours before serving. *Note:* Recipe can be doubled and both pasta and chicken mixtures can be prepared at the same time and mixed together the next day.

Perfect picnic fare!

Rochelle Mistretta

Broccoli Tortellini Salad

6-8 servings

1	(9-ounce) package cheese tortellini	2½	teaspoons chopped fresh basil *or* ¼ teaspoon dried basil
1	cup broccoli flowerets		
½	cup finely chopped parsley	½	teaspoon garlic powder
1	tablespoon chopped pimiento	½	cup prepared Italian dressing
1	(6-ounce) jar marinated artichoke hearts, undrained	5-6	cherry tomatoes, halved sliced ripe olives (optional) grated Parmesan cheese
2	green onions, sliced		(optional)

Cook tortellini according to package directions. Drain. Rinse with cold water. In a large bowl, combine all ingredients except cherry tomatoes, olives and Parmesan cheese. Cover and refrigerate 4-6 hours to blend flavors. Just before serving, add tomatoes, mix lightly. Garnish with olives, sprinkle with Parmesan cheese. Can be made ahead and refrigerated. Add broccoli and tomatoes just before serving to avoid discoloration.

This salad was served as the entrée at our 1991 "Pamper Yourself" Card Party/Luncheon/Fashion Show.

Women's Guild

Spatoni Pasta Salad

10-12 servings

1	(16-ounce) package spaghetti noodles	1	large red onion, chopped
3	cucumbers, chopped	1	(16-ounce) bottle Italian dressing
3	tomatoes, chopped	1	to 2 (2.62-ounce) bottles Salad Supreme Seasoning, *or* to taste
2	to 3 green bell peppers, chopped		

Cook spaghetti according to package directions. Drain and cool. Mix all ingredients together in a large bowl. Best if marinated overnight in refrigerator. Keeps well for several days.

A good pot luck salad for a large crowd.

Jill Gasperini

Tomato, Basil and Pasta Salad

8-10 servings

1 (12-ounce) package tricolor spiral pasta
½ cup extra virgin olive oil
4 tablespoons fresh lemon juice
3 tablespoon red wine vinegar
2 garlic cloves, minced
freshly ground black pepper

¼ cup chopped green bell pepper
¼ cup chopped pimiento
¼ cup grated carrots
¼ cup chopped spinach
½ cup cubed mozzarella cheese
3½ cups diced Italian plum tomatoes
1 cup chopped and firmly packed fresh basil

Cook pasta according to package directions. Drain. Whisk olive oil, lemon juice, vinegar, garlic, and pepper together. Add to pasta and toss. Refrigerate until cool. Add bell pepper, pimiento, carrots, spinach, and cheese. Toss in tomatoes and basil just before serving.

This colorful salad is great for a picnic or barbecue.

Nancy Barnwell

Dijon-Honey Dressing

1¼ cups

1 cup mayonnaise
¼ cup Dijon mustard
¼ cup honey
2 tablespoons vegetable oil

¾ teaspoon cider vinegar
⅛ teaspoon onion salt
⅛ teaspoon red pepper

Combine all ingredients in blender. Process until smooth. Cover and chill thoroughly. Will keep two weeks in refrigerator.

If you like Honey Mustard dressing at restaurants, you'll love this!

Karen Kerschen

Sweet And Sour Salad Dressing

2 cups

1 cup oil	pepper to taste
1 cup sugar	¼ teaspoon dry mustard
1 cup wine vinegar	1 small garlic clove,
½ teaspoon salt	crushed

Combine all ingredients in a glass jar. Shake to mix. Store in the refrigerator.

Especially good on bibb lettuce or a spinach salad.

Karen DouBrava

Dressing For Taco Salad

2 cups

¾ cup sugar	¼ cup taco sauce *or* salsa
¾ cup oil	sauce
½ cup vinegar	½ cup ketchup
2 teaspoons Worcestershire sauce	

Heat first 5 ingredients until sugar dissolves. Add ketchup. Keep in shaker jar or cruet in refrigerator. *Note:* The thickness and spiciness will depend on what kind of taco sauce you use.

Janet Hinrichs

 To keep eggs from cracking during boiling, pierce one end carefully with a pushpin, and ease eggs into simmering water.

Breads and Muffins

Coffee Cake

12 servings

½ cup chopped walnuts	1½ cups sugar
½ cup sugar	1½ teaspoons vanilla
1½ tablespoons unsweetened cocoa powder	4 eggs
	2¼ cups all-purpose flour
1 tablespoon cinnamon	1½ teaspoons baking powder
1 cup butter, softened	¾ cup raisins, dusted in flour
1 (8-ounce) package cream cheese, softened	(optional)

Preheat oven to 325°. Butter a 10-inch tube pan and sprinkle with nuts so that they stick to the pan. Combine ½ cup sugar, cocoa and cinnamon and set aside. Cream butter and cream cheese with sugar and vanilla. Beat well and add eggs one at a time. Stir in flour with baking powder and mix until batter is thick. Add raisins. Put half the batter into pan and sprinkle top with the sugar mixture. Spoon in remaining batter and smooth top evenly with a spoon. Bake 65-75 minutes. Cool 15 minutes, then remove from pan.

A treat even for the non-coffee drinker.

Mary Fehse

Pecan Coffee Cake

12-16 servings

5 cups all-purpose flour	3 eggs
6 tablespoons sugar	1 pound nuts, finely chopped
1 tablespoon salt	
1 package active dry yeast	¾ cup bread crumbs
½ cup margarine	½ cup honey
1½ cups milk	raisins (optional)

In a large bowl, sift together 2 cups flour, sugar, salt and dry yeast. In a saucepan over low heat, melt margarine in milk. Add eggs and milk mixture to flour. Beat with a wooden spoon. Add 3 cups flour, one at a time, beat until firm. Dust top of dough with just a sprinkle of flour. Cover and place in a draft-free area. Let rise until doubled in size. Punch down, divide dough in half, knead in a little bit of flour if dough is too sticky and roll in a rectangular shape to ½-inch thickness. Add nuts and bread crumbs to warm honey. Spread half the nut mixture on dough and sprinkle with raisins. Roll up jelly roll style and place in a greased 9x13-inch pan. Repeat with remaining dough and nut mixture. Cover and let rise until doubled in a draft-free place. Bake at 350° for 45 minutes. Cool on wire rack and slice.

This is a must at our house whenever family gathers. Excellent served cold or warmed slightly. Freezes well.

Florence Francis

Polish Placek (Polish Coffee Cake)

6 loaves

3	packages quick-rise active dry yeast	1	teaspoon salt	
9	to 10 cups all-purpose flour (depending on size of eggs used)	2	cups sugar	
		2½	cups milk	
		1	cup butter *or* margarine	
1¼	teaspoons nutmeg	6	eggs, room temperature	

Thoroughly mix yeast with ⅓ of flour (about 3 cups), nutmeg, salt and sugar. Heat milk and butter until very warm (butter will melt). Add liquid to flour mixture. Beat with electric mixer at medium speed for 2 minutes, scraping bowl often. Add ½ cup of flour and eggs. Beat on high speed for 2 minutes, scraping bowl often. Using spoon, mix in enough flour until batter breaks when spoon is lifted (dough at this point is too heavy for mixer). Place wax paper over bowl, then put damp towel on top of wax paper. Place in a draft-free area. Allow to rise until doubled in bulk. *Note:* An unheated oven is the perfect draft-free place. Place bowl with dough on upper rack with a bowl or pan of hot water on lower rack. Keep oven door closed. Replenish water as it cools.

Crumbs:

½	cup butter, softened	¾	cup sugar
¾	cup all-purpose flour		

Mix above ingredients with fork and then by hand until crumbly. After coffee cake batter has doubled in bulk, use a spoon to fill 6 well-greased 5x9-inch loaf pans ½ full. Disposable loaf pans can be used. Place crumb mixture on top of loaves. Cover with wax paper and damp towel. Return to draft-free area and let rise to ⅔ full. Bake at 400° for 30 minutes or until toothpick comes out clean.

This recipe has been in the family for generations. All the pinches, handfuls and dashes were carefully measured by my daughter when my mother was making it.

Florence Powell

 When separating an egg, if a bit of yolk gets into the white remove with a piece of eggshell.

Raisin Coffee Cake

9 servings

½   cup butter *or* margarine
1   cup sugar
2   eggs
1   teaspoon vanilla
1   cup sour cream
2   cups all-purpose flour
1½   teaspoons baking powder
1   teaspoon baking soda
¼   teaspoon salt
1   cup chopped walnuts
½   cup sugar
1½   teaspoons cinnamon
1   cup raisins

Preheat oven to 350°. Cream together butter and 1 cup sugar. Add eggs and vanilla; beat well. Blend in sour cream. Sift together flour, baking powder, soda and salt. Stir into creamed mixture; mix well. Spread half the batter in a greased 9x9-inch pan. Set aside. Mix nuts, ½ cup sugar and cinnamon. Sprinkle half of the nut mixture over batter. Top with raisins. Spoon remaining batter over raisins. Top with reserved nut mixture. Bake for 50-60 minutes. Serve warm.

Helen Bertelsen

Jewish Apple Cake

12-16 servings

2   teaspoons cinnamon
3   tablespoons sugar
6   apples, peeled, cored and thinly sliced
2½   cups sugar
1   cup oil
4   eggs
½   teaspoon salt
2½   teaspoons vanilla
⅓   cup orange juice
3   cups unsifted all-purpose flour
3   teaspoons baking powder
    powdered sugar

Preheat oven to 350°. Mix cinnamon and 3 tablespoons sugar and pour over apples. Stir to coat apples with mixture and set aside. In mixing bowl, beat sugar, oil, eggs, salt, vanilla and orange juice until creamy. Add flour and baking powder and beat until smooth. Grease and flour a bundt pan. Starting with batter, alternate 3 layers of batter and apples, ending with apples. Bake for 1 hour 45 minutes to 2 hours. Immediately turn out on rack to cool. When cool, sprinkle with powdered sugar.

A moist apple cake that is great morning, noon, or evening.

Beth Sturman

Raspberry Cream Cheese Coffee Cake

16 servings

2¼	cups all-purpose flour	1	egg
¾	cup sugar	1	(8-ounce) package cream
¾	cup margarine *or* butter		cheese, softened
½	teaspoon baking powder	¼	cup sugar
½	teaspoon baking soda	1	egg
¼	teaspoon salt	¼	cup raspberry preserves
¾	cup sour cream	½	cup sliced almonds
1	teaspoon almond extract		

Preheat oven to 350°. Lightly spoon flour into measuring cup. In a large bowl, combine flour and sugar. Using a pastry blender, cut in margarine until mixture resembles coarse crumbs. Reserve 1 cup of crumb mixture. To the remaining crumb mixture, add baking powder, baking soda, salt, sour cream, almond extract and egg; blend well with mixer. Spread batter over bottom and 2-inches up sides of greased and floured 9 or 10-inch springform pan. Batter should be about ¼-inch thick on sides. In a small bowl, combine cream cheese, sugar and egg; blend well. Pour over batter. Carefully spoon preserves evenly over cream cheese mixture. In a small bowl, combine reserved crumb mixture and sliced almonds. Sprinkle over preserves. Bake for 45-55 minutes. Cool 15 minutes. Remove sides of pan. Serve warm or cold. Refrigerate leftovers.

Treat yourself to this delicious almond-flavored coffee cake and you'll want to make it again and again. A great accompaniment to a special brunch menu.

Rita C. Leonard

Large eggs are the standard in recipes. Unless it specifies a size, a recipe means large eggs.

Banana Bread

1 loaf

1½	cups whole wheat flour	2	eggs, beaten
2	teaspoons baking powder	¼	cup milk
½	teaspoon baking soda	¼	cup vegetable oil
⅛	teaspoon salt	1	cup mashed ripe banana
½	cup firmly packed brown sugar	1	cup semi-sweet chocolate chips (optional)
½	teaspoon ground cinnamon		

Preheat oven to 350°. Combine flour, baking powder, soda, salt, brown sugar and cinnamon in a medium size mixing bowl; set aside. In a large bowl, combine eggs, milk and oil. Stir well. Stir in mashed banana. Add flour mixture, stirring until just moistened. Pour batter into a 9-inch loaf pan coated with vegetable cooking spray. Bake for 45 minutes or until a wooden toothpick inserted in center comes out clean. Cool in pan 10 minutes. Remove from pan and cool completely on a wire rack. *Note:* This bread is terrific with a cup of chocolate chips added to the batter.

Liz Gano

Pumpkin Bread

10-12 servings

3	cups sugar	1	cup vegetable oil
3½	cups all-purpose flour	¾	cup orange juice
1½	teaspoons salt	2	cups mashed pumpkin
2	teaspoons baking soda	4	eggs
1	teaspoon nutmeg	1	cup raisins
1	teaspoon cinnamon	1	cup chopped pecans

Preheat oven to 350°. Mix all ingredients together in a large mixing bowl, beat with electric mixer. Grease and flour 4 (1-pound) coffee cans. Fill each half full with mixture. (Bread will rise to top of can.) Bake for 1 hour. Remove from oven and cool for 20-30 minutes. Remove from can, cool completely and wrap in plastic wrap. Can be frozen.

Easy one bowl recipe. Travels well for picnics, trips, etc.

Lucille Stock

Rhubarb Bread

2 loaves

1½	cups brown sugar	2	teaspoons vanilla
1	egg	1½	cups peeled and thinly
1	cup buttermilk *or* sour		sliced rhubarb
	milk	½	cup chopped walnuts
⅔	cup cooking oil	⅓	cup sugar
2½	cups all-purpose flour	1	tablespoon margarine,
1	teaspoon baking soda		melted
1	teaspoon salt		

Preheat oven to 350°. With mixer, cream sugar and egg. Add buttermilk and oil. Mix dry ingredients together and add to creamed mixture. Stir in vanilla, rhubarb and walnuts. Pour in 2 greased loaf pans. Mix sugar and margarine; sprinkle mixture on top of loaves. Bake for 50 minutes or until bread tests done.

Rhubarb is the key ingredient that sets this bread apart. Wonderfully delicious!

Germaine Guerrette
Madawaska, Maine

Orange Poppy Bread

2 loaves

3	cups all-purpose flour	1½	teaspoons salt
1½	teaspoons baking powder	3	eggs, beaten
1½	cups milk	1⅛	cups oil
2¼	cups sugar	1½	teaspoons poppy seeds
1½	teaspoons vanilla	1½	teaspoons almond extract
1½	teaspoons butter flavoring		

Glaze:

½	teaspoon butter flavoring	½	teaspoon almond extract
½	teaspoon vanilla	¼	cup orange juice
¾	cup sugar		

Preheat oven to 350°. Mix all bread ingredients together. Beat on medium speed for 2 minutes. Pour into 2 greased loaf pans. Bake 1 hour. Mix glaze ingredients together. Pour over bread after it is baked and still hot. This bread may be frozen.

Pat Marr

115

Zucchini Bread

2 loaves

2	cups finely chopped zucchini, unpeeled	3	cups all-purpose flour
2	cups sugar	1	teaspoon baking soda
1	cup vegetable oil	1	teaspoon salt
3	eggs, lightly beaten	½	teaspoon cinnamon
2	teaspoons vanilla	1	cup chopped walnuts
		1	cup raisins (optional)

Preheat oven to 350°. Drain zucchini well and combine with sugar, oil, eggs and vanilla in a large bowl. Mix flour, soda, salt and cinnamon together. Add to zucchini mixture and blend well. Stir in nuts and raisins. Divide batter into 2 well greased 5x8-inch loaf pans. Bake for 70 minutes or until cake tester comes out clean. Cool in pans 10 minutes. Remove from pans and cool thoroughly on wire racks.

Mary Fehse

Bishop Bread

10-12 servings

6	eggs, separated	¾	cup semi-sweet chocolate chips
1½	cups sugar		
2⅔	cups all-purpose flour	1	cup chopped nuts
1	teaspoon vanilla		

In a mixing bowl, beat egg whites until foamy. Add egg yolks and sugar; beat well. Add flour and vanilla and beat in with a wooden spoon. Stir in chocolate chips and nuts. Turn batter into a greased and floured tube pan. Bake at 275° for 30 minutes. Raise oven temperature to 300° and continue to bake for an additional 40 minutes. Remove from oven and turn bread on wire rack to cool.

A different type of bread using no butter or oil.

Jan Harvey

If bread is browning too quickly, place a pan of water on the rack above it in the oven.

Monkey Bread

8-10 servings

4 cans biscuits (10 per can)	¾ cup margarine
⅔ cup sugar	1 cup brown sugar
1 tablespoon cinnamon	1 teaspoon cinnamon
½ cup crushed pecans	

Preheat oven to 350°. Cut each biscuit into 4 pieces. In a plastic bag, mix sugar with cinnamon. Place a few biscuit pieces at a time into bag and shake to coat. Grease bundt pan with margarine. Place a layer of biscuits in pan and add one layer of crushed pecans. Continue until all biscuits have been used. Melt margarine in saucepan. Add brown sugar and cinnamon. Mix well and pour over cake. Bake for 30 minutes. Immediately upon removal from oven, turn pan upside down on a large serving plate. Do not try to slice - just pick apart.

A pull-apart bread that is simply sensational.

Barbara Morphy

Orange Biscuit Ring

10-12 servings

1 cup sugar	2 (12-ounce) cans buttermilk
3 tablespoons grated	biscuits
orange rind	⅓ cup butter, melted

Preheat oven to 350°. Combine sugar and orange rind. Dip biscuits one at a time in butter and then in sugar mixture. Stand biscuits in a 9-inch greased tube pan. Bake for 30 minutes. Cool for 5 minutes and invert biscuit ring on serving plate. Drizzle icing over slightly cooled top.

Icing:

1 (3-ounce) package cream	½ cup sifted powdered sugar
cheese, softened	2 tablespoons orange juice

Beat together cream cheese and powdered sugar; add orange juice and blend well.

Treat your family to this delectable brunch bread and it will become an instant favorite. Your guests will love it too!

Rita C. Leonard

Cinnamon Rolls

about 32 rolls

1	package active dry yeast	6	to 7 cups all-purpose flour
½	cup milk		melted butter
1	teaspoon sugar		cinnamon sugar (2 tea-
½	cup all-purpose flour		spoons cinnamon
½	cup shortening		mixed with ½ cup
½	cup sugar		sugar)
2	cups milk		raisins and/or chopped
1	egg, beaten		pecans (optional)
2½	teaspoons salt		

Glaze:

2	cups sifted powdered sugar	3	to 4 tablespoons milk

Dissolve yeast in 1/2 cup lukewarm milk (115°). Add 1 teaspoon sugar and ½ cup flour. Mix well, cover and let rise for 30 minutes in warm place. While that is rising, heat shortening, ½ cup sugar and 2 cups milk on low heat, just until sugar and shortening are dissolved. Cool to lukewarm. Add 1 beaten egg and salt to yeast mixture and beat well. Pour in the lukewarm milk mixture and add enough flour (6 to 7 cups) to make dough. Grease dough lightly with melted butter and cover. Refrigerate overnight or let rise in warm place until doubled.

In the morning (or after doubled), knead on floured board until elastic, then divide in half. Roll out each half of dough to an 8x16-inch rectangle. Brush with melted butter and sprinkle with cinnamon sugar. If desired, sprinkle raisins and/or chopped pecans on top of cinnamon sugar. Then roll dough jelly roll style and pinch to seal. Slice into 1-inch slices and place in 3 or 4 greased 8-inch cake pans. Cover and let rise until doubled (about 2 hours). Bake at 375° for 12-15 minutes. Drizzle with powdered sugar glaze when still warm. *Note:* Use microwave temperature probe to warm milk to correct temperature of 115° to dissolve yeast. Dough rises beautifully in the oven: set oven temperature to "warm" for 60 seconds, then turn oven off.

These rolls are a delicious addition to your Christmas and Easter brunches. They can be baked 3 to 4 weeks in advance and frozen in air-tight freezer bags.

Gretchen Mattingly

Breakfast Pull Apart Rolls

8-10 servings

1 (5¼-ounce) package butterscotch pudding (not instant)	½ cup chopped walnuts
	1 (25-ounce) package frozen dinner rolls
½ cup brown sugar	½ cup butter, melted

In bowl, combine pudding, brown sugar and walnuts. Working quickly, so that butter does not harden on rolls thus preventing dry mixture from sticking to them, dip frozen rolls, one at a time, into melted butter and then coat with dry mixture. Drop rolls into a buttered 9-inch bundt pan. Top with any remaining butter and dry mixture. Put in unheated oven and allow to rise overnight or until rolls have risen above top of pan, about 7 hours. Bake 350° for 30 minutes. Cover top of pan lightly with aluminum foil if top of rolls begin to get too brown.

A great recipe for children to make to surprise mom.

Starla Smith
Temple Hughes

Apple Oat Muffins

12 muffins

1½ cups oat bran	¼ cup skim milk
½ cup whole wheat flour *or* all-purpose flour	1 egg *or* egg substitute
3 tablespoons brown sugar	2 tablespoons sunflower oil *or* vegetable oil
2 teaspoons baking powder	2 tablespoons honey
½ teaspoon salt	1 cup peeled, cored and diced cooking apples
1 teaspoon cinnamon	
½ cup apple juice	2 tablespoons raisins

Preheat oven to 400°. Grease a 12-cup muffin tin with margarine or use paper liners. Combine oat bran, flour, brown sugar, baking powder, salt and cinnamon; set aside. In a large mixing bowl, combine apple juice, milk, egg, oil and honey. Add flour mixture, apples and raisins and combine until just moistened. Fill muffin tin and bake for about 20 minutes or until golden brown and a cake tester comes out clean. Muffins may be frozen.

Down home goodness in every bite.

Barbara Martin

Blueberry Buttermilk Muffins

24-30 muffins

1	cup sugar	¼	to ½ teaspoon salt
½	cup butter *or* margarine, melted	1	cup buttermilk
2	eggs	1¼	cups blueberries (cleaned and drained)
2½	cups all-purpose flour	1	to 2 teaspoons sugar
2½	teaspoons baking powder		

Preheat oven to 375°. In mixing bowl, cream sugar and butter until smooth. Add eggs and blend. In separate bowl, combine flour, baking powder and salt. Add buttermilk and flour to the creamed mixture; mix until smooth. Do not overbeat. Gently stir in blueberries. Fill greased muffin tins about ¾ full, sprinkle lightly with sugar and bake for about 30 minutes. *Note:* Use fresh blueberries when available, otherwise use frozen berries. It is not necessary to thaw the frozen berries.

Judith W. Jones

Oatmeal Date Muffins

1 dozen

1	cup quick-cooking oats	1	cup light brown sugar
1	cup milk	1½	cups chopped dates
1	cup all-purpose flour	1	egg, beaten
2	teaspoons baking powder	4	tablespoons margarine, melted
½	teaspoon baking soda		
½	teaspoon salt		

Preheat oven to 400°. Oil muffin cups generously. Combine oats and milk in bowl and let stand for 8 minutes. In separate bowl, mix flour, baking powder, soda and salt. Add brown sugar and dates. Add egg and margarine to oatmeal mixture; stir well. Add dry ingredients and stir just enough to moisten. Fill prepared muffin cups ⅔ full. Bake for 15 minutes or until a wooden pick inserted in center comes out clean.

Makes a good wholesome snack. Recipe can also be doubled and frozen.

Pat Nelson
Dalhousie, New Brunswick, Canada

Pumpkin Pecan Muffins

12-15 muffins

½	cup brown sugar	¼	teaspoon salt
¼	cup dark molasses	1	teaspoon cinnamon
½	cup butter, softened	½	teaspoon ground nutmeg
1	egg, beaten	½	teaspoon ground allspice
1	cup mashed pumpkin	½	teaspoon ground ginger
1¾	cups all-purpose flour	¼	teaspoon ground cloves
1	teaspoon baking soda	½	cup whole pecans

Preheat oven to 375°. Oil muffin cups generously. Cream sugar, molasses, and butter. Stir in egg and pumpkin, blending well. Combine flour, baking soda, salt, and spices together. Add to pumpkin mixture. Fold in pecans. Fill prepared muffin cups ⅔ full with batter. Bake for 20 minutes or until a tester inserted comes out clean.

These muffins are wonderful anytime of year.

Nancy Barnwell

Mexican Muffins

17-20 muffins

2	cups biscuit mix	2	cups shredded sharp cheese
1	egg		
1	cup milk	½	onion, grated
½	cup margarine, melted		jalapeño pepper, seeded and minced (optional)

Preheat oven to 400°. Mix all ingredients together until just moistened. Spoon mixture into greased muffin tins. Bake approximately 20 minutes or until puffed and browned. *Note:* Pepper cheese can be substituted for all or part of required cheese. For a spicier muffin, a minced jalapeño pepper can also be added.

A wonderful tasty muffin that will complement any Mexican meal or egg dish.

Melba Fristick

Beat-The-Clock Buttermilk Biscuits

10-12 biscuits

2	cups all-purpose flour	¼	teaspoon baking soda
1	tablespoon baking	¼	cup vegetable oil
	powder	¾	cup buttermilk
½	teaspoon salt		

Preheat oven to 450°. Mix dry ingredients together in a bowl. Combine oil and buttermilk; add to flour mixture. Stir just until dough is formed. Gently knead dough, 3 or 4 times, on floured surface. Pat or roll dough out to ½-inch thickness and cut out biscuits. Place in well oiled 9x13-inch baking pan, flipping each biscuit over in the pan so that the tops are lightly coated with oil. Bake for 12 minutes.

These light and flaky biscuits are literally made in minutes.

Diana Wade

Daddy's Raisin Bread

20-24 servings

3	packages active dry yeast	3	eggs, slightly beaten
¾	cup warm water	10½	cups sifted all-purpose
¾	cup sugar		flour
3	teaspoons salt	1	(15-ounce) box golden
3	cups scalded milk, cooled		raisins
	to lukewarm	3	tablespoons vanilla
¾	cup butter, softened	1	egg, slightly beaten

In a bowl, dissolve yeast in warm (not hot) water. Add sugar and salt. In separate bowl, combine lukewarm milk, butter and eggs. Set aside and allow to cool to room temperature. When cooled, add to yeast mixture. Add flour and mix completely. Cover and let rise 1 hour. Wash and drain raisins and dust with flour. Add raisins and vanilla to flour mixture. Knead until hands come clean. Place dough in greased and floured 11x13-inch pan. Brush top of bread with slightly beaten egg. Cover and place pan on top rack of cold oven with a bowl or pan of boiling water on lower rack to aid rising. Let rise about 45 minutes or until doubled in bulk. Remove bread from oven. Preheat oven to 350° and bake for 45 minutes.

This bread has been an Easter favorite in my family for three generations.

Helen Bertelsen

Anadama Bread

2 loaves

7	cups all-purpose flour (approximately)	⅓	cup butter, softened
1½	cups cornmeal	2	packages dry yeast
2½	teaspoons salt	2¼	cups very warm water
		⅔	cup molasses

Mix together 2½ cups flour, cornmeal, salt, butter and yeast in a large bowl. Slowly add water and molasses to dry ingredients and beat 2 minutes at medium speed. Stir in enough flour to make a stiff dough. Knead dough until smooth and elastic, about 10 minutes. Place in a greased bowl turning once to coat top. Cover and let rise until doubled in bulk (about 1 hour). Punch down and divide in half. Shape and place in 2 greased 9-inch baking pans. Cover and let rise again until doubled in bulk, about 1 hour. Bake at 375° for 45 minutes or until done.

Angela Collins

Beer Bread

1 loaf

3	cups self-rising flour	1	(12-ounce) can warm beer (not light beer)
3	tablespoons sugar		melted butter

Preheat oven to 350°. In a large bowl, combine flour, sugar and beer together and stir until blended, it will be "gooey". Turn into a greased loaf pan and place pan on top of stove to allow to rise for 5 minutes. Bake for 35 minutes. Top with melted butter.

Wonderful, easy bread. Beer makes it rise.

Anne Reynolds

 When in doubt, always sift flour before measuring.

Nanny Gilchrist's Irish Soda Bread

1 loaf

3½	cups all-purpose flour	2	tablespoons caraway seeds
3	teaspoons baking powder		(optional)
½	teaspoon baking soda	1¾	cups buttermilk
2	teaspoons salt	2	tablespoons butter,
¾	cup sugar		melted
1¾	cups raisins	2	eggs, beaten

Preheat oven to 350°. Sift together flour, baking powder, soda, salt and sugar. Add raisins and caraway seeds. In separate bowl, combine buttermilk, butter and eggs. Stir into dry ingredients. Mix well. Grease a 9 or 10-inch round pan and dust with flour. Pour in batter. Dust top of batter with flour and make a deep cross on top. Bake for 1 hour. *Note:* 2 loaf pans may be used instead of 1 round pan.

Highlight your morning coffee with a slice of this moist and flavorful soda bread.

Christine Mahoney Goodwin
Valley Stream, New York

Easy Yeast Rolls

18 rolls

2	packages active dry yeast	½	teaspoon salt
1½	cups warm water	⅓	cup vegetable oil
4	cups all-purpose flour	1	egg
⅓	cup sugar		

In a large mixing bowl, dissolve yeast in warm water. Stir in 2 cups flour, sugar, salt, oil and egg. Beat with electric mixer for 2 minutes. Add remaining flour and beat for 2 minutes more. Cover bowl and keep in a warm draft-free place for about 30 minutes or until dough is doubled in size. Grease cups of a large muffin tin. Uncover dough and beat 25 strokes. Fill cups halfway, cover and let rise for ½ hour. Bake at 425° for 12 minutes.

Diana Wade

Kay's Refrigerator-Freezer Homemade Rolls

60 rolls or 3 loaves

1	cup boiling water	2	packages dry rapid rise
1	cup margarine		yeast
1	cup sugar	1	cup lukewarm water
1½	teaspoons salt	6	cups all-purpose flour
2	eggs, beaten		butter, melted

Combine boiling water, margarine, sugar and salt. Blend and cool. Add eggs after mixture is cool. Sprinkle yeast into lukewarm water; stir until dissolved. Combine yeast with egg mixture. With mixer, blend in flour. Cover and refrigerate for at least 4 hours. This will keep 7-10 days and can be used as needed. Shape dough into cloverleaf, parkerhouse or whatever shape rolls or bread desired. When shaping, dough may look a bit sloppy but baking turns them out perfect. In a greased pan or muffin tin, bake at 400° for 10-15 minutes. If making parkerhouse rolls, shape and dip in melted butter. A 9-inch round pyrex pan can also be used. *Note:* Rolls can be frozen. After dough is refrigerated for 4 hours, shape rolls in pan, brush with butter, cover tightly and freeze. Remove 5 hours before baking and let rise in a warm draft-free place. Bake at 400° for 10-15 minutes.

These rolls will melt in your mouth.

S. Kay Clifton

Maggie's Dinner Rolls

24 rolls

2	packages active dry yeast	1	cup scalded milk
¼	cup warm water	3½	cups sifted all-purpose
½	cup sugar		flour
½	cup butter *or* margarine	1	egg
½	teaspoon salt		

Soften yeast in warm water; set aside. In a large bowl, combine sugar, butter and salt. Pour hot milk over this mixture. Cool to lukewarm. With spoon, mix in 1½ cups flour. Mix in egg and yeast. Add remaining flour. Dough will be very soft. Turn out on heavily floured board and knead 20-30 times. You do not want a stiff dough. It should be very soft and fall over your hand when picked up. Place dough in an oiled bowl and keep in a warm and draft-free place. Let rise until doubled, about 60-90 minutes. Turn out on floured board and knead a few more times. Shape into desired form for type of rolls you like. Bake on greased baking sheets or muffin pans in a 400° oven for 12-15 minutes.

Margaret Kluthe

125

Herb Butter Sticks

8 servings

1	loaf French bread, uncut	1	teaspoon dried basil
1	cup butter *or* margarine, softened	½	teaspoon dried oregano
		1	teaspoon garlic powder
1	teaspoon dried chervil	½	teaspoon onion powder

Preheat oven to 425°. Cut loaf in half lengthwise and then across into 6-inch long thin bread sticks. Combine remaining ingredients in a medium bowl. Blend well. Spread butter mixture on all surfaces of the bread sticks. Bake for 8 minutes or until golden.

Great addition to pasta dishes.

Nancy Barnwell

Parmesan Pull Aparts

12 rolls

1	cup butter *or* margarine, melted	1	(11-ounce) package unbaked dinner rolls (Brown & Serve)
	pinch of basil	1	cup grated Parmesan cheese

Preheat oven to 350°. Combine butter and basil. Dip rolls individually in butter mixture, then roll in Parmesan cheese. Place on ungreased baking sheet. Bake 8-10 minutes or until lightly browned.

Quick and tasty way to serve instant rolls.

Pat Marr

Peel and mash over-ripe bananas and mix in a little lemon juice. Freeze in measured amounts. Thaw for making banana cake, bread or muffins.

Entrées

Barbecue Brisket

10-12 servings

1 (5-7 pound) flat beef brisket	dash garlic salt
1 cup soy sauce	paprika
1 (10½-ounce) can beef consommé	

Marinate brisket overnight in the next 3 ingredients. The next day, discard marinade and sprinkle brisket with paprika. Wrap brisket in heavy foil and place on a jelly roll pan. Bake at 350° for 3½-4 hours. When cool, slice thin and pour **Sauce** over meat.

Sauce:

1 cup ketchup	4 tablespoons brown sugar
4 tablespoons Worcestershire sauce	4 tablespoons vinegar
	2 tablespoons liquid smoke

In a small saucepan, mix first 4 ingredients and simmer for 10 minutes. Add liquid smoke and pour sauce over sliced meat. Rewrap meat in foil and bake at 300° for 30 minutes.

This brisket is great to fix ahead, just bake sliced meat with sauce when ready to serve.

Mary Helen Markee

Oven Barbecue — Texas Style

8-10 servings

1 (16-ounce) bottle oil-type Italian salad dressing	1 (8-ounce) bottle Texas Best BBQ sauce concentrate *or* your favorite
¼ cup Worcestershire sauce	
1 tablespoon minced garlic	
1 (3-4 pound) beef brisket brown sugar	1 cup 57 *or* A.1. sauce

Combine together Italian dressing, Worcestershire sauce and garlic; mix well. Marinate brisket overnight in sauce. Preheat oven to 400°. Pour a small amount of the marinade sauce in bottom of a 9x13-inch pan and place brisket on top. Rub brown sugar on brisket and brown in oven 20 minutes, fat side up and uncovered. Reduce oven temperature to 375°. Mix the 2 barbecue sauces together and pour ½ over brisket. Cook uncovered for 15 minutes. Reduce oven temperature to 325°. Turn meat over; cover liberally with remaining barbecue sauce, cover tightly and cook 2-3 hours or until brisket is tender. *Note:* Chicken, sausage or pork ribs can be included and cooked at the same time in large pan.

Anita Leathers

Brisket For Eight

8 servings

2 (5-ounce) jars horseradish
1 (5-6 pound) beef brisket

1 envelope dry onion soup
 mix
1 cup dry red wine

Preheat oven to 325°. Line a 9x13-inch baking pan with heavy duty aluminum foil. Spread one jar of horseradish on bottom. Place meat on top and spread with remaining horseradish. Sprinkle with soup and pour wine over all. Cover with foil and seal well. Bake for 5 hours. Slice at angle across grain and serve with juice. *Note:* Can be prepared the day before, slice and reheat before serving.

A favorite Texas recipe of ours.

Starla Smith

Reuben Casserole

4 servings

1¾ cups fresh *or* canned
 sauerkraut, drained
¼ pound thinly sliced cooked
 corned beef
1 cup shredded Swiss cheese
3 tablespoons Thousand
 Island dressing

2 medium tomatoes, thinly
 sliced *or* 2 cups
 canned tomatoes
4 tablespoons butter *or*
 margarine
1 cup crumbled seasoned
 rye wafers
¼ teaspoon caraway seeds

Preheat oven to 425°. Thinly layer sauerkraut in bottom of buttered 1½-quart casserole dish. Top with sliced corned beef, then shredded cheese. Dot dressing on top of cheese and add tomatoes. Dot with 2 tablespoons butter. Melt 2 tablespoons butter in small saucepan. Sauté crumbled rye wafers and add caraway seeds. Spread on top of ingredients and bake for 30 minutes or until bubbly.

Eva M. Edwards

Individual Beef Wellingtons

8 servings

2	tablespoons butter	5	to 6 ounces pâté foi gras
8	(6-8 ounce) beef		*or* liver pâté with
	tenderloins		truffles
¼	cup Madeira wine		salt
8	ounces fresh mushrooms,	1	egg mixed with 1 teaspoon
	minced		water
8	frozen puff pastry shells,		
	thawed		

Melt butter over high heat and sear steaks on both sides. Cook thick steaks a little longer. Add 4 tablespoons Madeira wine and simmer a minute, remove steaks and chill. Add mushrooms and remaining wine to skillet, cook until liquid evaporates. Roll out each pastry to a very thin 8-inch circle. Place ⅛ of mushroom mixture in center of pastry. Spread top of each filet with a little pâté, approximately 1 tablespoon and place pâté side down on mushroom mixture. Salt lightly and fold pastry around filet. Place on cookie sheet, cover and refrigerate, as long as overnight. Remove from refrigerator and baste with egg mixture. Bake in a 425° oven for 18-20 minutes or until golden brown. For the first 10 minutes, put pan on lowest rack in oven, then move to highest rack. Meat is rare to medium rare. Serve with **Bordelaise Sauce.**

Bordelaise Sauce: 2½ cups sauce

1	tablespoon chopped onion	1	teaspoon tarragon
8	ounces fresh mushrooms,	1	(10-ounce) can beef broth
	sliced	½	cup Madeira wine
2	tablespoons butter	1	tablespoon Kitchen
3	tablespoons all-purpose		Bouquet (optional)
	flour		

Sauté onions and mushrooms with butter. Add flour, stirring until blended. Gradually add rest of ingredients, stirring constantly, and simmer until thick. Sauce can be poured on plate and topped with Beef Wellington, poured over the Wellingtons or passed on the side.

When the occasion calls for elegance or festive dining, this entrée will meet all criteria.

Rita C. Leonard

Roast Beef Tenderloin

6-8 servings

1 onion, thinly sliced
1 (2½-pound) beef tenderloin, trimmed

½ cup margarine, melted
   salt and pepper

Preheat oven to 475°. Slice onion and place in a shallow roasting pan. Brush tenderloin with margarine and place on onions. Sprinkle generously with salt and pepper. Insert meat thermometer in center of raw roast so bulb touches the thickest part of meat. Roast until thermometer reaches desired temperature. Remove from oven and let rest for 5 minutes to redistribute juices. Slice thinly and serve.

Excellent served with béarnaise or horseradish sauce.

Darlene Ryan

Braised Beef Tips

4-6 servings

2 pounds beef roast, cubed
2 tablespoons shortening
1 cup beef broth
⅓ cup red wine
2 tablespoons soy sauce

1 garlic clove, minced
¼ teaspoon onion salt
2 tablespoons cornstarch
¼ cup water
   cooked rice *or* noodles

Brown beef cubes in shortening. Add beef broth, red wine, soy sauce, garlic and salt; bring to a boil. Reduce heat and simmer 1 hour. Combine cornstarch and water. Add to mixture to thicken. Serve over rice or noodles.

Starla Smith

Beef Burgundy

8-10 servings

3	pounds lean round steak	1	cup Burgundy wine
3	(10¾-ounce) cans cream of mushroom soup	1	(4-ounce) can button mushrooms
1	envelope dry onion soup mix	¼	teaspoon oregano
			cooked noodles

Preheat oven to 350°. Cut meat into 1-inch cubes. Combine all ingredients into a 2-quart casserole dish. Cover and bake for 3½ hours. Serve over hot noodles.

Variation: Use 2 pounds stew beef, 1 can mushroom soup, ½ cup wine, 2 cans mushrooms and omit oregano. Cook in crockpot on low for 8-10 hours.

A great make-ahead meal for the busy family.

Janet Hinrichs
Theresa Ellison

Beef Rolls Italian Style

8 servings

8	(¼-inch thick) slices round steak (about 3 pounds)	1	cup finely diced mozzarella cheese
1	teaspoon salt	10	thin slices salami, chopped
¼	teaspoon pepper		olive oil
2	cups dry bread crumbs	1	(27½-ounce) jar spaghetti sauce (flavored with meat)
4	tablespoons grated onion		
6	tablespoons grated Parmesan cheese		

With a meat mallet, pound steaks to tenderize and make thinner. Sprinkle with salt and pepper. In a large bowl, combine remaining ingredients except oil and spaghetti sauce; toss together to blend. Spread about ½ cup filling over each piece of meat. Roll up tightly, jelly roll style. Tie each end securely with twine or fasten with toothpicks. (Be sure you can find them later to remove.) In a large skillet, brown rolls on all sides in a few tablespoons olive oil. Transfer rolls to a large casserole dish and pour spaghetti sauce on top. Bake covered in a preheated 350° oven for 1½-2 hours or until tender. To serve, remove twine or toothpicks and cut each in half. Arrange on plates and spoon extra sauce from bottom of pan.

Serve this entrée at your next "Progressive Dinner" and wait for the compliments.

Janet Hinrichs

Burritos

8-10 servings

1 pound ground round	1 (⅜-ounce) envelope
1 small onion, chopped	enchilada sauce mix
2 (16-ounce) cans refried	8 ounces Monterey Jack
beans	cheese, shredded
1 (10-count) package flour	8 ounces shredded sharp
tortillas	Cheddar cheese
½ cup plain yogurt *or* sour	
cream	

Spray skillet with cooking spray and brown beef with onion. Drain well. Stir in beans. Place 2 heaping tablespoons of filling in center of each tortilla and top with about 1 tablespoon yogurt. Fold ends and overlap sides of tortillas; place seam side down in an 11x14-inch baking dish. Prepare sauce per envelope directions and spoon sauce over rolled tortillas, reserving about ½ cup. Bake for 15-20 minutes or until heated through. Sprinkle with shredded cheeses and top with remaining sauce. Bake for an additional 5 minutes or until cheese melts.

These tasty burritos are a snap to prepare and your family will love them.

Lorraine Leonard
Madawaska, Maine

Saralynn's Chili

4-6 servings

2 medium onions, chopped	½ to 1 tablespoon chili
2 tablespoons oil	powder
2 pounds ground chuck	1 (15-ounce) can pinto beans
1 (1.25-ounce) envelope dry	½ green bell pepper,
chili seasoning mix	chopped
2 (15-ounce) cans tomato	3 celery stalks, chopped
sauce	salt and pepper to taste
¼ teaspoon curry powder	shredded Cheddar cheese
	oyster crackers

Sauté onions in oil until tender. Add meat and brown; drain excess fat. Stir in chili seasoning, tomato sauce, curry and chili powder. Heat to boiling. Reduce heat; add beans, bell pepper and celery. Salt and pepper to taste. Simmer 1-2 hours, stirring occasionally. Garnish individual servings with shredded Cheddar cheese or oyster crackers.

This hearty dish is usually doubled, often tripled, to serve a hungry crowd.

Ann Couch

133

Eggplant And Ground Beef Casserole

6 servings

1	pound lean ground beef	2	(8-ounce) cans tomato
1	teaspoon salt		sauce *or* 2 cups
	pepper to taste		homemade sauce
2	tablespoons salad oil	½	to 1 teaspoon oregano
1	medium eggplant		light sprinkling of sweet
1	egg, beaten		basil (optional)
½	cup dried bread crumbs	½	cup Parmesan cheese
½	cup olive oil	1	cup grated Cheddar
			cheese

Preheat oven to 300°. Shape ground beef into 6 thick patties. Season to taste with salt and pepper. Brown in hot salad oil. Slice eggplant into 6 thick slices, do not remove skin. Dip into beaten egg, then roll in bread crumbs and brown in olive oil. Place coated eggplant slices into a shallow baking dish. Top each with browned beef patty and cover with tomato sauce. Sprinkle patties with oregano, sweet basil and Parmesan cheese. Top with grated Cheddar cheese and bake for 35 minutes.

Nita Vella

Marie's Rolled Meatloaf

4 servings

1	tablespoon margarine		water
1	medium onion, chopped	1	teaspoon salt
1	garlic clove, chopped	¼	teaspoon oregano
1	pound ground round		pepper
1	egg, beaten	2	tablespoons dry bread
2	slices white bread, crust		crumbs
	removed	2	cups mashed potatoes

Preheat oven to 350°. In a skillet, heat margarine and sauté onion and garlic. Remove to mixing bowl, add beef and egg. Add bread that has been softened in water and squeezed out. Add salt, oregano and pepper, mix well. Sprinkle a piece of waxed paper with bread crumbs. Press meat out on crumbs to make a rectangle about ½ inch thick. Spread potatoes on top of meat. Using waxed paper as a guide, roll meat and potatoes jelly roll style and place in a shallow pan or in a loaf pan. Bake about 1 hour. Serve with brown sauce made from drippings or any other sauce such as mushroom or tomato sauce.

A unique way to serve meatloaf!

Agnes Zodda

Poor Man's Stroganoff

8 servings

2	tablespoons margarine	3	tablespoons lemon juice
1	pound ground beef	1	(4-ounce) can chopped
1	medium onion, diced		mushrooms
	salt and pepper to taste	1	cup red wine
	garlic powder to taste	3	(5-ounce) packages tiny
3	(10¾-ounce) cans beef		noodles
	consommé	1	cup sour cream

In a large skillet, combine margarine, meat, onion and seasonings. Cook until meat is browned and onion is tender. Drain. Add consommé, lemon juice, wine and mushrooms. Cover and simmer 20 minutes. Add packages of noodles and stir well. Cover and simmer another 10-15 minutes. Fold in sour cream, cook another 5 minutes to heat through. Do not boil.

A hearty family-style dinner in a skillet.

Theresa Ellison

Tamale Pie

6 servings

1	pound ground round	1	teaspoon Worcestershire
¼	pound sausage		sauce
2	medium onions, chopped	1	(4-ounce) can ripe olives
½	green bell pepper,	2	(8-ounce) cans tomato sauce
	chopped	1	(16-ounce) can tomatoes
1	teaspoon chili powder	1	(16-ounce) can red kidney
			beans

In a large skillet, brown ground beef and sausage. Drain well. Add onions and green pepper; cook until tender. Stir in remaining ingredients and spoon into a 2½ to 3-quart casserole.

Cornbread mixture:

½	cup all-purpose flour	¾	cup cornmeal
1	teaspoon salt	⅔	cup buttermilk
1	teaspoon baking powder	1	egg, beaten
½	teaspoon baking soda	2	tablespoons salad oil

Preheat oven to 425°. In medium bowl, sift dry ingredients together. Combine liquid ingredients and stir into dry mixture just enough to moisten. Spread this on top of the meat mixture and bake for 20 minutes.

This one-dish meal is sure to become a family favorite.

Fran Batt

Quick Tamale Pie

6 servings

1 (10½-ounce) bag of corn chips
2 (10-ounce) cans chili with beans, heated

1 small red onion, chopped
1 cup grated Cheddar cheese

Preheat oven to 350°. In an 8x8-inch casserole dish, layer chips, chili, onion and cheese until pan is filled. Bake for 20 minutes or until cheese melts. Recipe can be doubled.

Serve with salad or slaw.

Jeane S. Lenzini

Beef-Caraway Stew

6 servings

2 to 2½ pounds lean chuck roast, cut into 1-inch cubes
salt and pepper
1 teaspoon paprika
2 tablespoons canola oil *or* other cooking oil
1 medium onion, chopped
2 beef bouillon cubes *or* 2 teaspoons beef instant bouillon

1½ cups boiling water
1 (10¾-ounce) can cream of mushroom soup
1 tablespoon prepared mustard
½ teaspoon caraway seeds
5 medium carrots, cut in 2-inch strips
1 (10-ounce) package frozen peas

Season beef cubes with salt, pepper and paprika. In a 4 to 6-quart Dutch oven, heat oil and brown beef cubes. Add onions and brown lightly. Dissolve bouillon in boiling water and blend with soup, mustard and caraway seeds; add to beef mixture. Add enough boiling water to barely cover meat. Cover and simmer for 2 hours. Add carrots and cook until tender. To preserve the color of the peas, cook separately for the time specified on the package, then add to stew just before serving. May be served with mashed potatoes, noodles or biscuits. **Note:** Do not omit any ingredients, as each is necessary to give this dish its special flavor.

A special flavored stew that is sure to please your taste buds.

Fran Batt

Simple Beef Stew

4 servings

1¼ pounds stew beef	4 average size carrots, sliced in chunks
1 large onion, chopped	2 (10¾-ounce) cans tomato soup
4 medium potatoes, quartered	

Preheat oven to 275°. Place all ingredients in 3-quart casserole. Bake covered for about 5 hours.

Serve with rolls for a hearty one dish meal.

Audrey R. McGovern

Five Hour Stew

8-10 servings

3 to 4 pounds stew beef	1 (4-ounce) can mushroom stems, undrained
3 carrots, sliced	1 (10¾-ounce) can tomato soup
4 celery stalks, chopped	½ cup Burgundy wine
2 onions, chopped	salt and pepper to taste
1 (16-ounce) can green beans, undrained	
2 large potatoes, peeled and sliced thick	

Preheat oven to 275°. In a Dutch oven, combine all ingredients together and stir to blend. Cover tightly and bake for 5 hours.

Don't peek while cooking! An easy one-pot meal your whole family will enjoy.

Pauline Cychowski

 Roux freezes well and you can be ready at any time to make a gumbo or stew.

Irish Stew

8 servings

1	cup Burgundy *or* other dry red wine	¼	cup olive oil
1	garlic clove, minced	2	(10½-ounce) cans condensed beef broth
2	bay leaves	6	carrots, cut into 2-inch slices
1	teaspoon salt		
½	teaspoon freshly grated pepper	12	small boiling onions
¼	teaspoon dried thyme	6	medium potatoes, peeled and halved
3	pounds lean stew beef, cut into 1-inch cubes		

Combine first 6 ingredients; pour over beef in a shallow dish. Cover and refrigerate 8 hours. Drain meat, reserving marinade. Discard bay leaves. Heat oil in a Dutch oven over medium heat; brown beef in oil. Add broth and reserved marinade; bring to a boil. Cover, reduce heat and simmer 1½ hours. Add carrots, onions and potatoes; cover and cook for an additional 30 minutes.

A tasty alternative to corned beef on St. Patrick's Day.

Pat O'Brien

Cherry Almond Glazed Pork Loin

10-12 servings

1	(4-pound) boneless pork loin	¼	teaspoon salt
1	(12-ounce) jar cherry preserves	¼	teaspoon ground cinnamon
		¼	teaspoon ground nutmeg
2	tablespoons light corn syrup	¼	teaspoon ground cloves
¼	cup red wine vinegar	¼	cup slivered almonds, toasted

Preheat oven to 325°. Rub roast with salt and pepper. Place on rack in shallow pan. Roast uncovered for 2-2½ hours. Combine remaining ingredients except almonds. Heat to boiling, stirring frequently, simmer 2 minutes. Add almonds and keep warm. The last 30 minutes of cooking time or when meat thermometer reaches 170°, spoon enough of mixture over the roast to glaze. Baste occasionally. Serve remaining sauce with roast.

The succulent flavor of lean pork blends well with the spiced cherry almond sauce.

Lois Poper

Iowa Pork Platter With Horseradish Sauce

8 servings

1	(12-ounce) can beer	½	teaspoon salt
2	tablespoons Worcestershire sauce	2	tablespoons brown sugar
1	tablespoon minced onion	1	(3-pound) boneless pork loin
1	teaspoon dry mustard		

For marinade, combine first 6 ingredients and mix well. Place marinade in a glass dish and marinate pork loin several hours or overnight in refrigerator. Roast at 350° for 2-2½ hours. Let roast sit at room temperature for 15 minutes before slicing. Serve with **Horseradish Sauce.**

Horseradish Sauce:

⅔	cup sour cream	2	tablespoons prepared horseradish

Combine sauce ingredients together. Serve sauce over sliced pork loin.

This entrée goes well with sliced tomatoes and coleslaw.

Lois Poper

Veal Parmesan

4 servings

½	cup corn flake crumbs	2	(8-ounce) cans tomato sauce
¼	cup Parmesan cheese		
½	teaspoon salt	½	teaspoon oregano
	dash pepper	¼	cup sugar
4	veal cutlets		dash onion salt
2	large eggs, slightly beaten	½	cup shredded mozzarella cheese
½	cup butter *or* margarine		

Preheat oven to 400°. Combine first 4 ingredients together in a bowl. Dip cutlets first in eggs and then in corn flake mixture. Melt butter in a 9x12-inch baking dish. Place cutlets in dish and bake for 20 minutes, turn cutlets over and bake another 20 minutes. Combine tomato sauce, oregano, sugar and onion salt together and heat to boiling. Pour sauce over cutlets after they have finished baking and top with mozzarella cheese. Return to oven and bake until cheese melts. Serve over noodles.

Theresa Ellison

Crispy Pork Medallions

4-6 servings

1	pound pork tenderloin		vegetable oil for frying

Marinade:

2	tablespoons water	1	teaspoon white vinegar
1	tablespoon soy sauce	2	garlic cloves, chopped
½	tablespoon salt	5	tablespoons cornstarch
1	teaspoon sugar		

Serving Sauce:

3	tablespoons chopped green onion	1½	teaspoons sugar
		3	tablespoons soy sauce
2	tablespoons grated ginger root	2	tablespoons white vinegar
1	tablespoon minced garlic	¼	teaspoon crushed red pepper

Slice pork into medallions and tenderize with mallet. Place in a 9x13-inch baking pan. Combine marinade ingredients and pour over pork. Cover and chill for at least 1 hour, turning occasionally. Make **Serving Sauce.** When ready to cook medallions, heat 1 inch of vegetable oil in large skillet until very hot. Add pork medallions slowly to oil; fry until crispy. You can remove pork and dip in marinade again and re-fry to make medallions crispier. (They will cook quickly). Drain on paper towels. Serve sauce on side as a dipping sauce or poured on the pork.

Delicious and pungent. Excellent with rice and broccoli.

Sarah W. D'Addabbo

Wiener Schnitzel

6 servings

6	veal cutlets, pounded thin	2	tablespoons cold water
	juice of ½ lemon	1	cup bread crumbs
½	cup all-purpose flour	5	tablespoons butter
2	large eggs	3	tablespoons vegetable oil

Sprinkle lemon juice over cutlets and let stand about 45 minutes. Pat dry and then dip cutlets into flour to coat both sides, shake off excess flour. In a shallow bowl, beat eggs with water. Dip cutlets into egg mixture to coat both sides, then dip into crumbs. In a large skillet, melt 3 tablespoons butter over medium heat. Add oil and sauté cutlets until golden, about 6 minutes on each side. Keep warm in oven until all cutlets are cooked. Add remaining butter to pan as needed. Serve with a wedge of lemon.

Cyndy Ortwein

Italian Sausage With Potatoes

6 servings

2 pounds Italian sausage
4 large potatoes, cut into
    fourths
1 cup sliced onions
1 (8-ounce) can tomato sauce
2 tablespoons chopped fresh
    parsley
1 teaspoon sweet basil
1 teaspoon oregano

garlic salt *or* powder
    (optional)
salt and pepper to taste
1 (16-ounce) can sweet peas,
    drained
1 (4-ounce) can mushrooms,
    drained (optional)
Parmesan cheese

Preheat oven to 325°. Cut sausage into 2-inch pieces and place in a lightly greased 9x13-inch baking dish. Add raw potatoes and onion slices; top with tomato sauce. Sprinkle parsley, basil, oregano and garlic salt over sauce. Season with salt and pepper. Bake covered for 1½ hours or until potatoes are tender. About 15 minutes before casserole is done, add peas and mushrooms. Top with a light sprinkling of Parmesan cheese.

A loaf of French bread completes this hearty one-dish meal.

Nita Vella

Stir-Fry Sauce

4 cups

2½ cups chicken broth
½ cup cornstarch
½ cup soy sauce
½ cup light corn syrup
½ cup dry sherry
¼ cup cider vinegar

2 garlic cloves, minced
2 teaspoons grated fresh
    ginger *or* ½ teaspoon
    ground ginger
¼ teaspoon ground red
    pepper

Combine all ingredients in a 1½-quart jar with tight-fitting lid. Shake well. Can be stored up to 3 weeks in refrigerator. Shake well before using.

Great with beef, chicken and vegetable stir-fry.

Nicki Knight

When using your microwave, leave wooden spoon in dish for recipes requiring frequent stirring.

Flank Steak Marinade

1 cup marinade

3	tablespoons honey	1½	teaspoons ground ginger
¼	cup soy sauce	½	cup vegetable oil
2	tablespoons vinegar	1	medium onion, chopped
½	teaspoon garlic salt		

Mix all ingredients in a blender and blend on high for 1 minute. Marinate flank steak overnight.

Maureen Kolb

Mustard Horseradish Sauce

6 servings

1½	tablespoons prepared horseradish sauce	1	cup sour cream *or* light sour cream
1	tablespoon prepared mustard	1	teaspoon lemon juice
		¾	cup sliced onions

Mix together all ingredients and blend well. Refrigerate.

A very different sauce for shrimp.

Margie Brennan

Ham Basting Sauce

1½ cups basting sauce

1	(16-ounce) can whole cranberry sauce	1	cup packed light brown sugar
2	teaspoons prepared mustard	½	cup Burgundy wine

Mix all ingredients together. Baste ham during the last 45 minutes of cooking time.

Maureen Kolb

Orange Mustard Glaze

1	cup packed light brown sugar	2	tablespoons orange marmalade
¼	cup orange juice	2	tablespoons dry mustard

Mix all ingredients together. Glaze during the last ½ hour of cooking time. Good with ham or pork.

Maureen Kolb

Easy Mustard-Honey Chicken

4 servings

¼ cup butter *or* margarine
½ cup honey
¼ cup prepared mustard
1 teaspoon curry powder
(or to taste)

½ teaspoon salt
4 large chicken breast halves, skinned

Preheat oven to 375°. Melt butter in an 8-inch square baking dish. Stir in honey, mustard, curry powder and salt. Place chicken, meaty side down, in baking dish and bake 20 minutes, basting once. Turn chicken and bake 20-30 minutes longer, until fork tender, basting twice. Spoon remaining pan juice over chicken before serving.

Florence Powell

Elegant Chicken Dijon

6 servings

6 chicken breast halves, skinned
¾ cup butter
1 garlic clove, minced
1 onion, sliced into rings
¾ cup all-purpose flour, seasoned to taste with salt and pepper

½ pound fresh mushrooms, sliced
1 tablespoon Dijon mustard
1 teaspoon tarragon
2 tablespoons chopped fresh parsley
1 lemon, very thinly sliced

Melt butter in a heavy skillet and lightly sauté garlic and onion rings. Remove onion and set aside. Pound chicken breasts until flattened. Dredge in flour seasoned with salt and pepper, shake off excess. Sauté chicken in butter and garlic mixture until lightly browned on both sides. Remove and set aside. Add mushrooms to same skillet and sauté until tender. Stir in mustard, tarragon and parsley. Return chicken breasts to skillet, top with mushrooms, onion rings and lemon slices. Cover and simmer about 15 minutes.

The finished dish is colorful as well as tasty with its lemon and parsley garnishes. It makes a delicious entrée and receives many compliments.

Anne Giannini

Pecan Chicken With Dijon Cream Sauce

4 servings

4	chicken breast halves, boned and skinned	1	cup finely chopped pecans
	salt and pepper to taste	2	tablespoons butter *or* margarine
½	teaspoon tarragon	1	tablespoon Dijon mustard
1	egg white, lightly beaten	1	cup heavy cream

Tenderize chicken pieces with meat mallet. Season with salt, pepper and tarragon. Let rest 30 minutes before cooking. Dip chicken in egg white, then roll in pecans. Sauté chicken in butter until golden on both sides. Remove chicken and keep warm. Stir in Dijon mustard and cream, simmer to reduce to sauce consistency. Place chicken on serving plates and spoon sauce over each breast.

Excellent served with rice.

Eva M. Edwards

Chicken With Lemon Butter

4-6 servings

6	chicken breast halves, boned and skinned	½	teaspoon salt
		¼	teaspoon pepper
2	eggs	1	cup fine, fresh bread crumbs
¾	cup all-purpose flour		
1	cup milk	4	tablespoons butter

Place each chicken breast between 2 pieces of plastic wrap and pound chicken with a mallet until thin. In bowl and with a wire whisk, mix eggs, flour, milk, salt and pepper. Place chicken in batter and let stand covered in refrigerator for 30 minutes or up to 3 days before using. When ready to cook, heat a heavy skillet over a low flame. With a pair of tongs, remove chicken from batter and coat each completely with bread crumbs. Add butter to hot skillet, it should sizzle and foam, but not darken. Lower heat so butter keeps its light color. Place 3 chicken breasts into skillet and sauté for about 6 minutes on each side. Sauté remaining 3. These may be kept warm in a 250° oven for about 30 minutes.

Lemon Butter:

½	cup butter	1½	tablespoons lemon juice

Melt butter over low heat and stir in lemon juice. Pour lemon butter over chicken before serving or put in small pitcher and let everyone pour their own.

Mary Fehse

Zesty Lemon Chicken

10-12 servings

12	chicken breast halves, boned and skinned	½	cup safflower oil
2	cups fresh lemon juice (9-10 lemons)	2	tablespoons grated lemon peel
1	cup all-purpose flour	⅓	cup packed light brown sugar
1½	teaspoons salt	¼	cup chicken broth
2	teaspoons paprika	2	lemons, sliced
1	teaspoon freshly ground pepper		minced fresh parsley

In large zip-lock bag, combine chicken breasts and lemon juice. Squeeze out air and seal. Refrigerate overnight, turning once. Remove chicken, reserving 2 tablespoons of marinade and pat dry. Put flour, salt, paprika and pepper in a plastic bag. Shake until well mixed. Put chicken breasts in bag, one at a time and shake to coat evenly. In large skillet, heat oil and fry breasts, a few at a time, until well browned, about 10 minutes. Arrange chicken in a single layer in large baking dish. Sprinkle evenly with lemon peel and brown sugar. Mix chicken broth with reserved marinade and pour around chicken. Bake at 350° for 20-30 minutes or until tender. Garnish with lemon slices and minced parsley.

Excellent hot and terrific cold. This is a treat for al fresco dining on your patio. And yes, you really do need 10 lemons!

Toni Kennedy

Chicken Dee-Licious

8 servings

2	whole chicken fryers, cut in pieces and skinned	1	(18-ounce) jar apricot preserves
1	package dry onion soup mix	1	(8-ounce) bottle Russian dressing cooked rice

Preheat oven to 350°. Spray a 9x12-inch baking dish with non-stick vegetable spray. Place chicken, skinned side down, in baking dish. Combine remaining ingredients, pour over chicken and bake uncovered for 1½ hours. Serve with rice.

Florence Powell

Chicken Curry

6-8 servings

4	slices bacon, chopped	½	cup applesauce
¼	cup chopped onion	1	tablespoon sugar
¼	cup chopped celery	2	chicken bouillon cubes
½	garlic clove, minced	¼	teaspoon salt
2	tablespoons vegetable oil	2	cups chopped cooked
¼	cup all-purpose flour		chicken *or* 2 (6½-ounce)
2½	tablespoons curry powder		cans chicken
3	tablespoons tomato paste		cooked white rice
1¼	cups water		chutney for topping
1	tablespoon lemon juice		

Condiments:
sweet pickles, raisins,   crumbled bacon,
bananas, peanuts,   cooked egg white,
apples, coconut,   cooked egg yolks, etc.

Over low heat, cook first 4 ingredients in oil for 10 minutes. Gradually add flour and cook another 5 minutes. Stir in remaining ingredients, except chicken, rice and chutney. Cover and cook over low heat for 45 minutes. Add chicken during last 15 minutes. Serve over rice with your choice of condiments and top with chutney. *Note:* Test of a good curry is that after mixing in the selected condiments, you should experience a different taste with each bite.

Great with ice cold beer and sherbet as a dessert.

Michal Farrar

 To clean aluminum pots when they are stained, merely boil with a little cream of tartar or vinegar.

146

Chicken Tikka

8 servings

½	cup butter	¼	to ½ teaspoon red pepper
1	teaspoon black pepper		or to taste
1	bay leaf	1	teaspoon paprika
1	(4-inch) cinnamon stick	1	teaspoon salt or to taste
3	to 4 whole cloves	½	teaspoon ground
2	large onions, chopped		coriander
1	(6-ounce) can tomato	½	teaspoon turmeric
	paste	8	chicken breast halves,
1½	cans water (9 ounces)		boned and skinned
1	teaspoon ground	½	teaspoon freshly grated
	cardamom		ginger root
1	teaspoon ground almonds	½	teaspoon crushed garlic
1	teaspoon black pepper	1	cup cream

In a 4-quart pot, sauté first 5 ingredients. Add onions and cook for about 30 minutes on medium heat. Stir frequently, until they are brown but not burnt. Add tomato paste to onions, followed by the next 9 ingredients. Cook over medium heat for a few minutes, than add the chicken and remaining ingredients except cream. Cook over medium heat for about 45 minutes, stirring frequently to prevent sticking. (Placing a grill between the burner and the pan will help reduce the danger of sticking and burning.) When chicken is tender, place chicken in a deep serving dish. Remove sauce from heat. Slightly warm up cream and stir cream into the sauce. (Cream should be just warm to the touch, not hot.) Pour sauce over chicken and place in warm oven until serving time.

Though this recipe may appear time consuming, it is not. It is delicious and well worth the effort! Excellent served with **Rice Pulao.**

Dorothy Joshi

If they are reasonably fresh when you buy them, eggs will last 30 to 40 days in the refrigerator.

147

Chicken Fricassée With Mushrooms

6 servings

3	tablespoons olive oil		salt and pepper to taste
2	tablespoons butter	1	(8-ounce) container fresh
1	cut up frying chicken *or*		mushrooms, sliced
	6 chicken breast	3	tablespoons canned
	halves		tomatoes, chopped

In heavy skillet, heat oil and butter. Brown chicken on both sides over medium heat. Season with salt and pepper. Add mushrooms and tomatoes, cover pan and cook 30-40 minutes until chicken is tender, turning occasionally. Remove chicken from pan. To serve, spoon sauce over chicken. *Note:* If sauce is too thin, bring to a boil and add ½ tablespoon of butter.

Good served with buttered noodles tossed with a bit of parsley, basil and a shake of garlic powder.

Sarah W. D'Addabbo

Chicken With Mushroom Sauce

6-8 servings

2	chicken fryers, cut up *or*	4	tablespoons chopped fresh
	8 breast halves,		parsley
	boned and skinned	¼	teaspoon garlic powder
2	(10¾-ounce) cans cream	2	tablespoons chopped
	of mushroom soup		onion
1	(10½-ounce) can beef	1	teaspoon thyme
	bouillon		pinch of rosemary
1	tablespoon Worcestershire	½	cup dry white wine
	sauce		cooked rice

Preheat oven to 350°. In a large skillet, brown chicken in a small amount of oil and butter. Drain and place chicken in a 9x13-inch baking dish. Add remaining ingredients to skillet and mix well. Bring mixture to a boil and scrape up browned bits from pan. Reduce heat, simmer a few minutes and pour sauce over chicken. (May be prepared ahead to this point and refrigerated.) Bake for 1 hour and if refrigerated, add an extra 30 minutes. Serve with rice.

A family favorite for 23 years. Cut chicken in bite-size pieces for a buffet.

Lois Poper

Gene And Ina Mae's Chicken

6-8 servings

8	chicken breast halves, boned and skinned	1	cup sour cream
1	(2.25-ounce) jar dried beef	¼	teaspoon curry powder
1	(10¾-ounce) can cream of mushroom soup	2	strips bacon, cut in 4 pieces (optional)
1	(6-ounce) jar sliced mushrooms, drained		fresh parsley sprigs

Preheat oven to 325°. Place chicken breasts between 2 sheets of waxed paper and pound to approximately ¼-inch thickness. Rinse dried beef under running water and pat to dry. Place 2 pieces dried beef on each chicken breast and roll. Place in a 9x13-inch casserole dish. Mix soup, mushrooms, sour cream and curry powder. Spread over chicken rolls. Top each roll with a small piece of bacon. Bake for 1½ hours. Garnish with fresh parsley sprigs and serve with wild rice and vegetables.

Lynda Edsall
Alpharetta, Georgia

Celestial Chicken

6 servings

4	to 5 chicken breast halves, boned and skinned	2	teaspoons salt
½	cup light cream	2	teaspoons paprika
1	cup all-purpose flour	2	teaspoons Accent
1	(2¾-ounce) bottle sesame seeds	¼	teaspoon pepper
		¼	cup parsley flakes
			oil for frying

Cut chicken into 1½-inch strips. Dip chicken in cream (can marinate in cream overnight in refrigerator). Combine flour with the next 6 ingredients and coat chicken in mixture. Fry chicken in 2-inches of hot oil until chicken is golden brown. Drain on paper towels. Serve with **Cream Sauce.**

Cream Sauce:

¼	cup butter		
¼	cup all-purpose flour	2	chicken bouillon cubes
1	teaspoon salt	1½	cups light cream
¼	teaspoon cayenne pepper	¾	cup water

Melt butter in saucepan. Add flour, salt, pepper and bouillon cubes. Stir constantly over medium heat. Add cream and water to desired consistency. Can be served in individual dishes for dipping or poured over chicken.

Linda D. Domer

Supremes De Volaille A L'orange En Pommes
(Chicken Breasts with Orange Sauce and Apples)

4 servings

7 tablespoons butter	4 chicken breast halves, boned and skinned
1 large apple, peeled, cored and chopped	1 cup chicken stock *or* canned broth
1 teaspoon honey	1 cup apple juice
1 teaspoon fresh lemon juice	½ cup orange juice
1 cup apple purée *or* applesauce	¼ cup orange liqueur *or* brandy
¾ cup all-purpose flour	1 (1-inch) cinnamon stick chopped fresh chives

Melt 2 tablespoons of butter in a small skillet. Add apple, honey and lemon juice; sauté until apple is tender, about 4 minutes. Add apple purée or applesauce and simmer an additional 2 minutes. Set aside. Place flour in a bowl and season to taste with salt and pepper. Dredge chicken in flour. Melt 2 tablespoons butter in large skillet, add chicken and cook until golden brown, about 4 minutes per side. Transfer to a warm plate and tent with foil. Add chicken stock, apple and orange juices, liqueur and cinnamon stick to same skillet and bring to a boil, scraping up any brown bits. Simmer until reduced to about ⅔ cup, about 15 minutes. Stir in apple mixture and remaining 3 tablespoons butter. Season with salt and pepper and discard cinnamon stick. Ladle sauce over chicken, sprinkle with chives and serve. *Note:* Apple purée can be made from canned apples.

C'est si bon!

Thomas M. Cox

Put your hand inside a waxed sandwich bag and you have a mitt for greasing your baking pans and casserole dishes.

Thousand Dollar Chicken

6 servings

6	chicken breast halves, boned and skinned	1	envelope from (2.4-ounce) package cream of chicken instant cup of soup
1	teaspoon Mrs. Dash (unsalted)		
2	teaspoons paprika	1	tablespoon onion flakes
½	teaspoon pepper	2	tablespoons parsley flakes
½	teaspoon Italian spices		juice of ½ lemon
2	tablespoons butter, melted	½	cup white wine
2	tablespoons olive oil (can substitute all oil for butter)	1	(4-ounce) can mushrooms, drained
		¼	pound snow peas (optional)
1	(10½-ounce) can chicken broth *or* bouillon		

Preheat oven to 350°. Wash and pat chicken dry; place in a 9x13-inch baking dish. Sprinkle both sides of breasts with first 4 seasonings. Combine butter and olive oil and drizzle mixture over chicken. Bake uncovered for 25 minutes before adding other ingredients. In a small saucepan, combine chicken broth and dry cream of chicken soup and blend well to dissolve. Add remaining ingredients except snow peas and simmer for several minutes. Pour over chicken and continue to bake for another 45 minutes or until chicken is tender, basting every 20 minutes. Add snow peas the last 20 minutes of cooking time.

Easy and fast to prepare since you don't have to brown the chicken and absolutely exquisite for your most discerning guests.

Geri Cuoghi

Six chicken breast halves equal 2⅔ cups diced cooked chicken.

Pollo Ala Tino

6-8 servings

4 pounds boneless chicken breasts, cut in 2-inch pieces	½ pound mushrooms, trimmed and sliced
1 cup all-purpose flour	1 (14-ounce) can artichoke hearts, drained
¼ cup vegetable oil	¼ cup fresh lemon juice
½ cup butter	salt and pepper to taste
1 garlic clove, finely chopped	1 tablespoon chopped fresh parsley
	¼ cup white wine (optional)

Dredge chicken in flour. In a large skillet, heat oil and sauté chicken until golden. Pour off oil, add butter, garlic and mushrooms. Let simmer for 5-10 minutes or until mushrooms are tender. Add artichokes, lemon juice, salt, pepper, parsley and wine. Simmer and stir gently or artichokes will break.

Directly translated, "Chicken with Insight". Tastes great with yellow rice and baby carrots.

Sarah W. D'Addabbo

Marie's Chicken Sherry

4 servings

1 cup sherry wine	½ cup margarine, melted
1 teaspoon seasoned salt	⅔ cup Parmesan cheese
3 teaspoons chopped fresh parsley	⅓ cup dry bread crumbs
2 teaspoons Worcestershire sauce	2½ to 3 pounds chicken breasts

Preheat oven to 350°. Grease an 8x12-inch baking dish. Mix wine, salt, parsley, Worcestershire and margarine. Place chicken in pan, pour mixture over chicken. Mix cheese and bread crumbs together and sprinkle over chicken and sauce. Cover pan and bake 1 to 1½ hours. *Note:* Broil for 2 minutes at end of cooking time for crusty chicken.

Mary Beth Harja

Chicken Cordon Bleu

6 servings

6	chicken breast halves, boned and skinned	2	(10¾ ounce) cans cream of chicken soup
1	egg, beaten		garlic salt *or* garlic powder to taste
6	tablespoons all-purpose flour		
1	teaspoon salt	1	cup dry white wine
½	teaspoon pepper	6	ham slices
4	tablespoons margarine	6	slices Swiss cheese

Preheat oven to 350°. Dip chicken in egg, then in flour mixed with salt and pepper. In a 10-inch skillet, melt margarine and lightly brown the chicken on both sides. Combine soup, seasonings and wine; pour over chicken that has been place in a 2-quart baking dish. Bake for 45 minutes, or until chicken is tender. Just before serving, top chicken with ham and cheese. Return to oven and bake until cheese is melted. Serve immediately. *Note:* When baking, cover lightly with foil if necessary.

A quick and easy recipe and everyone thinks you have gone to a lot of trouble. Good served with wild rice.

Virginia Heffernan

Chicken Monterey

8 servings

8	chicken breast halves, boned and skinned	½	cup Parmesan cheese
¼	cup margarine, melted	½	teaspoon oregano
¼	teaspoon oregano	¼	pound (8 slices) Monterey Jack cheese
1	teaspoon parsley flakes	5	tablespoons margarine, melted
½	cup dry bread crumbs		

Pound chicken to ¼-inch thickness. Combine melted margarine, oregano and parsley in a bowl. In a pie plate, stir together bread crumbs, Parmesan cheese and oregano. Brush herb-margarine mixture over top side of chicken. Place one slice of cheese on each chicken breast and roll up. Dip rolled chicken in melted margarine and roll in bread crumbs. Place seam side down in a 9x13-inch ungreased baking dish. Cover and refrigerate 4 hours or overnight. Preheat oven to 400° and bake uncovered for 20 minutes or until juice runs clear when pierced with a fork.

Great for company because you can prepare it the day before serving.

Jan Harvey

153

Cheesy Baked Chicken Breasts

8 servings

8	chicken breast halves, boned and skinned	⅓ cup dry white wine
8	(4x4-inch) slices Swiss cheese	1 cup herb seasoned stuffing mix, crushed
1	(10¾-ounce) can cream of chicken soup	¼ cup butter *or* margarine, melted

Preheat oven to 350°. Arrange chicken in a lightly greased 9x13-inch baking dish. Top with cheese slices. Combine soup and wine, stirring well. Pour sauce evenly over chicken and sprinkle with stuffing mix. Drizzle butter over crumbs. Bake for 45-55 minutes.

An elegant dish that can be prepared on the busiest day!

Rhonda Green
Agatha LaPaglia

Stuffed Chicken

2 servings

⅔	cup water	2 tablespoons all-purpose flour
1	cup flexible serving chicken-flavor stuffing mix	dash pepper
2	chicken breast halves, boned and skinned	2 tablespoons butter
		4 tablespoons dry white wine
		3 tablespoons water

In a small pan, bring water to a boil and stir in stuffing mix. Cover and remove from heat. Let stand for 5 minutes and fluff with a fork. With a meat mallet, pound chicken breasts very thin. Spoon stuffing on one end of cutlet and roll jelly roll style. Secure with a toothpick. Combine flour with pepper and roll cutlets in mixture. In a small skillet, melt butter and brown cutlets evenly. Add wine and water. Cover, reduce heat and simmer for 20 minutes, turning roll twice. **Note:** To pound chicken, always pound on the rough side of the meat. With flexible serving stuffing, you can make as many servings as you wish. This recipe is easily doubled, tripled, etc.

Meg Smerbeck

Crab-Stuffed Chicken Breasts

6 servings

6	chicken breast halves, boned and skinned	2	tablespoons all-purpose flour
	salt and pepper to taste	½	teaspoon paprika
3	tablespoons butter *or* margarine	2	tablespoons butter *or* margarine, melted
½	cup chopped onion	1	envelope hollandaise sauce mix
½	cup chopped celery		
3	tablespoons dry white wine	¾	cup milk
1	(7½-ounce) can crabmeat, drained and flaked	2	tablespoons dry white wine
½	cup herb-seasoned stuffing mix	½	cup shredded Swiss cheese

Preheat oven to 375°. Pound chicken to flatten and sprinkle with salt and pepper. In a medium-sized skillet, melt butter and cook onion and celery until tender. Remove from heat. Add the wine, crabmeat and stuffing; mix well. Place equal amount of mixture on each breast, roll up and secure. Combine flour and paprika, coat chicken. Place in a 7x11-inch baking dish, drizzle with 2 tablespoons butter. Bake uncovered for 1 hour. Transfer to serving platter. Blend sauce mix with milk in a medium saucepan. Cook and stir until thick. Add remaining wine and cheese, stir until cheese melts. Pour half the sauce over chicken and place remaining sauce in serving dish. *Note:* The chicken rolls may be prepared the day before and refrigerated.

An elegant entrée for your next special occasion.

Dorothy B. Watkins

Gravy made with cornstarch as a thickening agent instead of flour can be reheated many times without causing the grease to separate.

Italian Style Chicken Kiev

4-6 servings

½	cup margarine	6	chicken breast halves,
½	cup fine dry bread crumbs		boned and skinned
¼	cup Parmesan cheese	½	cup margarine, melted
½	teaspoon basil leaves	¼	cup white wine
½	teaspoon oregano leaves	¼	cup chopped green onions
½	teaspoon garlic salt	¼	cup chopped fresh parsley

Preheat oven to 350°. Melt margarine in bowl. In another bowl combine bread crumbs, cheese, basil, oregano and garlic. Dip chicken in margarine, then coat with crumb mixture. Place chicken in ungreased 9x13-inch baking dish. Cook for 45 minutes or until done. When chicken is done, combine remaining margarine, wine, onions and parsley. Pour margarine sauce over chicken and continue to bake about 5 more minutes. Serve with sauce.

Calma Hobson

Chicken With Walnuts

4-6 servings

1½	pounds chicken breasts,	½	teaspoon crushed red
	boned and skinned		pepper *or* to taste
3	tablespoons soy sauce	2	tablespoons cooking oil
2	teaspoons cornstarch	2	medium green peppers,
2	tablespoons dry sherry		cut into ¾-inch
1	teaspoon grated ginger		pieces
	root	4	green onions, bias sliced
1	teaspoon sugar		into 1-inch lengths
½	teaspoon salt	1	cup walnut halves
			cooked rice

Cut chicken into 1-inch pieces. Set aside. In a small bowl, blend soy sauce into cornstarch, stir in dry sherry, ginger root, sugar, salt and red pepper. Set aside. Preheat a wok or large skillet over high heat; add cooking oil. Stir-fry green peppers and onions in hot oil 2 minutes or until crisp tender. Remove from wok. Add walnuts, stir-fry 1-2 minutes or until just golden. Remove from wok. Add more oil as necessary. Add half the chicken and stir-fry 2 minutes. Remove from wok and stir-fry remaining chicken 2 minutes. Return all chicken to wok or skillet. Stir soy mixture and stir into chicken. Cook and stir until thickened and bubbly. Stir in vegetables and walnuts. Cover and cook 1 minute more. Serve at once with hot cooked rice.

A distinct flavored meal made the easy way by stir-frying.

Julie Angle

Chicken Scampi

4-6 servings

6	chicken breast halves, boned and skinned	¼	cup dry white wine
½	cup butter *or* margarine	1	tablespoon oregano
2	garlic cloves, minced	½	tablespoon parsley flakes
	salt and pepper to taste	1	teaspoon basil
⅛	cup lemon juice		cooked rice

Cut chicken into bite-size pieces. Melt butter in a large skillet over medium heat. Sauté garlic and chicken, seasoned with salt and pepper, for 10 minutes. Add the remaining ingredients and cook for about 15 minutes longer. Serve over rice.

Kathy Lynskey

Chicken Puffs

6 servings

1	(10-ounce) package frozen puff pastry shells, thawed	1½	teaspoons lemon pepper (or less)
⅓	cup crushed seasoned croutons	1	tablespoon lemon juice
¼	cup chopped pecans	1	cup diced cooked chicken
1	(3-ounce) package cream cheese, softened	1	(4-ounce) can mushrooms, drained
1	tablespoon margarine, softened	3	tablespoons margarine, melted

Preheat oven to 400°. Roll pastry shells between wax paper into fairly thin circles. Mix croutons and pecans and set aside. Mix remaining ingredients together, except 3 tablespoons margarine. Put 2-3 tablespoons chicken mixture in the middle of each round. Fold over ends and pinch together. Dip smooth side (bottom) in melted margarine and then crouton/pecan mixture. Place on oiled cookie sheet, margarine side up and bake for 15-20 minutes. Watch that the top doesn't get too brown. *Note:* Recipe is easily doubled and can be frozen. Thaw and reheat in 400° oven for about 15 minutes covered with foil.

Eva M. Edwards

157

Chicken Squares

4 servings

1 (6-ounce) can white chicken meat
1 (3-ounce) package cream cheese, softened
3 tablespoons butter, melted

1 tablespoon onion flakes
½ teaspoon seasoned salt
1 (8-count) package crescent rolls

Mix chicken, cream cheese, butter, onion flakes and salt together. Press 2 triangular rolls together to form a square, seal perforations. Fill with 1½ to 2 tablespoons chicken mixture. Bring four corners together at top and seal. Repeat for other 3 squares. Bake according to directions on crescent roll can. *Note:* Can be made the night before and baked when ready to serve.

Great for a ladies luncheon, serve with a green salad and fruit.

Rhonda Green

Easy Chicken Dinner

6-8 servings

1 cup uncooked rice
1 (10¾-ounce) can cream of celery soup
1 (10¾-ounce) can water
6 to 8 chicken pieces, skinned

1 (10-ounce) package frozen broccoli spears
1 envelope dry onion soup mix

Preheat oven to 350°. Spread rice in a 9x13-inch casserole dish. Pour soup and water over rice and mix thoroughly. Place chicken on top of rice mixture and place broccoli spears on top of chicken. Sprinkle dry onion soup mixture on top of chicken and broccoli. Cover pan tightly with foil and bake for 1 hour 45 minutes - 2 hours. Do not remove foil until ready to serve.

Meg Smerbeck

To find out whether an egg is cooked, spin it on its side. If the egg wobbles, it is raw. If it spins smoothly, it is cooked.

Artichoke And Chicken Casserole

8-10 servings

2	(14-ounce) cans artichokes	1	cup mayonnaise
2⅔	cups diced, cooked chicken *or* turkey	1	teaspoon lemon juice
		½	teaspoon curry powder
2	(10-ounce) cans cream of chicken soup	1¼	cups grated sharp Cheddar cheese
		1½	cups bread crumbs

Preheat oven to 350°. Drain artichokes, cut in quarters and arrange in casserole. Then spread chicken. Combine rest of ingredients except cheese and crumbs. Pour over chicken and artichokes. Sprinkle cheese and crumbs on top. Bake for 25 minutes.

Artichokes give an aristocratic flair to this traditional casserole.

Sue Chris Gauthreaux

Chicken and Broccoli Casserole

8-10 servings

2	(10-ounce) packages frozen broccoli spears	1	teaspoon lemon juice
3	whole chicken breasts, cooked and diced	½	teaspoon curry powder
		1	cup shredded sharp Cheddar cheese
2	(10¾-ounce) cans cream of chicken soup	½	cup Ritz cracker crumbs
1	cup mayonnaise	2	tablespoons margarine, melted

Preheat oven to 350°. Cook broccoli in small amount of boiling water until tender. Drain and arrange in an 8x12-inch buttered casserole dish. Place chopped chicken on top. Combine soup, mayonnaise, lemon juice and curry powder. Pour over chicken. Sprinkle with cheese. Combine cracker crumbs and margarine and top with crumb mixture. Bake for 25 minutes.

Virginia Heffernan

Donna's Tasty Chicken Casserole

6-8 servings

4   whole chicken breasts,
    boned and skinned
3   cups water
2   bay leaves
1   chicken bouillon cube
1   (10¾-ounce) can cream
    of chicken soup

1   (10¾-ounce) can cream
    of mushroom soup
1⅓ cups milk
1   (8-ounce) bag of
    herb-seasoned
    stuffing mix
1   cup butter
1   cup chicken broth

Boil chicken breasts in 3 cups water with bay leaves and bouillon cube for 20 minutes. Remove chicken from water and cut into bite-size pieces, saving 1 cup of broth. Combine soups, milk and add chicken. Spread mixture in 9x13-inch casserole dish. Right before baking, spread stuffing over top of chicken. Melt butter in the 1 cup of reserved broth and pour over stuffing. Baked covered at 350° for 45 minutes and uncovered for an additional 15 minutes.

Mary Fehse

Cornish Hens

16 servings

2   teaspoons salt
2   teaspoons dried basil
2   teaspoons dried tarragon
2   teaspoons ground savory
½   teaspoon pepper
16 (1 to 1¼-pound) Cornish
    hens

1   cup butter, melted
1   cup orange marmalade
    watercress and peeled
    orange slices
    cooked rice

Preheat oven to 325°. Combine seasonings, stir well and sprinkle cavity of hens. Brush skins of each hen with melted butter and sprinkle with seasonings. Truss hens and place breast side up on a rack in a shallow roasting pan. Pour water into pan to cover bottom (about ⅛ inch deep). Bake for 45 minutes. Baste hens with orange marmalade during the last 10 minutes of baking. Serve over rice on large platter with watercress, orange slices and flowers (violets) in the center.

Very simple but elegant.

Margie Brennan

Chicken Enchiladas

6 servings

2	tablespoons butter	1	teaspoon coriander
¾	cup chopped onion	½	teaspoon salt
½	cup chopped green bell pepper	3	cups chicken broth
		1	cup sour cream
2	cups chopped cooked chicken	1½	cups shredded Monterey Jack cheese
3	tablespoons butter	12	(6-inch) flour tortillas
¼	cup all-purpose flour		parsley

Preheat oven to 350°. Melt 2 tablespoons butter in a large skillet and sauté onion and pepper. Combine with chicken and set aside. In the same skillet, melt the 3 tablespoons butter and blend in flour, coriander and salt. Stir in 2½ cups of broth, reserving ½ cup and cook until thick and bubbly. Remove from heat and stir in sour cream and ½ cup cheese. Stir half of this sauce into the chicken mixture. Dip tortillas in remaining sauce and fill each tortilla with ¼ cup of the chicken mixture. Roll up and place in a 9x13-inch casserole dish, seam side down. Mix reserved ½ cup broth with remaining sauce and pour over enchiladas. Sprinkle with 1 cup cheese and bake for 25-30 minutes. Garnish with parsley. Freezes very well.

A delicate flavored dish your whole family will enjoy.

Beth Sturman

When stuffing poultry, fill cavity only ¾ full since stuffing will expand.

Enchilada Casserole

4-6 servings

1 (10-12 count) package
corn tortillas
1 cup chopped onion
2 cups diced cooked chicken
2 cups grated Cheddar
cheese (reserve ½
cup for topping)

1 (10-ounce) can Rotel
tomatoes
1 (10¾-ounce) can cream
of chicken soup
½ cup milk
additional cheese
salsa
sour cream

Preheat oven to 350°. Grease a 2½ to 3 quart baking dish. Tear tortillas into quarters. Line dish using ⅓ of the tortilla pieces. Add ½ of the onion, chicken, cheese and ½ of the combined tomatoes, soup and milk. Repeat process, ending with ⅓ of the tortilla pieces. Cover and bake for 45 minutes. Remove cover and top with reserved cheese. Return to oven for another 5-10 minutes or until cheese melts. Serve with additional cheese, salsa and sour cream.

Variation: 1 pound cooked ground beef or turkey can be substituted for the chicken. Monterey Jack cheese can be substituted for half or all the Cheddar cheese.

Pat Smith

Sour Cream Chicken Enchiladas

8-10 servings

1 (8-ounce) package Mon-
terey Jack cheese with
jalapeños, shredded
1 (8-ounce) package shredded
Cheddar cheese
1 whole cooked chicken,
boned, skinned and
cut up (about 4 cups)
2 cups sour cream

2 (10¾-ounce) cans cream
of mushroom soup
1 medium onion, chopped
1 (4-ounce) can chopped
green chilies
2 (8-10 count) packages
flour tortillas
salsa sauce

Preheat oven to 325°. Mix all ingredients together except tortillas and salsa in large bowl. Place equal amount of filling in center of each tortilla, roll and place seam side down in a 9x13-inch baking pan. Reserve enough of the filling to coat top of each tortilla, about 1 tablespoon. Bake for 30 minutes or until heated through. To serve, place salsa on top of each enchilada.

Ever popular Mexican ingredients blend together in this delicious dinner.

Helen Applegate

Tortilla Casserole

6-8 servings

8 chicken breast halves, cooked, boned and skinned
2 (10¾-ounce) cans cream of mushroom soup
2 cups sour cream
1 cup diced onions
1 (4-ounce) can green chilies, chopped
1 tablespoon butter

2 dozen tortilla chips, crushed
1 pound pasteurized process cheese, shredded *or* ½ pound pasteurized process cheese and ½ pound shredded sharp Cheddar cheese

Preheat oven to 300°. Cut cooked chicken in medium size chunks and set aside. Mix soup and sour cream, set aside. Sauté onions and chilies in butter, add to soup mixture. In a 9x13-inch baking dish, layer half crushed chips, chicken, soup mixture and cheese. Repeat layers and end with cheese. Bake covered for 1½ hours; cover can be taken off during the last 30 minutes of baking time.

Pat O'Brien

Chicken Chimichangas

5-6 servings

2½ cups chopped cooked chicken
⅔ cup mild picante sauce
⅓ cup chopped green onions
¼ to 1 teaspoon cumin
½ teaspoon oregano
Condiments:
shredded lettuce
chopped tomatoes

10 to 12 (6-inch) flour tortillas
¼ cup butter, melted
1 cup shredded Cheddar cheese
1 cup shredded Monterey Jack cheese

sour cream
refried beans

Preheat oven to 475°. Combine chicken, picante sauce, green onions, cumin and oregano. Brush 1 side of each tortilla with butter. Spoon about ⅓ cup chicken mixture on unbuttered side, top with 1 tablespoon of each cheese. Coat a 9x13-inch baking dish with vegetable spray. Roll tortilla and place seam side down in dish. Top with any leftover cheese and bake for 13 minutes or until crisp and golden brown. Serve with shredded lettuce, chopped tomatoes and sour cream. Also good with refried beans.

A great way to use leftover chicken!

Pauline Cychowski

163

Southwest Turkey Pie

4 servings

Basic Marinara Sauce:

2	tablespoons olive oil	1	tablespoon crushed basil
1	medium onion, chopped	1	teaspoon sugar
2	garlic cloves, finely chopped	1	teaspoon crushed oregano
1	(28-ounce) can tomatoes, crushed	¼	teaspoon salt

Heat oil in medium-size skillet over medium heat. Add onion and garlic; cook until tender, about 6 minutes. Add remaining ingredients, cover and cook over medium heat 20 minutes.

Turkey Pie:

1	medium onion, chopped	1½	cups *Basic Marinara Sauce*
½	sweet red bell pepper, chopped (optional)	1	cup frozen corn kernels, thawed
½	sweet green bell pepper, chopped	¼	teaspoon salt (optional)
12	ounces ground turkey	2	ounces shredded Cheddar cheese
½	teaspoon ground cumin	1	(8½-ounce) package cornbread mix
2	teaspoons chili powder		

Preheat oven to 400°. Cook onion and peppers in a non-stick skillet coated with cooking spray for 4 minutes. Crumble turkey into skillet, add cumin and chili powder; cook until meat is no longer pink. Add sauce, corn and salt. Bring to a simmer. Remove from heat and add cheese. Pour into a 10-inch deep-dish pie plate. Prepare cornbread according to package directions. Spoon over turkey mixture. Bake for 25 minutes. *Note:* You can double this recipe (turkey pie portion) and freeze one pie, minus the cornbread topping. Then when thawed, just mix cornbread and proceed as directed. This is a good way to use the other half of the marinara sauce recipe and have a meal in the freezer.

Beth Sturman

When milk is slightly soured, add a pinch of soda and it can be used as fresh milk.

Crawfish Etouffée

6 servings

¾ cup vegetable oil
1 cup all-purpose flour
1 cup chopped onion
1 tablespoon chopped fresh parsley
1 tablespoon chopped green onions
2 teaspoons chopped celery
2 teaspoons chopped green bell pepper

3 pounds crawfish tails (can substitute shrimp *or* lump crabmeat)
water
2 teaspoons paprika
Tabasco® sauce to taste
salt and pepper to taste
2 cups cooked rice

Using cooking oil and flour, make a small semi-dark roux. Refer to **Roux** recipe for instructions. Add chopped onion, parsley, green onions, celery and bell pepper. Cook until tender. Add cleaned crawfish tails and cook 15-20 minutes. Add very little water, 1 tablespoon at a time. Your etouffée should be very thick. Add paprika. Season to taste with Tabasco®, salt and pepper. Serve over cooked rice.

A zesty Cajun-style dish.

S. Kay Clifton

Cajun Blackened Fish

6 servings

1 cup unsalted butter
1 tablespoon sweet paprika
1 teaspoon onion powder
1 teaspoon garlic powder
1 teaspoon cayenne pepper
½ teaspoon dried oregano leaves
2 teaspoons salt

¾ teaspoon white pepper
¾ teaspoon black pepper
½ teaspoon dried thyme leaves
6 (8 to 10-ounce) fish fillets, ½-inch thick (redfish, channel bass, pompano *or* flounder)

Melt butter in a small saucepan and set aside. Heat heavy skillet over high heat until it is beyond smoking stage, at least 10 minutes. Combine all seasonings together and mix well. Sprinkle seasoning mix generously and evenly on both sides of fillets, patting it by hand. Place in hot skillet and pour 1 teaspoon butter on top of each fillet. (May flame up.) Cook until it looks charred, about 2 minutes. Turn fish over, pour 1 teaspoon butter on top and cook until done, about 2 minutes. Serve piping hot.

Seasonings can be made ahead and kept on hand to blacken chicken, catfish or steaks.

S. Kay Clifton

165

Fish For Guests

6-8 servings

2   pounds fresh *or* frozen sole   ¼   teaspoon garlic salt
    or haddock fillets,   ½   teaspoon grated onion
    thawed   ½   teaspoon Worcestershire
1   (10¾-ounce) can cream of   sauce
    shrimp soup   1¼   cups Ritz cracker crumbs
¼   cup butter *or* margarine,
    melted

Preheat oven to 375°. Place fish in a greased 9x13-inch baking dish. Spread with soup. Bake for 20 minutes. Combine butter and seasonings. Mix with cracker crumbs. Sprinkle over fish and bake an additional 10 minutes.

Elizabeth S. Moody

Company Scrod-Baby Cod

6 servings

2   pounds scrod *or* baby cod   1   teaspoon garlic powder
1   packet Ritz crackers,   4   tablespoons butter,
    crushed   melted
12 ounces grated sharp   paprika
    Cheddar cheese

Preheat oven to 425°. Divide scrod into 6 pieces and place on buttered cookie sheet. Mix crushed crackers, cheese and garlic powder together in a bowl. Sprinkle cracker mixture on top of fish and drizzle butter over crumbs. Sprinkle with paprika and bake for 15-20 minutes.

An entrée that's been made many times and is wonderful for company.

Joan Foote

Crabmeat Delight

4 servings

1   cup chopped green onions   ¾   cup butter, melted
    (include green tops)   1   pound fresh lump crabmeat
¾   pound fresh mushrooms,   ½   cup cream sherry
    sliced

Sauté onions and mushrooms in butter until tender. Add crabmeat and sherry and cook until thoroughly heated. Serve as an entrée with rice.

My own variation of a recipe from my favorite restaurant in Mobile.

Gretchen Kaemmer Smith

Crab Stuffed Fillet Of Sole

4 servings

½	to 1 tablespoon butter *or* margarine	1	tablespoon Italian bread crumbs
¼	cup diced fresh mushrooms	1½	teaspoons minced chives
½	garlic clove, minced	4	(2½ to 3-ounce) sole fillets
¼	cup fresh crabmeat, cleaned		additional melted butter *or* margarine paprika

Preheat oven to 325°. Melt butter in a medium-size skillet and sauté mushrooms and garlic until soft, about 5 minutes. Remove from heat, add crabmeat, bread crumbs and chives. Wash and dry fish fillets. Brush with additional melted butter on one side and spread each fillet with crab mixture. Carefully roll up fillets and place seam side down in a 1½-quart casserole dish that has been sprayed with non-stick vegetable spray. Drizzle melted butter over each fillet and sprinkle with paprika. Bake 30-35 minutes depending on thickness of fillets. Baste a couple of times with butter from the bottom of the casserole.

This sensational entrée will make a fish lover out of you!

Peg Kottke

Jane's Crab Cakes

4 servings

1	egg		dash Tabasco® sauce
2	tablespoons mayonnaise	1	pound backfin crabmeat (lump crabmeat), picked for shells
1	teaspoon dry mustard		
½	teaspoon black pepper		
1	teaspoon Old Bay seasoning (no substitutions)	¼	cup cracker crumbs vegetable oil for frying
2	teaspoons Worcestershire sauce		

In a blender or mixing bowl, combine the egg, mayonnaise, mustard, pepper, Old Bay, Worcestershire and Tabasco®. Mix until frothy. Place crabmeat in a bowl and pour the mixture over top. Sprinkle in cracker crumbs and toss gently, taking care not to break up the lumps of crabmeat. Form the cakes by hand into 3-inch wide, 1-inch thick rounded mounds. Do not pack the crab cake batter together too firmly. Heat oil in a deep skillet to 375°. Deep-fry crab cakes a few at a time, until golden brown on all sides, about 3 minutes. Remove with a slotted spoon to a paper towel. Serve at once.

Wonderful Maryland recipe!

Jane Reynolds

Boiled Shrimp (Peel-Em And Eat-Em)

5 pounds cooked shrimp

½ cup lemon juice
4 yellow onions, quartered
1 (3-ounce) package crab boil
2 tablespoons liquid crab
  and shrimp boil
1 teaspoon red pepper

2 teaspoons black pepper
3 tablespoons salt
5 pounds medium shrimp
  with shells, rinsed
  and drained
cocktail sauce

Fill large stockpot with twice as much water as shrimp and bring to a boil. Add all ingredients except shrimp, cover and continue boiling for 15 minutes. Add shrimp and boil 5 minutes or more. Test; shrimp should be tender, not soft nor tough. Remove stockpot from burner and immediately add 2 handfuls of ice cubes. This will force shrimp at bottom to soak up seasonings. Allow to sit for 10 minutes. Drain and separate shrimp from seasonings. Cool and then refrigerate until ready to serve. Serve chilled with cocktail sauce and plenty of napkins.

For a complete meal, serve with corn-on-the cob, slaw and new potatoes boiled in water seasoned with the same spices as shrimp. Or simply peel-em and eat-em.

Nicki Knight

Shrimp Scampi

6 servings

2½ pounds large fresh shrimp,
    peeled and deveined
1 cup butter, melted
¼ cup olive oil
1 tablespoon parsley flakes

1 tablespoon lemon juice
¾ teaspoon salt
¾ teaspoon garlic powder
¾ teaspoon dried basil
½ teaspoon dried oregano

Preheat oven to 450°. Place shrimp in a single layer in a 10x15-inch jelly roll pan. Set aside. Combine remaining ingredients; pour over shrimp. Bake for 4 minutes or until shrimp are done.

This is a very easy and delicious way to prepare shrimp. It can be tossed with pasta or served over rice. A green salad and crusty rolls complete the meal.

Gretchen Mattingly

Fresh fish will float when placed in cold water.

Baked Stuffed Shrimp

4 servings

2	tablespoons butter, melted	½	pound bay scallops
2	cups Ritz cracker crumbs		dry sherry
1	teaspoon minced onion	1	pound large shrimp,
½	cup butter, melted		shelled and deveined

Preheat oven to 450°. Spread melted butter in bottom of a 10x14-inch baking dish. In a large bowl, mix cracker crumbs with minced onion, stir in melted butter. Add bay scallops. Stir in enough of the dry sherry (2-3 tablespoons or more) to lightly mold a heaping tablespoon of stuffing mixture to a shrimp. Hold shrimp on its side and <u>lightly</u> press stuffing on top side of shrimp. Place stuffed shrimp in prepared pan and bake for 20 minutes. *Note:* If shrimp are large enough, butterfly shrimp and lightly place stuffing between cut area.

Elegant and wonderfully delicious. A perfect "company's coming" entrée that is easy and quick to prepare.

Rita C. Leonard

Tequila Lime Prawns

4-6 servings

1	to 2 pounds large shrimp,	½	teaspoon salt
	shelled and deveined	½	teaspoon crushed red chili
3	tablespoons butter		pepper
1	tablespoon olive oil	3	tablespoons coarsely
3	to 4 large garlic cloves,		chopped cilantro
	minced		lime wedges
¾	cup tequila		hot cooked rice
¼	cup lime juice		

Pat shrimp dry with a paper towel. Heat butter and oil in large skillet over medium heat. When butter is melted, add garlic and cook 30 seconds. Add shrimp, cook 2 minutes stirring occasionally. Stir in tequila, lime juice, salt and chili pepper. Cook 2 minutes or until shrimp are pink and glazed. Add cilantro and cook 10 seconds. Garnish with lime wedges. Serve over hot cooked rice.

An exquisite dish for a special evening that is quick and easy to prepare.

Geri Murtagh

 Cooking shrimp in shells helps retain the flavor.

Shrimp Rice

4-6 servings

½	cup butter	1	(10¾-ounce) can French
½	green bell pepper,		onion soup
	chopped	1	(4-ounce) jar sliced
1	cup rice		mushrooms, undrained
1	pound shrimp, shelled		water
	and deveined		salt and pepper to taste

Preheat oven to 350°. Melt butter in skillet. Sauté green pepper. Add rice and shrimp, sauté until shrimp turn pink, about 5 minutes. Add soup. Place undrained mushrooms in measuring cup and add water to measure ¾ cup. Add to other ingredients in skillet and stir to blend. Season with salt and pepper. Turn mixture in a greased casserole dish, cover and bake for 1 hour.

Rice takes on a new look in this quick main dish.

Lisa Zeringue

Creamy Shrimp Dish

4-6 servings

2	(10¾-ounce) cans cream of	1	(16-ounce) package frozen
	shrimp soup		cooked shrimp,
2	(8-ounce) packages cream		thawed, rinsed and
	cheese		drained
1	tablespoon parsley flakes	1	(8-ounce) can sliced water
2	teaspoons lemon juice		chestnuts, drained
¼	teaspoon garlic salt	3	cups hot cooked rice
¼	teaspoon paprika		(optional)
		1	(10-ounce) package frozen
			puff pastry shells
			(optional)

In a medium saucepan over medium heat, mix together the first 6 ingredients to make a creamy sauce. Add shrimp and heat thoroughly. Add water chestnuts 2 minutes before serving to maintain their firmness. Serve over rice or baked pastry shells. *Note:* You can substitute crabmeat, scallops or other seafood for shrimp.

For an elegant presentation, serve this savory shrimp sauce over baked pastry shells.

Karen Breunig

170

Tuna Casserole

6 servings

1	(12-ounce) package wide noodles	2	cups small broccoli flowerets
1	cup sour cream	⅓	cup chopped green bell pepper
1	cup mayonnaise		
½	cup milk	¼	cup chopped green onions
½	cup Parmesan cheese	1	(12½-ounce) can tuna, drained and flaked
1	teaspoon Dijon mustard		salt and pepper to taste

Preheat oven to 350°. Cook noodles according to package directions, drain. In a large bowl, combine sour cream, mayonnaise, milk, Parmesan cheese and Dijon mustard. Add hot noodles, broccoli, peppers, onions and tuna. Mix well. Add salt and pepper to taste. Place in ungreased 2-quart baking dish. Bake covered 40-45 minutes or until hot and bubbly.

Real good — wonderful flavor.

Judy Baker

Crab Noodle Casserole

6 servings

1	(6 to 8-ounce) package frozen crabmeat, thawed *or*	2	tablespoons butter
		1	cup sour cream
1	(6½ to 7½-ounce) can crabmeat, drained	1	cup cottage cheese
		1	cup grated sharp Cheddar cheese
6	ounces fine noodles		
⅓	cup chopped onion	¼	teaspoon salt
½	cup chopped celery	⅛	teaspoon pepper
¼	cup chopped green bell pepper	½	cup bread crumbs
		2	tablespoons butter, melted
1	garlic clove, minced		

Preheat oven to 350°. Drain crabmeat and slice if necessary. Cook noodles according to package directions and drain. Sauté onion, celery, green pepper and garlic in 2 tablespoons of butter. Combine with crabmeat, drained noodles, sour cream, cottage cheese, grated cheese and seasonings. Spoon into a buttered 9x13-inch casserole dish. Mix bread crumbs with the melted butter and sprinkle on top of casserole. Bake for 35 minutes.

With this elegant casserole, you only need a green salad and hot rolls to complete the menu.

Sue Burnett

171

Fettuccine Alfredo With Peas, Shrimp And Prosciutto

4 servings

½	cup butter	½	pound tiny shrimp, shelled, deveined and cooked
2	garlic cloves, minced		
	salt and pepper to taste		
1	cup Parmesan cheese	½	pound prosciutto, shaved
1	cup half-and-half	½	teaspoon dried parsley flakes
1	egg yolk		
10	ounces tiny frozen peas	12	ounces fettuccine

In a large skillet, melt butter, add garlic, salt, pepper and cheese. Stir over very low heat until blended. Slowly add half-and-half, stirring constantly. Lightly beat egg yolk; take several tablespoons of hot cheese mixture and add to yolk. Slowly add yolk mixture to saucepan and stir to blend. After sauce is mixed, add peas, cooked shrimp and prosciutto. Keep warm. Cook fettuccine according to package directions and drain. Toss warm pasta with sauce. Serve immediately.

A simple but elegant meal that is prepared in minutes.

Sarah W. D'Addabbo

Scallops Fettuccine Regatta

6 servings

1	cup thinly sliced green onions	1	cup chopped parsley
½	cup butter	½	cup butter, melted
1½	pounds bay scallops	½	cup all-purpose flour
2	cups dry white wine		salt and pepper to taste
1	cup grated Parmesan cheese	2	cups light cream
		2	(9-ounce) packages fresh spinach fettuccine

In a large skillet, sauté green onions in butter until soft, 2-3 minutes. Add scallops and sauté lightly. Add white wine and simmer for 5 minutes. Stir in Parmesan cheese and parsley. Thicken with a paste made from ½ cup melted butter and flour. Over medium heat, slowly stir paste in sauce, stirring constantly, until sauce thickens. Season and slowly add cream, stirring constantly. Heat through but do not boil. Cook fettuccine according to package directions; drain. Serve sauce over fettuccine noodles.

This rich entrée has a succulent and unique flavor. Incredibly indulgent but worth every calorie!

Rita C. Leonard

Fettuccine Pie

6-8 servings

1	pound bulk Italian sausage	1	(4-ounce) can sliced
1	medium onion, chopped		mushrooms, drained
¼	cup chopped celery	1	(8-ounce) package
2	tablespoons oil		fettucine
½	teaspoon oregano	1	(3-ounce) package cream
½	teaspoon basil		cheese, softened
1	(16-ounce) can tomatoes,	½	teaspoon garlic salt
	chopped	½	teaspoon salt
1	(6-ounce) can tomato paste	¼	cup Parmesan cheese

Preheat oven to 350°. Sauté sausage, onion and celery in oil. Drain any excess fat. Add seasonings, tomatoes, tomato paste and mushrooms. Simmer for 30-45 minutes. Cook fettucine according to package directions and drain. Mix cream cheese with salts. Add fettucine and mix until noodles are well coated. Pat fettucine mixture around the sides and bottom of a 10-inch glass pie plate. Pour tomato mixture on top and sprinkle with Parmesan cheese. Bake uncovered for 30 minutes. Cut into pie wedges.
Note: Can be made ahead, but cook 15 minutes longer if refrigerated.

A simple and tantalizing variation of a classic pasta dish.

Jennie Hart
Buffalo, New York

Pork Primavera

4 servings

12	ounces fettuccine	½	pound fresh pea pods,
2	garlic cloves, minced		trimmed and strings
1	pound pork tenderloin,		removed
	cut into strips	8	to 10 cherry tomatoes,
1	tablespoon olive oil		halved and drained
4	green onions, sliced	½	teaspoon oregano
1	zucchini, coarsely grated	½	cup dry white wine
		¼	cup grated Romano/
			Parmesan cheese

Cook fettuccine according to package directions and drain. In a large skillet, sauté garlic and pork in oil until lightly browned. Add vegetables and oregano. Simmer for a few minutes, stirring until moisture is gone. Add wine and simmer to reduce liquid. Pour over fettuccine. Toss with cheese and serve immediately.

This dish is as colorful as it is quick and easy. Wonderfully delicious as well.

Pat O'Brien

Japanese Fried Spaghetti

4-6 servings

1	(7-ounce) package thin spaghetti	7	to 8 scallions, chopped (green parts only)
½	pound bacon	6	to 8 cups finely shredded cabbage
2	to 3 garlic cloves, chopped	3	tablespoons soy sauce

Cook spaghetti according to package directions and drain. Do not overcook spaghetti. Chop bacon and fry until crisp; remove from pan and discard all but 2 tablespoons bacon drippings. Stir-fry garlic and scallions in bacon fat for 1 minute. Add cabbage and stir-fry 2 minutes. Add cooked spaghetti and bacon to cabbage mixture and toss well. Add soy sauce and toss again to combine all ingredients.

A delicious and unusual way to serve spaghetti.

Mary Stasul
Little Neck, New York

Cavatini

4 servings

4	ounces curly egg noodles	1	(4-ounce) can mushrooms
8	ounces ground beef	2	ounces pepperoni, chopped
16	ounces spaghetti sauce	4	(1-ounce) slices mozzarella cheese
1	(8-ounce) can tomato sauce		

Cook noodles according to package directions and drain. Cook ground beef in skillet until brown and crumbly; drain. Add spaghetti sauce, tomato sauce, mushrooms, and pepperoni. Stir until well mixed. Combine with noodles in 5x7-inch casserole. Top with cheese. Bake at 350° for 20 minutes or until cheese melts.

A quick and easy dish that is quite tasty.

Karen Kerschen

Seafood Lasagna

12 servings

8	lasagna noodles	1	(8-ounce) package
1	cup chopped onion		imitation crabmeat,
2	tablespoons butter		chopped *or* 1 (7½-
1	(8-ounce) package cream		ounce) can crabmeat,
	cheese, softened		drained, flaked and
1½	cups creamy cottage		cartilage removed
	cheese	1	pound shelled shrimp,
1	egg, beaten		cooked and halved
2	teaspoons dried basil		lengthwise (if frozen,
½	teaspoon salt		thaw and drain well)
⅛	teaspoon pepper	¼	cup grated Parmesan
2	(10¾-ounce) cans cream		cheese
	of mushroom soup	½	cup shredded sharp
⅓	cup milk		Cheddar cheese
⅓	cup dry white wine		

Cook lasagna noodles according to package directions and drain. Arrange 4 noodles in bottom of greased 9x13-inch baking dish. Cook onion in butter until tender, blend in cream cheese. Stir until melted, remove from heat. Stir in cottage cheese, egg, basil, salt and pepper. Spread half of this mixture on top of noodles. Combine soup, milk and wine. Stir in crabmeat and shrimp. Spread half of this mixture on top of the cheese layer. Repeat the 3 layers. Sprinkle with Parmesan. Bake uncovered in a 350° oven for 45 minutes. Top with Cheddar and bake 2-3 minutes more, until cheese is melted and bubbly. Let stand for 15 minutes before serving. *Note:* Dish can be prepared ahead and refrigerated.

This savory dish is sure to become an instant favorite with your family and friends.

Rita C. Leonard

Fish odor should never be strong, only mild and fresh. Buy moist firm textured fish.

175

Sweet Lasagna

8 servings

1	pound sweet *or* hot Italian sausage	2	(6-ounce) cans tomato paste
½	pound ground beef	½	cup water
½	cup finely chopped onion	12	curly lasagna noodles
2	garlic cloves, minced	1	(15-ounce) container ricotta cheese *or* cottage cheese
2	tablespoons sugar		
1	tablespoon salt		
1½	teaspoons dried basil	1	egg, slightly beaten
½	teaspoon fennel seed	½	teaspoon salt
¼	teaspoon pepper	1	(3-ounce) jar Parmesan cheese
¼	cup chopped fresh parsley		
1	(35-ounce) can Italian-style tomatoes *or* 4 cups canned tomatoes, undrained	¾	pound mozzarella cheese, thinly sliced

Remove sausage from casing and chop. Break up ground beef; sauté sausage, beef, onion and garlic. Cook 20 minutes and drain well. Add sugar, salt, basil, fennel seed, pepper and half of parsley; mix well. Add tomatoes and mash; stir in tomato paste and water. Bring to a boil, reduce heat and simmer covered for 1½ hours, stirring occasionally. Cook noodles according to package directions. Drain and rinse with cold water, dry on paper towels. In a large bowl, combine ricotta, egg, salt and remaining parsley. Mix well.

In a 9x13-inch pan, spoon 1½ cups sauce on bottom of pan. Layer with 6 noodles lengthwise and overlap to cover. Spread with half the ricotta mixture and top with ⅓ mozzarella cheese. Spoon 1½ cups sauce over cheese and sprinkle with ¼ cup Parmesan. Repeat layering starting with noodles and ending with 1½ cups sauce sprinkled with Parmesan cheese. Spread with remaining sauce and top with remaining mozzarella and Parmesan. Cover with foil and bake at 375° for 25 minutes. Remove foil and bake uncovered for an additional 25 minutes. Cool 15 minutes before cutting.

The fennel seed sets this lasagna apart with its sweet distinctive flavor.

Pat O'Brien

Beef Noodle Bake

2 (6-serving) casseroles

1½	pounds lean ground beef	1	(8-ounce) package cream cheese, softened
1	medium onion, chopped		
1	(6-ounce) can tomato paste	2	cups small-curd cottage cheese
1½	cups hot water		
1	teaspoon salt	⅔	cup thinly sliced green onions
1	garlic clove, minced		
½	teaspoon dried basil	1	teaspoon salt
¼	teaspoon sugar	12	ounces broad noodles, cooked and drained

Preheat oven to 375°. Cook beef and onion until beef loses its color and onions are limp. Drain well. Add tomato paste, hot water, salt, garlic, basil and sugar; stir to combine. Simmer 10 minutes. In a medium bowl, combine cream cheese, cottage cheese, green onions and salt. Lightly grease two 9x9-inch casserole dishes. Place ¼ of the cooked noodles into each casserole. Top with half the cheese mixture, then the remaining noodles. Spoon meat sauce over noodles in both casseroles. Cover 1 casserole, bake for 15 minutes. Uncover and bake 15 minutes longer, until bubbling hot. Cover, seal and label second casserole. Freeze. To serve, bake 30 minutes, covered, then 15-20 minutes uncovered.

A definite crowd pleaser.

Florence Powell

Lowfat cooking tip:
Try different kinds of oils, such as olive, peanut, sesame and chili oils to add flavor to vegetables, meats, sauces, and stir-fry.

Lena's Meatballs And Sausage In Sauce

6 servings

1	pound Italian sausage links	¼	teaspoon pepper
2	garlic cloves, minced	1	tablespoon salt
1	tablespoon olive oil	1	teaspoon oregano
1	(28-ounce) can Italian tomatoes, puréed in blender	1	teaspoon basil
		1½	cups water
1	(6-ounce) can tomato paste	1	(16-ounce) package spaghetti or pasta of your choice
2	(8-ounce) cans tomato sauce		

With a fork, poke holes in sausage. In a large saucepan over low heat, brown sausage and garlic in oil. Mix in remaining ingredients except pasta. Bring to a boil and then reduce heat. Simmer with cover ajar about 2½ hours. Stir occasionally.

Meatballs:

1	pound ground sirloin	½	cup dry bread crumbs
½	teaspoon garlic powder	½	cup finely grated Locatelli, Pecorino or Parmesan cheese
1	teaspoon salt		
⅛	teaspoon pepper		
1	egg, slightly beaten	2	to 3 pieces white bread, crumbled
1	teaspoon parsley flakes		
¼	cup milk		oil

In medium bowl, combine all ingredients, except oil. Mix well with hands to combine. Shape mixture into meatballs; making approximately 10. In medium skillet, heat enough oil to cover bottom of pan. Add meatballs and cook just enough meatballs at one time to cover bottom of skillet. Cook until crispy brown all over. Remove meatballs and drain on paper towels. After all meatballs are browned, add them to the sauce and continue simmering until sauce is done. Serve over spaghetti or pasta of your choice.

A favorite Italian dinner served every Sunday when I was growing up.

Agnes Zodda

178

Mama Lucy's Spaghetti And Meatballs

10-12 servings

Gravy (Sauce):

½ cup olive oil	4 (6-ounce) cans tomato paste
1 bulb garlic, minced	8 (6-ounce) cans water
1 medium onion, chopped	1 tablespoon sugar
2 (28-ounce) cans tomato sauce	1 (2-pound) package spaghetti, cooked al dente
1 (28-ounce) can water	

In a small skillet, heat oil and sauté garlic and onion until tender. Set aside. In a large saucepan, combine tomato sauce with water. In another large saucepan, combine tomato paste with water. Cook sauce and paste mixtures in different saucepans for 1 hour on low. Add sugar to the tomato sauce mixture. Pour half of the garlic and onion mixture into the tomato sauce and the other half into the tomato paste. Then mix the 2 sauce mixtures together in 1 large saucepan and cook for 3 more hours on low. While gravy is cooking, prepare **Meatballs.**

Meatballs:

4 pounds ground chuck	1 (8-ounce) jar grated Romano cheese
½ (24-ounce) loaf white bread, soaked in water and squeezed out	1 dozen eggs
	parsley flakes to taste
1 bulb garlic, finely chopped	salt and pepper to taste

Mix ingredients in the order they are listed. Knead 100 times. Pinch off amount of mixture that will fit in the palm of your hand and shape into a ball. Heat enough oil in a large skillet to cover the bottom. Drop meatballs into hot oil and brown on all sides, making sure they stay rounded. When done, load meatballs in a large spoon and gently put it down in the gravy. Pour any leftover oil from frying into gravy. Serve meatballs and gravy over spaghetti. *Note:* If you leave meatballs too long in the sauce, they will soak up too much of the gravy. When stirring, use wooden spoon and gently touch sides of saucepan only. Never rinse pasta. If desired, cooked meat such as chops, chicken or steak can be added to the gravy for flavor.

This is my grandmother's recipe. She came to America from Palermo, Sicily and had her own restaurant. This recipe was her specialty.

Nancy Jackson

Asparagus With Pasta

4 servings

1	(8-ounce) package any flat pasta	1	cup chopped tomatoes
4	to 6 ounces bacon, chopped and all fat removed	1	tablespoon tomato paste
4	tablespoons olive oil	4	ounces chicken broth
2	garlic cloves, chopped	4	ounces dry white wine
1	bunch fresh asparagus, trimmed and cut into 1-inch pieces	1	tablespoon basil
		1	tablespoon parsley flakes
		3	tablespoons grated Parmesan cheese

Cook pasta according to package directions and drain. Meanwhile in a large frying pan, cook bacon until crisp. Drain all bacon drippings. Keep bacon in pan; add oil, garlic and asparagus. Sauté for 4 minutes. Add remaining ingredients, except cheese, and simmer for 10 minutes. Toss pasta with sauce and cheese.

Tantalize your palate with this exquisite dish.

Cyndy Ortwein

Blue Cheese Sauce With Pasta

4 servings

1	(8-ounce) package fettuccine *or* linguine	4	ounces dry white wine
4	tablespoons butter	6	ounces cream
4	tablespoons olive oil	6	to 8 ounces blue cheese
2	garlic cloves, minced	6	tablespoons grated Parmesan cheese
½	red bell pepper, chopped	2	tablespoons chopped fresh parsley
4	green onions, chopped		

Cook pasta according to package directions and drain. Meanwhile, heat butter and oil in a saucepan and sauté garlic, pepper and green onions 2-3 minutes. Add remaining ingredients, except for the cheese and parsley and simmer 8 minutes, stirring constantly. Add blue cheese and simmer a few more minutes. Toss pasta with sauce, Parmesan cheese and parsley.

Cyndy Ortwein

Eileen's Italian Artichokes And Chicken With Pasta

6 servings

1 (16-ounce) package tricolored pasta
6 chicken breast halves, boned and skinned
1 garlic clove, minced
2 tablespoons margarine
1 (10¾-ounce) can cream of chicken soup
1 (8-ounce) carton sour cream

½ cup shredded mozzarella cheese
½ cup dry white wine
2 tablespoons grated Parmesan cheese
1 (6-ounce) jar marinated artichoke hearts, drained and halved

Cook pasta according to package directions and drain. Rinse chicken, pat dry. In a 12-inch skillet, cook garlic in margarine for 15 seconds. Add chicken, cook for 5 minutes or until light brown. Turn once. Meanwhile, in medium mixing bowl, stir together soup, sour cream, mozzarella, wine and Parmesan cheese. Add to skillet, cover and cook 5-7 minutes or until chicken is tender. Remove chicken to a platter. Keep warm. Stir sauce in skillet; add artichokes, cover and cook 1-2 minutes or until heated through. Serve over cooked pasta.

An exquisite dish that is simple to prepare.

Agnes Zodda

Pasta With Sun-Dried Tomato Sauce

4 servings

10 sun-dried tomatoes water, enough to cover tomatoes
2 tablespoons olive oil
2 garlic cloves, chopped

1 to 2 teaspoons tomato paste
1 teaspoon parsley flakes
1 pound thin spaghetti *or* capellini
Romano cheese

Soak tomatoes in water for at least 2 hours. Remove and chop roughly. Save liquid. Heat oil in skillet and sauté garlic. Add tomatoes and ½ of reserved liquid. Simmer for 15 minutes. Swirl tomato paste into pan to thicken slightly. Stir in parsley. Cook pasta according to package directions. Serve sauce over pasta; sprinkle with cheese. *Note:* This sauce is best prepared in advance to allow flavors to blend. If you want a thicker sauce, use a bit more tomato paste.

Sarah W. D'Addabbo

181

Marie's Pasta With Vodka Sauce

4 servings

4	tablespoons olive oil	1	(35-ounce) can plum
5	fresh sage leaves		tomatoes, chopped
3	garlic cloves, minced	¼	teaspoon basil
4	slices Canadian bacon, diced	¼	teaspoon oregano
			salt and pepper to taste
1	medium onion, diced	½	to ¾ cup heavy cream
¼	cup vodka	1	(16-ounce) package pasta

Place olive oil in a large saucepan, sauté sage, garlic, bacon and onion until tender. Carefully flame with vodka. Add tomatoes, basil, oregano, salt and pepper. Cook for 45 minutes. Add cream, simmer 5 minutes. Cook pasta according to package directions and drain. Serve sauce on pasta.

A must for your next special occasion.

Agnes Zodda

Gratineed Ziti And Spinach Parmesan

4-6 servings

1	medium onion, chopped	¾	teaspoon salt
3	medium garlic cloves, finely chopped	¼	teaspoon ground pepper
		10	ounces ziti
2	tablespoons extra virgin olive oil	1	pound fresh spinach, stemmed, leaves washed, dried and coarsely chopped
1	(28-ounce) can Italian peeled tomatoes, chopped and undrained	6	ounces mozzarella cheese, diced
¼	teaspoon crushed red pepper	1	cup freshly grated Parmesan cheese

In a large skillet, cook onion and garlic in oil over moderate heat until onion softens, about 5 minutes. Add chopped and undrained tomatoes. Stir in red pepper. Increase heat to moderately high and boil the sauce, stirring, until most of the liquid evaporates, about 8 minutes. Season with salt and pepper. Cook ziti according to package directions, drain and return to pot. Stir in spinach, mozzarella, and ⅓ cup of Parmesan cheese. Add tomato sauce and toss. Transfer to a lightly greased 10x14-inch baking dish and sprinkle with remaining Parmesan cheese. Broil 1-2 minutes until brown. Serve at once.

A green salad and French bread is all you need to complement this tasty dish. For dessert, serve vanilla ice cream with amaretto.

Robin Chandler

Rotini With Anchovy Paste

2 servings

2	tablespoons olive oil	1	teaspoon dried oregano leaves
1	medium onion, chopped	¼	teaspoon dried red pepper flakes
3	garlic cloves, minced		salt and pepper to taste
½	medium green bell pepper, chopped	1	(10-ounce) package rotini noodles, cooked al dente
1	(10-ounce) can tomatoes, undrained		freshly grated Romano cheese
2	to 4 anchovy fillets *or* 1 table-spoon anchovy paste		
1	teaspoon dried basil leaves		

Heat olive oil in skillet. Add chopped onion and garlic. Simmer 3-4 minutes, stirring occasionally. Add bell pepper and continue to simmer until ingredients have softened. Add tomatoes and break apart with wooden spatula or spoon. Add remaining ingredients except noodles and cheese; cook for 20 minutes, seasoning with salt and pepper to taste. Serve over cooked rotini noodles and sprinkle with Romano cheese.

Anchovy fillets melt when cooked. This can be served in smaller portions as an appetizer.

Thomas M. Cox

Leniwe Pierogi

6 servings

1	(16-ounce) box twisted noodles, cooked	8	ounces fresh mushrooms, sliced
½	cup butter *or* margarine	1	(32-ounce) jar sauerkraut, undrained
2	medium onions, diced		white pepper to taste

Cook noodles according to package directions and drain. Melt margarine in frying pan and sauté onions until clear. Add mushrooms and cook until tender. Pour in sauerkraut with liquid and cook with onions and mushrooms until hot. Add noodles and stir until mixed. Add pepper to taste.

Served several times at the Knights of Columbus "Polish Night" by request. You will love it!

Florence Powell

Pasta

Linguine Case

4 servings

¼	cup olive oil	1	tablespoon capers, drained
¼	cup butter	1	pound shrimp, cooked
1	tablespoon all-purpose flour	3	tablespoons grated Parmesan cheese
1	cup chicken broth, hot	1	teaspoon oregano
3	garlic cloves, crushed	1	pound linguine
2	teaspoons lemon juice	2	tablespoons olive oil
½	teaspoon chopped parsley	1	tablespoon butter, softened
	salt and pepper	¼	teaspoon salt
¼	pound fresh mushrooms, sliced and sautéed		additional Parmesan cheese (optional)

In a large heavy skillet, heat olive oil and butter over moderately low heat. Add flour and cook 3 minutes, stirring constantly. Stir in heated chicken broth and increase heat to moderately high and cook 1 minute. Add garlic, lemon juice, parsley, salt and pepper to taste. Cook over moderately low heat for 5 minutes, stirring occasionally. (Can be made ahead to this point. Finish just before serving.)

Add sautéed mushrooms and capers. Cook covered for 5 more minutes. Add cooked shrimp and 2 tablespoons of cheese. Sprinkle with oregano. Cook 3 minutes. Remove from heat. Meanwhile, cook linguine according to package directions and drain in colander. In the same pot used to cook linguine, combine olive oil, butter, salt and remaining Parmesan cheese. Return drained linguine to pot and toss. Serve linguine in individual bowls, top with shrimp sauce and additional Parmesan cheese if desired.

A rich and totally satisfying meal. Hot crusty Italian bread and a green salad is all that is needed to round out this dinner.

Phyllis Schwarzmann

Linguine With Spicy Tomato-Cream Sauce

4-6 servings

2	tablespoons olive oil	1	pound linguine
1	tablespoon minced onion	¼	cup fresh basil *or* ½
2	garlic cloves, crushed		teaspoon dried basil
¼	to ½ teaspoon red pepper flakes		freshly grated Romano cheese
1	(14-ounce) can whole tomatoes, undrained		freshly grated black pepper
½	cup light cream *or* half-and-half		salt to taste

Heat oil in heavy skillet. Add onion, garlic, pepper flakes; cook over medium heat, stirring often, until tender, about 5 minutes. Add tomatoes. Cook over high heat, crushing tomatoes with back of spoon, until almost dry, about 8 minutes. Stir in cream and boil for 1 minute. Cook linguine according to package directions. Drain. Toss with sauce and basil. Serve with Romano cheese, freshly grated black pepper and salt to taste.

Sarah W. D'Addabbo

Stuffed Pasta Shells

8 servings

32	jumbo pasta shells	2	eggs, slightly beaten
2	(10-ounce) packages frozen chopped spinach, thawed and squeezed dry	1	cup Parmesan cheese
		2	teaspoons dried basil
		2	garlic cloves, minced
1	(15-ounce) container ricotta cheese		salt and pepper to taste
			spaghetti sauce (your own *or* commercial)

Preheat oven to 350°. Cook shells according to package directions and drain. In a bowl, combine spinach, ricotta, eggs, ½ cup Parmesan, basil and garlic. Season with salt and pepper; blend well. Spread ½ cup sauce into bottom of 9x13-inch baking dish. Fill each shell with spinach/cheese mixture. Place shells, filling side up, into baking dish. Cover with sauce and remaining Parmesan. Cover loosely with foil and bake for 30 minutes.

A delightful meatless entrée everyone will enjoy.

Rae P. Podgorski

Tuna Stuffed Shells

5 servings

20	jumbo shells	4	tablespoons snipped
1	(6½-ounce) can tuna,		parsley
	drained and flaked	1	teaspoon lemon juice
1	cup soft bread crumbs	1	(10¾-ounce) can cream
¼	cup finely chopped onion		of celery soup
1	egg, beaten	½	cup milk
			paprika

Preheat oven to 350°. Cook shells according to package directions and drain. Rinse in cold water and drain again. In a bowl, combine tuna, bread crumbs, onion, egg, 2 tablespoons parsley and lemon juice. Fill each shell with about 1 tablespoon tuna mixture. Arrange stuffed shells in a baking dish. In a saucepan, heat together soup, milk and remaining parsley. Pour over prepared shells. Sprinkle with paprika. Cover and bake for 20-30 minutes or until bubbly.

Regina O. Scruggs

Kahlua-Cinnamon Fruit Dip

approximately 1½ cups dip

2	(3-ounce) packages cream	6	tablespoons sour cream
	cheese, softened	8	teaspoons coffee liqueur
6	tablespoons powdered	½	teaspoon cinnamon
	sugar		

In small bowl, beat cream cheese with electric mixer until fluffy. Add remaining ingredients, blending thoroughly. Serve with assorted fresh fruits of your choice.

This fruit embellishment is a sheer delight!

Diane O'Shea

Lowfat cooking tip:
In place of sour cream or mayonnaise, use plain
lowfat yogurt in dips or sauces.

Fruit Dip

2 cups

1 (8-ounce) package cream
cheese, softened
1 (7-ounce) jar marshmallow
creme

½ teaspoon cinnamon
½ teaspoon nutmeg
fresh fruit

Blend the first 4 ingredients until well blended. Serve with fresh fruits of your choice, such as fresh whole strawberries, pineapple wedges or melon balls.

Sheila Van Auken

Caramel Apple Dip

10 servings

1 (8-ounce) package cream
cheese, softened
¾ cup brown sugar
¼ cup white sugar

1 teaspoon vanilla
½ cup chopped nuts
red apples, sliced in
wedges

Blend first 5 ingredients together with mixer until well blended. Chill. Serve with crisp red apple slices. *Note:* Dip sliced apples in lemon juice to prevent discoloration.

Yummy!

Theresa Ellison

Strawberries Extraordinaire

20 servings

20 large strawberries,
washed and patted
dry

6 ounces chocolate chips
1 tablespoon vegetable oil

Melt chocolate chips in double boiler; stir in oil and reduce heat to low. Dip strawberries in melted chocolate and allow to harden on waxed paper. Do not refrigerate. Use the same day. *Note:* Pretzels or bananas may also be dipped.

Sheila Van Auken

To release molds easier, pour water into empty mold, drain and fill with mixture to be chilled.

Scalloped Pineapple

8 servings

½ cup margarine, melted
4 cups fresh bread cubes
3 eggs
½ cup sugar

½ cup evaporated milk
1 (20-ounce) can
    unsweetened crushed
    pineapple, undrained

Combine margarine and bread cubes, stirring well; set aside. Combine eggs, sugar and milk; beat at low speed until just blended. Add bread mixture and pineapple, stirring well. Pour into lightly greased 8-inch square baking dish. Bake, uncovered, at 350° for 1 hour. Shield with aluminum foil the last 10 minutes, if necessary.

Great with ham and chicken.

Jan Harvey

Pineapple-Cheese Surprise

6-8 servings

1 (20-ounce) can pineapple
    tidbits
½ cup sugar
3 tablespoons all-purpose
    flour

1 cup shredded sharp
    Cheddar cheese
½ cup Ritz cracker crumbs
¼ cup butter, melted

Preheat oven to 350°. Drain pineapple, reserve 3 tablespoons liquid. Combine sugar and flour. Stir in reserved liquid. Add mixture to cheese and pineapple. Turn into a well greased 1-quart casserole. Sprinkle cracker crumbs on top and drizzle melted butter on top. Bake for 30 minutes.

Makes a great accompaniment to ham or pork.

Phyllis Schwarzmann

Banana-Berry Compote

4 servings

½ cup orange marmalade
¼ cup orange juice
⅛ teaspoon ground allspice

2 medium bananas, sliced
1 pint strawberries, halved
1 cup blueberries

In a large bowl, mix marmalade, juice and allspice. Add fruit; gently toss together. Spoon into dessert bowls.

Gretchen Mattingly

Cranberry Compote

12 servings

3 cups peeled, cored and chopped apples	3 (1-ounce) envelopes cinnamon and spice instant oatmeal
2 cups fresh whole cranberries	¾ cup chopped nuts
2 teaspoons all-purpose flour	½ cup all-purpose flour
1 cup sugar	½ cup brown sugar
	½ cup butter, melted

Preheat oven to 350°. In large bowl, mix chopped apples and cranberries. In small bowl, combine flour and sugar. Mix flour mixture with apples. Place apples in a 2-quart casserole dish. In separate bowl, mix oatmeal, nuts, flour, sugar and butter. Sprinkle mixture over apples and pat down. Bake uncovered for 45 minutes. *Note:* Can be frozen. Thaw and bake as mentioned above.

Great with ham and turkey.

Mary Limbacher

Strawberry Microwave Jam

2 cups

2 cups diced strawberries	1½ cups sugar
1½ tablespoons lemon juice	½ teaspoon margarine

Combine all ingredients in a 2-quart glass measure or a 3-quart casserole dish. Let mixture sit until juices form, about 30 minutes. Microwave, uncovered, on high (100% power) for 6 minutes or until mixture begins to boil. Stir. Microwave on high for 10-13 minutes, stirring every 2-3 minutes. Spoon 1 tablespoon into a cup and refrigerate for 15 minutes. If jam is too thin, microwave mixture for another 2 minutes. Test again, repeat until you get the consistency you like. Refrigerated, the jam will keep for several months. Can be frozen.

Aline Tatro

Italian Zucchini Pie

6 servings

4	cups thinly sliced, unpeeled zucchini	¼	teaspoon oregano
1	cup coarsely chopped onion	2	eggs, well beaten
½	cup margarine *or* butter	8	ounces shredded mozarella cheese
2	tablespoons parsley flakes	1	(10-inch) pie shell *or* 1 (8-ounce) can refrigerated crescent dinner rolls
½	teaspoon salt		
½	teaspoon black pepper		
¼	teaspoon garlic powder	2	teaspoons Dijon mustard
¼	teaspoon sweet basil leaves		

Preheat oven to 375°. In 10-inch skillet, cook zucchini and onion in margarine until tender, about 10 minutes. Stir in parsley and seasonings. In large bowl, blend eggs and cheese. Stir in vegetable mixture. Spread crust with mustard, pour vegetable mixture into crust and bake for 18-20 minutes. *Note:* If using crescent rolls, separate dough into 8 triangles, firmly press perforations to seal and place into 10-inch pie pan.

Anne Giannini
Agnes Zodda

Sausage Deep Dish Pie

6 servings

1	(10-inch) pastry shell, unbaked	2	tablespoons all-purpose flour
½	pound hot bulk sausage	2	eggs, beaten
½	cup chopped onion	⅔	cup evaporated milk
1	tablespoon oil	2	teaspoons parsley flakes
1½	cups shredded sharp Cheddar cheese	½	teaspoon salt
		¼	teaspoon garlic powder
		¼	teaspoon pepper

Preheat oven to 375°. Brown sausage and drain well. Remove sausage to paper towel. Sauté onion in oil until tender. Spread sausage in pie shell and top with onion. Mix cheese with flour and sprinkle over onion. Mix remaining ingredients and pour over sausage mixture. Bake for 45 minutes.

Kids love this quiche! Can also be served as an appetizer, just cut in small squares rather than wedges.

Kay Gordan

Spinach Pie (Spanakopeta)

12-14 servings

2	(10-ounce) packages fresh spinach, stemmed and chopped	1½	tablespoons all-purpose flour
1	bunch scallions, chopped, including tops	½	cup milk
1	pound cottage cheese	1½	cups butter, melted salt to taste
½	pound feta cheese, crumbled	1	pound frozen phyllo sheets, thawed plain yogurt (optional)
6	to 7 eggs		

Preheat oven to 400°. In a large bowl, combine spinach, scallions, cottage cheese, feta cheese, eggs, flour, milk, 4 tablespoons melted butter and salt. Mix thoroughly. Place all but 7 phyllo sheets in a well buttered 16-inch round baking pan or in a 10x15 or 12x17-inch baking pan. The larger the pan, the thinner the pita. Brush each sheet of phyllo with melted butter and overlap each sheet, leaving edge of each sheet hanging over sides of pan. Place spinach filling in pan, spreading evenly and cover with the remaining 7 phyllo sheets; brushing each with melted butter, overlapping each and allowing the edge of the sheet to hang over sides of the pan. Brush top with melted butter; turn edges of sheets in and all around and again brush edges with butter. Place in oven and immediately lower temperature to 350°. Bake 1 hour or until golden in color. Remove from oven; place a large flat tray over pita, invert and slide back into pan. *Note:* May be served hot or at room temperature. Often served topped with plain yogurt. To save on calories, butter every other phyllo sheet and use butter flavored cooking spray on the alternates.

Excellent, even if you do not care for spinach. Great for a luncheon.

Lemonitra K. Finning

Fresh eggs sink in water, stale eggs float.

Classic Quiche

6-8 servings

1	(9-inch) deep dish pastry shell, baked	4	eggs, slightly beaten
12	slices bacon, cooked crisp and crumbled	¾	teaspoon salt (optional)
1	cup shredded Swiss cheese	⅛	teaspoon black pepper
		2	cups half-and-half
			pinch nutmeg (optional)

Place crumbled bacon on bottom of baked pie shell, sprinkle cheese on top of bacon, set aside. In a large bowl, combine eggs, salt, pepper and half-and-half. Stir until well blended. Pour over bacon and cheese. Sprinkle with nutmeg. Bake at 425° for 15 minutes, reduce heat to 300° and bake for another 30-40 minutes or until knife inserted in center comes out clean. *Note:* Can be prepared the day before, reheat in microwave.

A classic recipe that continues to be a favorite. Serve with pastries or bran muffins, fruit and juice.

S. Kay Clifton

Spinach Quiche

4-6 servings

1	(9-inch) deep dish pastry shell, unbaked	¾	cup heavy cream
1	(10-ounce) package frozen chopped spinach	½	teaspoon salt
3	eggs	¼	teaspoon pepper
2	tablespoons all-purpose flour	8	ounces shredded Cheddar cheese
		4	slices bacon, cooked crisp and crumbled

Preheat oven to 375°. Cook spinach according to package directions, drain and squeeze dry. Set aside. Mix eggs, flour, cream, salt and pepper. Blend in spinach and cheese. Place crumbled bacon in bottom of unbaked pie shell. Pour spinach mixture over bacon. Bake for 45 minutes or until a knife inserted in center comes out clean. Let cool 10 minutes before cutting. Cut in wedges.

Great for brunch or anytime.

Mary Fehse

 Salmonella food poisoning has been linked with raw or undercooked eggs. Cook eggs well to destroy salmonella; do not eat raw eggs.

Green Chile Quiche

6 servings

1	(4-ounce) can diced green chilies, drained	¼	cup milk
½	pound Cheddar cheese, grated	4	tablespoons all-purpose flour
½	pound Monterey Jack cheese, grated	5	eggs
		1	teaspoon salt

Preheat oven to 325°. Line quiche pan with chilies. Layer grated cheeses on chilies. In a mixing bowl, combine remaining ingredients and beat until well mixed. Pour over cheese and chilies. Do not stir. Bake for 30 minutes. Remove from oven and let rest 30 minutes. Cut into wedges and serve.

An unusual brunch main dish!

Shona Moore

Cheese 'n Chicken Quiche

6 servings

1	(9-inch) deep dish pie shell, unbaked	1½	cups chopped, cooked chicken
4	eggs	1	cup shredded Swiss cheese
1	cup heavy cream *or* whipping cream	2	tablespoons chopped pimiento, drained
½	cup creamy Italian dressing		

Preheat oven to 400°. Bake pie shell for 10 minutes, remove from oven. Reduce heat to 375°. In large bowl, beat eggs. Blend in cream, creamy Italian Dressing, chicken, cheese and pimiento. Pour into prepared shell. Bake for 40-50 minutes or until quiche tests done. Garnish with additional pimiento if desired.

Lela Wiseman

Pizza Quiche

6 servings

2	(9-inch) pastry shells	1	(3-ounce) package sliced pepperoni, chopped
½	pound hot Italian sausage	¼	cup grated Parmesan cheese
1	cup ricotta *or* cream-style cottage cheese	2	tablespoons milk
3	eggs		commercial pizza sauce (optional)
1	cup shredded mozarella		

Line a 9-inch pie plate with 1 pastry shell; flute edges. Bake at 450° for 5 minutes. Remove from oven; reduce oven temperature to 350°. Remove casings from sausage. Cook sausage in a medium skillet until browned, stirring to crumble; drain well and set aside. Combine ricotta cheese and eggs; beat well. Stir in sausage, mozzarella cheese, pepperoni and Parmesan cheese. Spoon into partially baked pie crust. Roll out remaining pastry to an 8-inch circle; cut into 7 wedges. Arrange on top of filling. Bake at 350° for 20 minutes. Brush milk over top of pastry; bake an additional 20 minutes or until golden brown. Let cool 10 minutes. Serve with warm pizza sauce if desired.

Something different that's a hit with the entire family!

Nicki Knight

Noodle Pudding Soufflé

12 servings

1	(8-ounce) package medium size noodles	2	cups sour cream
½	cup margarine, softened	½	teaspoon salt
½	cup sugar	2	teaspoons vanilla
1	cup cottage cheese	5	eggs
			cinnamon

Cook noodles 8-10 minutes until tender and drain. In bowl, beat margarine and sugar. Add cheese, sour cream, salt and vanilla. Mix in eggs one at a time, beating after each addition. Stir in cooked noodles. Pour into greased 9x13-inch baking dish. Sprinkle top with cinnamon. Bake at 350° for 50-55 minutes, until golden brown. Let stand 5 minutes before cutting into squares. May be frozen and reheated.

This is a wonderful dish when serving a buffet-style meal. Makes a great brunch dish too as the noodle pudding tastes like bread pudding.

Mary Fehse

Salmon Quiche

6 servings

Crust:

1	cup whole wheat flour	½	teaspoon salt
⅔	cup shredded sharp	¼	teaspoon paprika
	Cheddar cheese	6	tablespoons vegetable oil
¼	cup chopped almonds		

Combine wheat flour, cheese, almonds, salt and paprika in a bowl. Stir in oil. Reserve ½ cup of the crust mixture. Press remaining mixture into bottom and up the sides of a 9-inch deep dish pie plate. Bake crust in a 400° oven for 10 minutes. Remove from oven. Reduce oven temperature to 325°.

Filling:

1	(15½-ounce) can salmon	1	tablespoon finely chopped
3	eggs, beaten		onion
1	cup sour cream	¼	teaspoon dill weed
¼	cup mayonnaise	3	drops Tabasco® sauce
½	cup shredded sharp		
	Cheddar cheese		

Drain salmon, reserving liquid. Add water to reserved liquid, if necessary, to make ½ cup liquid. Flake salmon, removing bones and skin; set aside. In a bowl, blend together eggs, sour cream, mayonnaise, and reserved salmon liquid. Stir in salmon, ½ cup cheese, onion, dill weed and Tabasco® sauce. Spoon filling into crust. Sprinkle with reserved crust mixture. Bake at 325° for 50 minutes, or until knife inserted in center comes out clean.

The crust for this quiche is anything but ordinary and the filling is equally as exquisite.

Rita C. Leonard

Cheese Apple Omelet

4 servings

6	eggs, separated	2	medium cooking apples,
½	teaspoon salt		thinly sliced
3	tablespoons water	½	pound Swiss cheese,
2	tablespoons butter		shredded
1	tablespoon butter		parsley

Preheat oven to 400°. In a large bowl, beat egg whites at high speed until stiff peaks form. In a small bowl, beat egg yolks, salt and water at high speed until very thick. Fold egg yolk mixture into beaten egg whites. In 12-inch skillet with oven-safe handle, melt 2 tablespoons butter over medium heat. Pour egg mixture into skillet and cook until top is puffy and bottom is golden, about 3 minutes. Place skillet in oven and bake until top of omelet is golden, about 5 minutes. Meanwhile, in a 10-inch skillet, melt 1 tablespoon butter over medium-high heat. Add ⅔ of the apple slices and cook for 5 minutes. To serve, place cheese and cooked apples over half of omelet, fold omelet over filling, and lift omelet onto warm platter. Garnish with parsley and remaining apples.

Great dish for your next brunch.

Margie Brennan

Sausage And Rice Casserole

8-10 servings

1	onion, finely chopped	2	(10¾-ounce) cans cream
2	pounds pork sausage		of chicken soup
	(medium *or* hot)	½	to 1 cup sour cream,
1	pound fresh mushrooms,		to taste
	sliced	3	cups cooked rice

Preheat oven to 350°. Sauté onion with pork sausage. Add mushrooms and simmer about 20 minutes. Drain. Add cream of chicken soup and sour cream. Combine with 3 cups cooked rice and mix well. Pour into a 2-quart casserole. Bake for 45 minutes.

Excellent for brunch!

Calma Hobson

 To remove onion odor from your hands, rub them with celery.

Chili Huevos

6 servings

3	(4-ounce) cans whole green chilies, drained and seeds removed	⅛	teaspoon white pepper (optional)
6	ounces Monterey Jack cheese, sliced (or grated if preferred)	½ 2	teaspoon salt to 3 drops hot pepper sauce (optional)
6	eggs	1	to 1½ cups grated
1	tablespoon all-purpose flour		Cheddar cheese paprika salsa sour cream

Preheat oven to 350°. Butter generously an 8-inch square glass baking dish. Layer ½ the chilies and ½ the Monterey Jack cheese. Repeat. In bowl, whisk eggs, flour, pepper, salt and hot sauce. Pour over chilies and cheese. Top with Cheddar cheese. Dust well with paprika. Bake for 30 minutes or until set. Remove from oven and let sit for 10 to 15 minutes for easier cutting. Serve with salsa and sour cream. *Note:* For an appetizer, use a 9-inch square dish. Cool and cut into 1-inch squares. This is called Texas Fudge.

Good brunch dish. Prepare hot sausage and a fruit salad. Don't forget the sangria!

Pat Smith

Sausage Apple Ring

8-10 servings

2	pounds bulk sausage	½	cup minced onion
1½	cups cracker crumbs	1	cup finely chopped apples
2	eggs, slightly beaten		scrambled eggs
½	cup milk		parsley

Preheat oven to 350°. Combine all ingredients except eggs and parsley. Mix well and press lightly into a greased 6-cup ring mold to shape. Turn out in a shallow baking pan. Bake for 30 minutes. Drain excess fat from pan and continue baking another 30 minutes. To serve, fill center of ring with scrambled eggs and garnish platter with parsley. To prepare in advance, bake 30 minutes, refrigerate overnight and finish baking for 30 minutes the morning of the brunch.

A unique way to prepare and serve favorite brunch fare.

Jennie Hart
Buffalo, New York

197

Sausage Roll

36 servings

1 pound highly seasoned pork bulk sausage

recipe for rolled biscuits on Bisquick box *or* 2 individual packages Bisquick

Roll out sausage between 2 sheets of wax paper into a thin rectangular shape. Make biscuit dough according to package directions. Roll out into a long rectangular shape slightly larger than sausage roll. Lay sausage on top of dough and roll up jelly roll style. Wrap in freezer paper and freeze for a little while for easier slicing or chill overnight in refrigerator. When ready to serve, cut into thin slices, about ¼-inch thick and bake at 400° for 10 minutes. If additional browning is necessary, place under broiler for 30 seconds. *Note:* Can be prepared ahead and frozen. Thaw at room temperature until right consistency to slice.

Great as an appetizer or for brunch.

Sharon Amos

Favorite Pancakes

24 pancakes

2 cups all-purpose flour
6 teaspoons baking powder
¼ cup sugar
1 teaspoon salt

2 eggs
2 cups milk
⅓ cup vegetable oil

Place all ingredients in a blender and blend for 1 minute. Pour batter onto greased griddle and flip to lightly brown on both sides. Makes 24 medium-sized pancakes. Serve with your favorite toppings. Recipe can be halved. Refrigerate leftovers and reheat in toaster or microwave.

These light and fluffy pancakes will disappear fast.

Solange Guerrette
Enfield, Connecticut

Mini Blintzes

10-12 servings

2	(8-ounce) packages cream cheese, softened	¼	cup brown sugar
½	cup sugar	1	teaspoon cinnamon
2	egg yolks	2	loaves white bread (thin sliced)
1	cup butter		sour cream (optional)

In a small mixing bowl, beat cream cheese and sugar until light and fluffy. Add egg yolks, blend well. Melt butter, stir in brown sugar and cinnamon. Trim crusts from bread and flatten each slice with a rolling pin. Spread slices with a thin layer of the cream cheese mixture. Roll up and dip in butter mixture. Place on a cookie sheet and freeze. When frozen, transfer to freezer bag. When ready to serve, cut in thirds and bake frozen in a preheated 350° oven for 12-15 minutes or until lightly browned. Can be served with sour cream. *Note:* Can be halved if serving a smaller group.

Delicious make-ahead recipe. Great for brunch or as appetizers.

Jill Gasperini

Basic Crêpes

approximately 2 dozen

4	eggs	2¼	cups whole milk
¼	teaspoon salt	¼	cup butter, melted
2	cups all-purpose flour		

Combine all ingredients in blender; blend 1 minute. Scrape down sides and blend an additional 15 seconds. Cover and refrigerate for at least 1 hour. Brush a 6-inch non-stick pan with butter. Heat pan over medium-high heat. Add 2-3 tablespoons crêpe batter. Quickly swirl pan to cover bottom with batter. When batter loses glossy look, turn crêpe with spatula. Cook for a few seconds and remove. *Note:* Crêpes may be used immediately, refrigerated overnight or frozen. To freeze, stack cooled crêpes between waxed paper. Wrap in aluminum foil, place in air-tight freezer bag and freeze no longer than 3 months. Thaw wrapped crêpes at room temperature about 1 hour.

Nancy R. Willingham

Peach Melba Crêpes

6 servings

1 (10-ounce) package frozen raspberries
¼ cup currant jelly
2 tablespoons butter
¼ teaspoon almond extract
1 (16-ounce) can peach slices, drained
1 pint vanilla ice cream

6 crêpes (see *Basic Crêpe* recipe)
½ cup whipping cream, whipped with 1 tablespoon sugar
¼ cup slivered almonds, toasted

Thaw raspberries, force through sieve. In medium saucepan, combine raspberry purée, currant jelly, butter and almond extract. Bring to boil over moderate heat. Stir in peaches; cool. Spoon about ⅓ cup ice cream into center of each crêpe; fold sides over. Spoon peaches and sauce over each crêpe. Pipe whipped cream over each serving. Sprinkle with toasted almonds.

Dazzle your family and treat them to these delectable filled crêpes for your next Sunday brunch.

Nancy R. Willingham

Creamy Strawberry Crêpes

8 servings

1 (8-ounce) package cream cheese, softened
1¼ cups sifted powdered sugar
1 tablespoon lemon juice
1 teaspoon grated lemon rind
½ teaspoon vanilla

1 cup heavy cream, whipped
8 (8-inch) crêpes (see *Basic Crêpe* recipe)
3½ cups sliced fresh strawberries

In mixing bowl, combine cream cheese, sugar, lemon juice, rind and vanilla. Mix until well blended. Fold in whipped cream. Fill each crêpe with about ⅓ cup fruit and about ⅓ cup cream cheese mixture; roll up. Top with remaining fruit.

Include these irresistible crêpes on your next brunch menu.

Sheila Van Auken

Florentine Crêpe Cups

12 crêpe cups

12 crêpes (see *Basic Crêpe* recipe)
1 (6-ounce) package shredded sharp Cheddar cheese
3 tablespoons all-purpose flour

1 (10-ounce) package frozen chopped spinach, thawed and well drained
6 slices bacon, cooked crisp and crumbled
3 eggs, beaten
⅔ cup mayonnaise
⅛ teaspoon pepper

Preheat oven to 350°. Combine cheese and flour; toss. Stir in remaining ingredients, except crêpes, mixing well. Grease a full size muffin tin and carefully place 1 crêpe in each cup, smoothing the bottom and overlapping sides as necessary. Divide spinach mixture among 12 crêpe-filled muffin cups. Bake for 35-40 minutes. Serve as a brunch dish or vegetable side dish.

Absolutely wonderful and very easy when you have crêpes made up ahead of time.

Judy Tribe
Dalhousie, New Brunswick, Canada

Lowfat cooking tip:
Try stir-fry. Use a wok or sauté pan and a very small amount of oil.

Sausage-Filled Crêpes

8 servings

Crêpes:

3	eggs, beaten	1	cup all-purpose flour
1	cup milk	½	teaspoon salt
1	tablespoon oil		

Filling:

1	pound sausage	1	(3-ounce) package cream
¼	cup chopped onion		cheese, softened
½	cup shredded Cheddar cheese		

Topping:

½	cup sour cream	½	cup butter, softened

Combine eggs, milk, oil, flour and salt. Beat until smooth. Allow to stand one hour at room temperature. Grease a 6-inch skillet and preheat on medium heat. Pour 2 tablespoons of batter into skillet; tilt pan until batter coats bottom of pan. Cook on one side only. Invert on a paper towel. Repeat until 16 crêpes are made. Meanwhile, cook sausage and onion until browned. Drain and crumble. Add cheeses and mix well. Set aside. Combine sour cream and butter. Set aside. Place 2 tablespoons of sausage mixture in each crêpe, roll up and place in a 9x13-inch baking dish, seam side down, and chill. Bake covered in preheated 375° oven for 20 minutes. Remove from oven. Spoon topping mixture over crêpes and bake uncovered for 5 more minutes. *Note:* Filled crêpes can be prepared the day before. Refrigerate and bake when ready to serve. Crêpes can be made ahead and frozen. Place waxed paper between each crêpe, wrap in plastic wrap and store in airtight freezer bag. These can be frozen for several months.

Well worth the trouble to prepare!

Rae P. Podgorski

Vegetables

Asparagus Supreme

4-6 servings

4 cups fresh asparagus, trimmed and cut up or 2 (8-ounce) packages frozen cut asparagus
1 (10¾-ounce) can cream of shrimp soup
½ cup sour cream
2 tablespoons coarsely shredded carrots (optional)

1 (4½-ounce) can tiny shrimp (optional)
1 teaspoon grated onion
⅛ teaspoon pepper
½ cup herb-seasoned stuffing mix
1 tablespoon butter or margarine, melted

Preheat oven to 350°. Cook fresh asparagus in boiling salted water 5-6 minutes or until crisp tender. (Cook frozen asparagus per package directions.) Drain well. Combine soup, sour cream, carrots, shrimp, onion and pepper; fold in asparagus. Turn into an ungreased 1-quart baking dish. Combine stuffing mix with melted butter. Sprinkle around edge of asparagus mixture. Bake uncovered for 30-35 minutes.

Sure to be included in your list of "favorite" recipes.

Mary Beth Harja

Baked Beans

8-10 servings

½ pound sliced bacon
2 large onions, chopped
1 medium green bell pepper, chopped
1 (16-ounce) can kidney beans, drained
1 (16-ounce) can lima beans, drained

1 (16-ounce) can pork and beans, drained
⅓ cup brown sugar
¼ cup vinegar
1 tablespoon dry mustard
1 cup ketchup
1 tablespoon Worcestershire sauce

Preheat oven to 350°. In large casserole or Dutch oven, fry bacon until crisp. Remove bacon, drain on paper towel and crumble. Sauté onions and green pepper in bacon drippings until tender. Drain well. Add all remaining ingredients and stir well. Stir in crumbled bacon. Bake for 45 minutes.

A nice change from the traditional! Great with barbecue, especially pork.

Nicki Knight

3 Bean 2 Cheese Casserole

6-8 servings

1	(16-ounce) can kidney beans, drained	1	(14-ounce) can tomatoes, undrained
1	(16-ounce) can navy beans, drained	3	tablespoons soy sauce
1	(15-ounce) can chick peas, drained	1	teaspoon chili powder
1	tablespoon oil	1	teaspoon oregano
1	medium onion, chopped	½	teaspoon dry mustard
1	small green bell pepper, chopped	1	teaspoon paprika
		1	cup grated Cheddar cheese
		1	cup grated Monterey Jack cheese
			cooked rice

Preheat oven to 350°. In a large bowl, combine drained beans and set aside. Sauté onion and green pepper in oil and add to beans. Stir in tomatoes and seasonings; mix well. Grease a 2-quart casserole dish and pour in bean mixture. Sprinkle cheese on top and bake for 25 minutes.

Serve over rice for a vegetarian main dish the whole family will enjoy.

Diane Werve

Green Beans With Mushrooms

6 servings

2	garlic cloves, minced	1	pound fresh green beans, trimmed
1	medium red onion, cut into thin strips	1	teaspoon dill weed
¼	pound small fresh mushrooms, trimmed and sliced		dash black pepper
1	tablespoon butter *or* margarine	2	tablespoons almonds, toasted

Sauté garlic, onion and mushrooms in butter until tender. Set aside. Steam or cook beans in small amount of water until crisp tender. Drain. Combine beans and mushroom mixture, add dill weed and pepper. Garnish with nuts. Serve immediately.

Nicki Knight

Elegant Green Bean Casserole

10-12 servings

½	cup butter *or* margarine	⅛	teaspoon Tabasco® sauce
2	(4-ounce) cans mushrooms, drained	½	teaspoon salt
		½	teaspoon pepper
1	medium onion, chopped	4	(16-ounce) cans whole green beans, drained
¼	cup all-purpose flour		
2	cups milk	1	(8-ounce) can sliced water chestnuts, drained
1	cup half-and-half		
2	cups shredded sharp Cheddar cheese	1	(4-ounce) package sliced almonds

Preheat oven to 375°. Melt butter and sauté mushrooms and onion; add flour and cook until smooth. Add milk, half-and-half, cheese and seasonings; stir constantly until mixture is smooth. Do not boil. Mix in beans and water chestnuts. Pour into an 11x14-inch baking dish. Sprinkle almonds on top. Bake for 30 minutes.

Charlotte Sharpe

Swiss Beans

3-4 servings

1	(10-ounce) package frozen cut *or* French style green beans	1	teaspoon sugar
		½	teaspoon grated onion
		½	cup sour cream
2	tablespoons butter	1	cup grated Swiss cheese
½	teaspoon salt		paprika
⅛	teaspoon pepper		

Preheat oven to 350°. Cook green beans according to package directions and drain. Combine beans with butter, salt, pepper, sugar, onion and sour cream. Place in greased 1-quart casserole. Top with grated cheese and paprika. Bake for 35 minutes.

Karen DouBrava

Hollow out vegetables such as bell peppers, cabbage, or artichokes and use as containers for dips.

Broccoli Casserole

8-10 servings

2	(10-ounce) packages frozen chopped broccoli	1	medium onion, chopped *or* 1 tablespoon onion flakes
2	eggs, slightly beaten	1	cup grated sharp Cheddar cheese
1	cup mayonnaise	1	cup bread crumbs *or* Ritz cracker crumbs
1	(10¾-ounce) can cream of mushroom soup	2	tablespoons butter, melted

Preheat oven to 350°. Cook broccoli, drain well and set aside. In a large bowl, mix together eggs, mayonnaise and soup. Stir in onion and cheese. Add broccoli, mix well and turn into a greased casserole dish. Bake for 45 minutes or until bubbly. Mix crumbs with melted butter and sprinkle on top of casserole the last 15 minutes of cooking time.

A family favorite.

Pauline Cychowski

Broccoli & Rice Casserole

6 servings

1	(10-ounce) package frozen chopped broccoli, cooked and drained	½	cup milk
		½	cup pasteurized process cheese, cubed *or* grated Cheddar cheese
1	onion, finely chopped		
2	tablespoons butter *or* margarine	½	cup cooked rice
1	(10¾-ounce) can cream of chicken soup *or* cream of mushroom soup		

Preheat oven to 275°. Sauté onion in butter. Add soup and milk; mix well. Add cheese and stir until melted. Add rice and broccoli; turn into a casserole dish. Bake for 1 hour.

Variation: Omit onion and butter, use 1 cup grated Cheddar cheese, 3 cups cooked rice, add 1 teaspoon salt and dash of pepper. Bake at 325° for 30 minutes.

Quick and easy to prepare.

Rae P. Podgorski
Sandra Lenzini Parish

Sweet & Sour Brussels Sprouts

6-8 servings

3	cups fresh *or* 2 (9-ounce) packages frozen Brussels sprouts	2	teaspoons sugar
		1½	teaspoons salt
		¼	teaspoon garlic powder
8	slices bacon	⅛	teaspoon black pepper
2	tablespoons vinegar		

Wash and trim sprouts, cook 10 minutes in lightly salted water or per package directions. Drain. Fry bacon until crisp. Remove bacon, crumble and set aside. Drain fat, leaving ¼ cup drippings in pan. To drippings add vinegar, sugar, salt, garlic powder and pepper. Add sprouts, stir and heat through. Serve topped with crumbled bacon.

Good, even for those not terribly fond of Brussels sprouts.

Mary Beth Harja

Zesty Carrots

4-6 servings

6	to 8 carrots, sliced diagonally and cooked until crisp tender	½	cup mayonnaise
		½	teaspoon salt
		½	teaspoon pepper
½	cup liquid from cooked carrots	¼	cup cracker crumbs *or* bread crumbs
2	tablespoons grated onion	1	tablespoon butter, melted
2	tablespoons horseradish		dash paprika

Preheat oven to 375°. Grease a 2 quart shallow casserole dish with non-stick cooking spray. Mix carrot liquid, onion, horseradish, mayonnaise, salt and pepper. Pour over carrots. Mix cracker crumbs with butter and sprinkle over top. Sprinkle paprika over cracker crumbs. Bake for 15-20 minutes.

Karen DouBrava

Anything that grows under the ground start off in cold water – potatoes, beets, carrots, etc. Anything that grows above ground, start off in boiling water – greens, beans, etc.

Marinated Carrots

6-8 servings

5	cups sliced carrots	1	cup sugar
1	small green bell pepper, cut in round slices	½	cup salad oil
		1	teaspoon salt
1	medium red *or* white onion, cut in round slices	1	teaspoon pepper
		1	teaspoon prepared mustard
1	(10¾-ounce) can tomato soup	1	teaspoon Worcestershire sauce
¾	cup vinegar		

Cook carrots until almost done, drain and cool. The carrots are better if they are still a bit crunchy. Add the pepper and onion slices to the cooled carrots. Mix the remaining ingredients and pour over vegetables. Cover and marinate 12 hours or longer. Drain and serve. Carrots will last approximately 2 weeks in refrigerator.

The delicately spiced and slightly sweetened sauce make these carrots anything but ordinary.

Nancy R. Willingham

Shredded Carrots

6-8 servings

6	cups finely shredded carrots	4	tablespoons butter
2	cups finely sliced green onions	¾	teaspoon dried fennel
		2	tablespoons orange flavored liqueur
	chicken stock for simmering (about 1 cup)		chopped fresh parsley
		2	tablespoons grated orange rind

Simmer carrots and onions with enough stock to cover over low heat, stirring occasionally, for 2-4 minutes or until liquid has cooked away completely. Add butter and fennel and mix well. Just before serving, stir in liqueur and sprinkle with parsley and grated orange rind.

An excellent vegetable dish to accompany any entrée.

Trudy S. Eissler

Easy Corn Casserole

8-10 servings

1 (11-ounce) can whole kernel corn with liquid	1 cup sour cream
	2 eggs, slightly beaten
	1 (8½-ounce) box corn muffin mix
1 (16-ounce) can cream style corn	1 cup shredded Cheddar cheese
8 tablespoons margarine, melted	

Preheat oven to 350°. Spray a 9x13-inch baking dish with a non-stick cooking spray. Mix together first 5 ingredients. Pour in corn muffin mix and stir well. Pour into prepared dish and bake for 30-40 minutes or until center is almost set. Then sprinkle with cheese and bake 10 to 15 minutes longer, until center is set and cheese is melted.

This always gets a rave review at potluck or sit down dinners.

Pamela M. Richert

Mushroom Casserole

6-8 servings

2 pounds fresh mushrooms	¼ teaspoon ground nutmeg
¼ cup butter *or* margarine	¼ teaspoon pepper
3 tablespoons all-purpose flour	8 ounces sour cream
1 teaspoon salt	¼ cup minced fresh parsley
2 teaspoons Dijon mustard	¼ cup minced onion

Preheat oven to 325°. Clean and slice mushrooms. Set aside. Using electric beaters, cream butter, flour, salt, mustard, nutmeg and pepper. Add remaining ingredients except mushrooms. In a 2-quart baking dish sprayed with cooking spray, place half of mushrooms in bottom of pan. Spread with half the sour cream mixture. Repeat layers. Bake covered for 45 minutes, uncover and bake for an additional 15 minutes. Remove from oven and let sit to firm up. *Note:* Buy ready to use mushrooms from salad bar to save time.

Great with red meat. Make it once and you'll be sold!

Rosalie A. Johnson

Sensational Stuffed Eggplant

8-10 servings

4	cups plain dry bread crumbs	8	ounces grated mozzarella cheese
2	cups all-purpose flour, sifted	½	cup freshly grated Parmesan cheese
4	eggs	2	cups chopped fresh parsley
¼	cup milk		spaghetti sauce (about 5
2	large eggplants, peeled olive oil		cups, your own *or*
2	(15-ounce) containers ricotta cheese		commercial)

Preheat oven to 450°. Combine crumbs and flour in a large shallow pan. Beat eggs and milk in a large bowl. Cut eggplant lengthwise into ⅛-inch thickness. Dip eggplant slices into egg mixture then dredge with flour mixture, shaking off excess. In a large skillet, sauté slices in olive oil until golden, about 1 minute per side. Drain on paper towels. In a large bowl, combine together the ricotta, mozzarella and Parmesan cheese. Add parsley. Spread 2 to 3 tablespoons cheese mixture on one side of each eggplant slice. Roll up jelly roll style. Spread 1 cup spaghetti sauce over bottom of each of 2 (9x13-inch) baking dishes. Arrange rolls seam side down in a single layer in pans. Spoon remaining sauce over rolls. Bake uncovered for 30 minutes or until sauce is bubbly.

Even those who "don't like eggplant" come back for seconds. This dish is always *a hit and people always want the recipe.*

Rebecca G. Cox

Vidalia Fried Onion Rings

6-8 servings

1½	cups all-purpose flour	1	tablespoon vegetable oil
2	egg yolks	1	teaspoon salt
1½	cups beer (active *or* flat; cool *or* room temperature)	3	to 4 large Vidalia onions
		3	to 4 cups vegetable oil salt

Mix flour, egg yolks, beer, oil and salt in a mixing bowl. Cover and allow batter to sit at room temperature for 3-4 hours. Peel onions and cut into ¼-inch slices. When batter is ready, heat oil in deep fryer, dip onion rings into batter and drop rings into oil. Cook until browned. Drain on paper towels. Sprinkle with salt. Serve hot.

Dolores W. Mistretta
Fort Myers, Florida

Vidalia Onion Pie

6-8 servings

1	(9-inch) deep dish pie shell, unbaked	3	eggs, slightly beaten
3	to 4 large Vidalia onions, chopped	½	teaspoon salt
		¼	teaspoon paprika
2	tablespoons butter	2	cups milk

Preheat oven to 375°. Sauté onions in butter until transparent. Put onions in pie shell. Combine eggs, salt, paprika and milk together. Pour over onions and bake for 35-45 minutes or until golden brown. Serve hot or cold.

A unique way to serve this sweet and delicious onion.

Maureen Kolb

Marinated Artichokes And Mushrooms

6-8 servings

¾	cup vinegar	½	teaspoon thyme
½	cup vegetable oil	½	teaspoon oregano
¼	cup olive oil	1	onion, sliced into rings
2	garlic cloves, crushed	1	pound fresh mushrooms
1	teaspoon seasoned salt	2	(7-ounce) cans artichoke
¼	teaspoon salt		hearts, split
½	teaspoon freshly ground pepper		fresh parsley, minced

Combine all ingredients except mushrooms, artichokes and parsley in a saucepan. Bring to a boil. Add whole mushrooms and split artichokes to mixture. Return to a boil, reduce heat, cover and simmer for 10 minutes. Add parsley. Remove from heat. Refrigerate overnight in a covered dish. Drain before serving.

Very elegant and always gets a lot of compliments.

Rebecca G. Cox

Use up the end crusts of your bread by putting them on top of pots in which you are cooking cauliflower, cabbage or greens. It will absorb cooking odors.

English Pea Casserole

4-6 servings

1 small onion, chopped	1 (10¾-ounce) can cream
1 cup sliced celery	of mushroom soup
½ cup margarine, melted	1 (2-ounce) can chopped
2 (8½-ounce) cans small	pimiento, drained
English peas (sweet	1 (8-ounce) can water
and young peas)	chestnuts, drained
	½ cup Ritz cracker crumbs

Preheat oven to 300°. Sauté onion and celery in margarine until tender. Remove from heat. Drain peas and reserve ½ cup liquid. Combine soup and reserved liquid together and add to onion mixture. Stir in peas, pimiento and water chestnuts. Turn into a buttered 2-quart casserole dish. Sprinkle with cracker crumbs and bake for 15-20 minutes or until bubbly.

June Haley

Dominic's Peppers

4 servings

2 tablespoons olive oil	1 (8-ounce) can tomato
3 garlic cloves, coarsely	sauce
chopped	1 cup water
1 cup chopped onion	1 teaspoon salt
½ cup chopped pepperoni,	½ teaspoon pepper
ham or any smoked	1 teaspoon basil
meat (optional)	1 teaspoon oregano
½ cup sliced celery	garlic powder to taste
4 green bell peppers, cut in	
slices	

Put oil in warm skillet. Add garlic and onion; cook until clear. Add pepperoni or smoked meat and celery. Cook for a few minutes until soft. Add peppers, tomato sauce and water. Stir in seasonings, more or less to taste. Simmer until done; approximately 30 minutes. This can be used as a side dish, or served over rice as a main dish. The meat is for added flavor and seasoning and can be omitted. Freezes well. *Note:* You can use more or less of any or all ingredients.

A very colorful and tasty dish.

Catherine E. Motta
Washington, D. C.

213

Spinach Stuffed Squash

8 servings

4	yellow crookneck squash	1	teaspoon salt
1	tablespoon butter, melted	1	cup sour cream
	salt and pepper to taste	2	teaspoons red wine
	grated Parmesan cheese		vinegar
½	cup chopped onion		bread crumbs
½	cup margarine		grated Parmesan cheese
2	(10-ounce) packages frozen		butter
	chopped spinach,		
	cooked and well		
	drained		

Preheat oven to 350°. Cook whole squash in boiling salted water for about 10 minutes or until tender. Very carefully cut each squash into halves and scoop out seeds. Brush each shell with butter and sprinkle with salt, pepper and Parmesan cheese. Place shells in a lightly buttered 9x13-inch baking dish. For spinach stuffing, sauté onion in butter until tender. Add spinach, salt, sour cream and vinegar; blend well. Stuff each squash shell with spinach mixture. Sprinkle each with additional Parmesan cheese and bread crumbs, dot with butter. Bake for 15 minutes or until hot.

A simple and elegant vegetable that is sure to please your taste buds.

Sue Land

Gloria's Squash Casserole

8-10 servings

3	pounds yellow squash, sliced	1	teaspoon salt
½	cup chopped onion	½	teaspoon pepper
½	cup butter *or* margarine	¼	teaspoon garlic powder
2	eggs, beaten *or* equivalent egg substitute	½	teaspoon thyme
¾	cup herb seasoned dressing, lightly crushed	2	tablespoons grated Parmesan cheese (optional)

Preheat oven to 350°. Cook squash, covered, in a small amount of boiling salted water 10-15 minutes or until tender. Drain well and mash. Set aside. Sauté onion in butter until tender. Add onion, eggs, herb dressing and seasonings to squash. Spoon mixture into a lightly greased 2-quart casserole. Bake uncovered for 20 minutes. If desired, sprinkle with Parmesan cheese during the last few minutes of baking. *Note:* This casserole freezes well uncooked. Thaw completely and cook according to directions, allowing about 10 extra minutes if ingredients are cold.

Gloria Arnold

Jo's Spinach & Ricotta Dumplings

about 2 dozen dumplings

2 tablespoons margarine	¾ cup ricotta cheese
2 tablespoons chopped onion	⅔ cup all-purpose flour
2 tablespoons chopped ham	2 egg yolks
1 (10-ounce) package frozen chopped spinach, thawed	1 cup Parmesan cheese
	¾ teaspoon pepper
	chicken broth *or* water

Sauté onion in margarine until golden. Add ham and stir 1 minute. Press thawed spinach against sides of strainer to remove excess water. Add to skillet and sauté 5 minutes or until no excess liquid remains. Place spinach mixture in a large bowl. Add ricotta and flour. Mix thoroughly with wooden spoon. Add egg yolks, cheese and pepper. Mix well. Shape into small balls. Work quickly and try to keep dumplings as small as you can so they cook fast and stay soft. Dust hands with flour if needed. Bring broth or water to a boil, using enough broth or water to cover dumplings. Drop 3 or 4 dumplings in at a time and cook 3-4 minutes. Remove with slotted spoon and serve in soup or as a vegetable. Top with melted butter. *Note:* The chicken broth they were cooked in can also be used for soup.

Helen Bertelsen

Spinach Casserole

6-8 servings

3 (10-ounce) packages frozen chopped spinach	1 envelope dry onion soup mix
1 cup sour cream	grated Parmesan cheese

Preheat oven to 350°. Cook spinach according to package directions. Drain well. Mix with remaining ingredients and place in buttered casserole with grated cheese on top. Bake until bubbly and heated through, about 20 minutes.

Elizabeth S. Moody

Spinach Madeline

6-8 servings

2 (10-ounce) packages frozen chopped spinach
4 tablespoons butter
2 tablespoons all-purpose flour
2 tablespoons chopped onion
½ cup evaporated milk
½ cup reserved vegetable liquid

½ teaspoon black pepper
¾ teaspoon celery salt
¾ teaspoon garlic salt
   salt to taste
1 teaspoon Worcestershire sauce
1 (6-ounce) roll jalapeño cheese, cut in small pieces
   buttered bread crumbs (optional)

Cook spinach according to package directions. Drain well and reserve ½ cup liquid. Melt butter in saucepan over low heat. Add flour, stirring until blended and smooth, but not brown. Add onion and cook until soft but not brown. Add milk and reserved liquid slowly, stirring constantly to avoid lumps. Cook until smooth and thick, continue stirring. Add seasonings and cheese and stir until melted. Combine with cooked spinach. Serve immediately or put into a casserole dish and top with buttered crumbs. The flavor is improved if the latter is done and kept in refrigerator overnight. Bake at 350° for 20-30 minutes or until heated through.

This spinach dish is our children's favorite and they often ask for it. Goes well with beef tenderloin.

Sharon Amos

Never soak vegetables after slicing, you will lose much of the nutritional value.

Cascades Ratatouille

8-10 servings

8	medium tomatoes	½	cup butter
1½	pounds zucchini squash, trimmed and sliced	3	garlic cloves, minced
		1	tablespoon dried oregano
3	celery stalks, sliced	1	tablespoon dried basil
1	large green bell pepper, cut in 1-inch pieces	1	tablespoon salt
		1	teaspoon pepper
1	large eggplant, cubed	4	tablespoons grated Parmesan cheese
1	large onion, cut in 1-inch pieces		

Preheat oven to 350°. Grease a large shallow casserole dish. Scald tomatoes in boiling water for 60 seconds, drain, remove skin, and cut in half. Squeeze out and discard tomato juice and cut each half into 4 pieces. Reserve. In boiling salted water, blanch until barely tender, the zucchini, celery, green pepper and eggplant. Drain and reserve. Sauté onions in butter for 4 to 5 minutes. Add garlic and seasonings; continue to sauté until onions are transparent. Combine all ingredients in prepared casserole and sprinkle with Parmesan cheese. Bake for 20-25 minutes or until bubbly.

Excellent served with grilled chicken!

Sue Luscomb

Stuffed New Potatoes

40 pieces

20	small red potatoes	2	tablespoons chopped fresh parsley
2	celery stalks, diced		
2	scallions, diced		white pepper to taste
1	medium carrot, diced	½	teaspoon salt
2	hard-cooked eggs, diced	1	cup mayonnaise
2	tablespoons pickle relish	1	cup sour cream
2	tablespoons dill weed		dill weed

Boil potatoes until tender; drain and cool. Cut in half and cut a tiny slice off bottom to stand upright. With a tiny scoop, scoop out center, leaving a strong shell. Cut scooped out centers into small pieces. Gently toss potato pieces with celery, scallions, carrot, eggs, relish, dill, parsley, pepper and salt. Mix mayonnaise and sour cream together. With a rubber spatula, gently fold in potato mixture. With small spoon, mound salad inside potato shells. Refrigerate for 2 hours. Sprinkle with dill weed for garnish.

Excellent addition to an "Open House" buffet table.

Eva M. Edwards

217

Stuffed Pumpkin

8 servings

1 small whole pumpkin, about 10-inches in diameter
boiling salted water
salt
2 tablespoons salad oil
2 pounds ground beef
1 large onion, finely chopped
1 medium green bell pepper, finely chopped
2 teaspoons salt
2 teaspoons oregano

1 teaspoon vinegar
freshly ground pepper to taste
2 garlic cloves, mashed
¾ cup seedless raisins
pimiento-stuffed green olives
2 teaspoons capers
1 (8-ounce) can tomato sauce
½ cup red wine
3 eggs, beaten

With a sharp knife, cut a circular top about 5-inches in diameter out of the pumpkin. Save top to use as a lid. Scoop out pumpkin seeds and scrape inside of pumpkin clean. Place in a large kettle and cover with boiling salted water, cover kettle. Bring water to a boil, lower heat and simmer for about 30 minutes until pumpkin meat is almost tender. The pumpkin should still be firm enough to hold its shape well. Carefully remove from water and drain well. Dry the outside and sprinkle a little salt on the inside. Set aside.

In a heavy skillet with a cover, heat salad oil. Add ground beef, onion and green pepper. Cook until beef is browned and crumbly. Drain. Remove from heat and add salt, oregano, vinegar, pepper and garlic. Stir in raisins, olives and capers, then gradually add tomato sauce and red wine. Cover skillet, return to heat and simmer for about 15 minutes, stirring occasionally. Cool slightly and add beaten eggs, mixing thoroughly. Fill cooked pumpkin with meat stuffing, pressing to pack firmly. Cover loosely with pumpkin lid and place in a greased shallow baking pan. Bake for 1 hour. Allow to cool for 10-15 minutes before serving. To serve, carefully lift stuffed pumpkin onto a serving plate. Slice from top to bottom in flat wedges, spooning more meat filling onto each slice.

Try this recipe and be surprised, it is as good as the best squash and the presentation is beautiful.

Trudy S. Eissler

Hash Brown Potato Casserole

10-12 servings

½ cup butter *or* margarine, melted
½ to 1 teaspoon salt
¼ teaspoon black pepper
¼ teaspoon garlic powder
¼ teaspoon Mrs. Dash
2 cups shredded Cheddar cheese
½ cup finely chopped onion
2 cups sour cream
1 (10¾-ounce) can cream of chicken soup
1 (32-ounce) package frozen hash brown potatoes, thawed
½ to 1 cup Ritz cracker crumbs

Preheat oven to 350°. In a large bowl, combine first 9 ingredients together and blend well. Fold in hash browns and turn into a buttered 9x13-inch baking dish. Top with cracker crumbs. Bake for 45-60 minutes.

Variation 1: Omit pepper, garlic powder, Mrs. Dash and cracker crumbs.

Variation 2: Omit all seasonings and use 1 cup crushed corn flakes for topping.

Variation 3: Omit garlic powder, Mrs. Dash, use 12 ounces pasteurized process cheese and ½ cup milk. Melt cheese, milk and soup together in microwave, blend in remaining ingredients, use 2 cups corn flake crumbs with ¼ cup melted butter for topping.

Nicki Knight
Rae P. Podgorski
Paula Hlobik
Peg Kottke

Tasty Potato Casserole

8-10 servings

10 large red potatoes
½ cup grated Cheddar cheese
1 cup mayonnaise
½ cup finely chopped onion
1 pound bacon, cooked crisp and crumbled

Boil unpeeled potatoes and slice after they are cooked. Combine cheese, mayonnaise and onion. Gently stir into potatoes. Place in a greased casserole dish and top with bacon. Bake at 350° for 20-30 minutes or until heated through and bubbly.

Mary Fehse

New Potatoes Florentine

6 servings

1 (10¾-ounce) can Cheddar
  cheese soup
1 (16-ounce) can tomatoes,
  chopped
1 (10-ounce) package frozen
  chopped spinach,
  thawed and squeezed
  dry
½ cup minced onion *or*
  finely sliced

1 tablespoon chopped fresh
  parsley *or* 1 teaspoon
  parsley flakes
4 ounces fresh mushrooms,
  sliced
1 garlic clove, minced
  dash pepper
2 cups shredded Swiss
  cheese
½ teaspoon marjoram
4 cups sliced unpeeled new
  potatoes

Preheat oven to 350°. Butter a 2-quart baking dish. Mix all ingredients together except potatoes and reserve ½ cup cheese. Blend well and fold in potatoes. Turn into a baking dish, cover and bake 75 minutes or until potatoes are tender. Uncover and sprinkle with remaining cheese and bake an additional 15 minutes.

If you're in the mood for something different to complement your entrée, try this.

Peg Kottke

Potatoes Romanoff

10 servings

6 medium potatoes
2 cups sour cream
1½ cups shredded sharp
  Cheddar cheese
1½ teaspoons salt

¼ teaspoon pepper
1 bunch green onions,
  chopped
  paprika

Boil potatoes in jackets until fork tender. Peel and mash in large bowl. Stir in sour cream, 1 cup of the cheese, salt, pepper and onions. Turn mixture into a buttered 9x9-inch casserole dish. Top with remaining cheese and sprinkle with paprika. Cover and refrigerate overnight. Bake uncovered at 350° for 30-40 minutes. Allow to settle 15 minutes before serving.

Something to take the place of a baked potato. Excellent for company.

Calma Hobson

Crab Stuffed Potatoes

4 servings

4	medium baking potatoes	1	teaspoon salt
	salad oil		dash pepper
6	ounces frozen crabmeat,	4	teaspoons grated onion
	thawed	1	cup shredded Cheddar
½	cup butter, melted		cheese
½	cup half-and-half		paprika

Preheat oven to 425°. Wash potatoes and rub skins with oil. Bake at 425° for 45 minutes or until done. Allow potatoes to stand until cool to touch. Slice skin away from top of each potato. Scoop out pulp, leaving shells intact. Mash pulp. Combine potato pulp and remaining ingredients except paprika, stirring well. Stuff potato shells. Sprinkle with paprika. Bake in foil for 30 minutes at 350° or until heated through. Freezes well.

Elizabeth Blaylok

Aunt Dess' Sweet Potato Casserole

10 servings

2	(16-ounce) cans yams,	¼	cup dry sherry
	drained	½	teaspoon salt
1	cup crushed pineapple,	½	teaspoon pepper
	drained		butter
2	ripe bananas		miniature marshmallows

Preheat oven to 350°. In a bowl, mash yams and pineapple with bananas. Add sherry, salt and pepper. Whip together until smooth. Place in a buttered 2-quart casserole. Dot with additional butter and marshmallows. Bake uncovered for 45 minutes or until bubbly.

Phyllis Schwarzmann

Always tear lettuce in bite-size pieces, never cut with a knife.

221

Stella's Sweet Potato Soufflé

8-10 servings

5	to 6 sweet potatoes, cooked, peeled and mashed	1	teaspoon cinnamon
1	cup sugar	½	teaspoon nutmeg
2	eggs, beaten	1	cup crushed corn flakes
½	cup milk	½	cup brown sugar
½	cup butter *or* margarine, melted	1	cup chopped nuts
		¼	cup butter *or* margarine, melted

Preheat oven to 350°. Using an electric mixer, beat first 7 ingredients together and pour into a lightly greased 2-quart casserole. Bake uncovered for 30-35 minutes. Meanwhile, prepare topping by combining corn flakes and remaining ingredients together. Mix well until crumbly. Sprinkle topping over baked sweet potatoes and return to oven for an additional 10 minutes. *Note:* Potatoes can be left in warm oven until serving time, it makes the topping extra crunchy.

This delicious casserole is our family's favorite and is served every holiday. The recipe is always doubled!

Nancy R. Willingham

Spiced Rice

6 servings

1	cup uncooked rice		freshly ground pepper to taste
2	cups boiling salted water		
1	(1-inch) piece of fresh ginger, peeled	½	teaspoon ground nutmeg
		2	teaspoons minced shallots
¼	cup seedless raisins	1	tablespoon lemon juice
¼	cup currants	½	teaspoon coriander
2	ounces dried apricots, chopped	1	tablespoon olive oil
		½	cup toasted pine nuts

Cook rice with peeled ginger in boiling salted water, until done, about 25 minutes. While rice is cooking, soak raisins, currants and chopped apricots in hot water to cover, then drain when plump. When rice is ready, remove ginger and place rice in a warm serving casserole. To the rice, add pepper, nutmeg, shallots, lemon juice, coriander and olive oil. Gently fold in plumped raisins, currants and apricots. Keep warm until ready to serve. Just before serving, sprinkle with pine nuts.

A colorful and tasty rice. Perfect accompaniment to leg of lamb, roast ham or pork.

Trudy S. Eissler

Rice Pulao

8 servings

1	cup Basmati rice (found in Asian food stores)	2¼	cups water
½	cup butter	½	teaspoon salt *or* to taste (optional)
1	medium onion, chopped	¼	teaspoon garum masala
3	whole peppercorns		(found in Asian food
2	whole cloves		stores) (optional)
1	handful sliced almonds		

Indian Basmati rice has excellent flavor. Accept no substitutes grown elsewhere. This rice must be washed before using because it is not processed as much as domestic rice and is dusty. To wash, cover it with water, stir gently with your fingers and slowly pour out water. If this rice is roughly handled, the grains will break. Wash 3 times or until you are satisfied rice is clean. Set aside.

In a 2-quart saucepan, melt butter. Sauté onion in butter, then add peppercorns, cloves and almonds. Add rice and stir gently until it is coated with butter. This helps the grains be more separate when cooked. Add water and remaining ingredients. Cook on medium high heat to bring rice to a boil. Reduce heat and simmer for 20 minutes, stirring once after 5 or 10 minutes of cooking. Serve immediately. *Note:* If you wish, after washing rice, add 2¼ cups water to rice and let it soak until you are ready to cook it. This results in a longer, fluffier grain. About 25-30 minutes before serving, add sautéed ingredients and seasonings to rice and its water and cook.

*Excellent served with **Chicken Tikka.***

Dorothy Joshi

A pair of scissors are great for slivering celery, onion, meats, and cheese.

Blue Cheese Rice

6 servings

1	cup rice, uncooked	2	hard-cooked eggs, chopped
2	tablespoons butter, melted	¾	cup sour cream
2	tablespoons lemon juice	½	teaspoon salt
½	teaspoon dry mustard	¼	teaspoon pepper
¼	cup sliced scallions	4	ounces blue cheese, crumbled
½	cup sliced black olives		

Cook rice according to package directions. Combine rice, butter, lemon juice and mustard. Add scallions, olives, eggs, sour cream, salt and pepper. Stir in blue cheese. Place in a greased 8x8-inch casserole dish. Bake at 350° for 30 minutes. *Note:* Can be made ahead and refrigerated before baking.

A wonderful cheese-flavored rice. Great with grilled steaks.

Maureen Kolb

Ricardo's Rice

4-6 servings

½	cup butter	1	green bell pepper, chopped
1	cup long grain white rice	1	diced fresh tomato
1	onion, chopped	2	cups chicken broth *or* stock
2	garlic cloves, minced		

In a large pan, melt butter, add rice and stir until rice turns clear. Add vegetables and stir for 1 minute. Add liquid, stir and cover. Simmer over low heat for 20 minutes.

This recipe was given to us by a bartender at the Buccaneer Hotel, St. Croix, Virgin Islands in 1979.

Sarah W. D'Addabbo

Red Beans And Rice Cajun Style

10-12 servings

1	pound dried red beans	½	garlic clove, minced
1	pound ham hocks, smoked sausage *or* hot sausage	¼	cup chopped fresh parsley
		2	bay leaves
		¼	cup butter
1	ham bone		salt to taste
1	large onion (or more), chopped		cayenne pepper *or* Tabasco® sauce to taste
1	cup chopped green onions	2	cups cooked rice

Most Cajun cooks like to bring their beans to a rolling boil for a couple of minutes, then let them soak in that same water overnight. In the morning, brown sausages or fat meat first to remove some of the grease. Rinse soaked beans and add enough water to just cover beans. Bring beans and ham bone to a boil and add all other ingredients, except rice. Reduce heat and simmer for at least 3 hours. Beans should be very creamy. Serve over hot fluffy rice. *Note:* Addition of a ham bone adds real flavor not possible to achieve otherwise.

Red Beans and Rice was usually served on Mondays because this was the day everyone washed and cleaned. They let them simmer most of the day, stirring occasionally.

S. Kay Clifton

Toss avocado slices in lemon juice to keep from turning brown.

Creole Rice Dressing

10-12 servings

2	cups rice, uncooked	1	large onion, finely
3	cups finely chopped		chopped
	celery	3	tablespoons bacon drippings
1	bunch green onions,	1	pound lean ground chuck
	finely chopped	1	pound hot bulk sausage
2	large green bell peppers,		salt and pepper to taste
	finely chopped	1	tablespoon Worcestershire
1	small bunch parsley,		sauce
	finely chopped	2	to 3 cups chicken broth

Preheat oven to 325°. Cook rice according to package directions and set aside. In large Dutch oven, sauté vegetables in bacon drippings until tender. In separate skillet, brown the ground meat and sausage. Drain excess fat. Add meats, seasonings and rice to vegetables and mix well. Gradually add chicken broth to moisten dressing mixture. Bake covered in a large casserole dish for 1 hour. *Note:* Cooked, chopped chicken giblets can be added for extra flavor and texture.

This dressing can be used separately as a side dish or used as a stuffing for fowl, green bell peppers, eggplant or tomatoes.

Dot Ryland

A teaspoon of sugar for every 3 cups of water used in cooking peas, carrots, cabbage or onions will improve the flavor.

Sausage And Spinach Bread Stuffing

16 servings

1	pound bulk pork sausage	½	cup milk
3	cups sliced fresh	1½	teaspoons basil
	mushrooms	½	teaspoon oregano
1½	cups chopped onion	½	teaspoon poultry
½	cup shredded carrots		seasoning
3	garlic cloves, minced	¼	to ½ teaspoon crushed red
8	cups dry bread cubes *or*		pepper
	1 (16-ounce) package		carrot curls (optional)
	seasoned stuffing mix		spinach leaves (optional)
1	(10-ounce) package frozen		
	chopped spinach,		
	cooked and drained		

Preheat oven to 325°. In skillet, cook sausage until brown. Remove to paper towels, reserving 2 tablespoons drippings. Cook mushrooms, onion, carrots, and garlic in drippings until tender. Drain off fat. Combine bread cubes, sausage, cooked vegetables, poultry seasoning and red pepper. Mix well. Form into balls, using ½ cup mixture for each. Place on greased baking sheet. Bake for 25 minutes. Serve arranged on spinach-lined serving platter with turkey and garnish with carrot curls. *Note:* Stuffing can be used to stuff a 14-16 pound turkey or place stuffing in a greased casserole dish and bake for 30-35 minutes. If a more moist stuffing is desired, add drippings from turkey, up to 1 cup or desired consistency and pour in casserole dish.

This stuffing is a traditional Thanksgiving favorite at our house.

Rita C. Leonard

Vegetable Marinade

1½ cups marinade

1	cup vinegar	1	tablespoon salt
½	cup vegetable oil	1	teaspoon pepper
1	tablespoon dill weed	1	to 2 garlic cloves, crushed

Mix all ingredients together. Use to marinate vegetables such as mushrooms, quartered carrots, broccoli and cauliflower flowerets. Marinate vegetables 24 hours. Drain ½ hour before serving.

Maureen Kolb

Lemon-Herb Marinade

1½ cups marinade

⅔   cup olive oil
⅓   cup fresh lemon juice
⅓   cup dry vermouth
2   tablespoons dried
    rosemary

1   tablespoon dried thyme
½   teaspoon sugar
½   teaspoon salt
½   teaspoon pepper.

Combine all ingredients and blend well. Use mixture to marinate fresh sliced vegetables such as zucchini, yellow squash, carrots, etc., for at least 20 minutes. Steaks can also be marinated for at least 1 hour. Grill vegetables for 10 minutes. Grill steaks according to weight and taste. *Note:* Marinade can be made 2 days ahead.

Roxanne Morris

As soon as your tomatoes get home from the market, drop them into hot water before storing them in the refrigerator. They will not spoil as easily and will be ready for peeling when needed.

Light and Luscious

Ways To Reduce Dietary Fat

- Select lean meat, poultry and fish. Remove skin from chicken.
- Eat more rice, pasta, beans, potatoes, grains and vegetables. These foods should be the centerpiece of your meal.
- Drink skim milk. You can wean yourself gradually by going from whole milk to 2% to 1% to skim.
- Eat whole-grain breads and rolls. These have more flavor and you don't need the butter or margarine to make them taste good.
- Use jams and jelly on muffins and toast instead of butter, margarine or cream cheese.
- Use lowfat or fat-free salad dressings on your salads.
- When snacking, choose fresh fruits and vegetables, plain popcorn, pretzels, or rice cakes instead of cookies, ice cream or potato chips.
- Substitute ice milk, lowfat frozen yogurt or sherbet for ice cream. Try frozen juice bars or popsicles.
- Eat a vegetarian meal at least once a week.
- For dessert, choose fruit, sponge cake or angel food cake. Top with fruit purée.
- Substitute 2 egg whites, or ¼ cup egg substitute product for 1 whole egg.

Fat Free Mexican Dip

6 cups dip

24 ounces fat-free cottage cheese	¼ cup skim milk
4 green onions, sliced	1 (12-ounce) jar picante sauce
1 teaspoon garlic powder	sliced green onion tops
½ teaspoon chili powder	fresh vegetables *or* light
12 ounces fat-free cheese slices	tortilla chips

Combine first 4 ingredients in food processor; blend until smooth. Melt cheese slices, milk and picante sauce in microwave on medium low setting, stirring often. Add to food processor and blend until smooth. Refrigerate to blend flavors. Garnish with sliced green onion tops. Serve with fresh veggies or light tortilla chips.

Low fat and heart smart recipe. Also good on a baked potato.

Peg Kottke

Dieter's Delight

2-4 servings

1	(12-ounce) container low fat cottage cheese	½	carrot, chopped
2	green onions, chopped	½	tomato, chopped
½	green bell pepper, chopped	½	cucumber, chopped
			salt and pepper to taste

Combine all ingredients. Prepare ahead of time to bring out the flavor.

Serve with fruit and crackers for a nice light and healthy lunch.

S. Kay Clifton

Diane's Breakfast

6-8 servings

½	pound turkey sausage roll	12	ounces egg substitute
10	slices bread, cubed	2	cups skim milk
½	cup sliced mushrooms	⅛	teaspoon salt
½	cup diced green bell pepper	⅛	teaspoon pepper
12	ounces shredded low-fat Cheddar cheese		

Cook turkey sausage until brown and drain well. Mix sausage, bread, mushrooms, green pepper and cheese. Spread mixture in a greased 9x13-inch baking pan. Combine eggs, milk, salt and pepper. Pour over mixture, cover with foil and refrigerate overnight. Bake at 350° for 45 minutes.

A tasty low cholesterol brunch dish that must be prepared the night before. Great for overnight company.

Patricia Jean Vrabel

Light Vegetable Soup

6 servings

½	pound fresh green beans	2	cups peeled and cubed potatoes
1	(46-ounce) can no-salt tomato juice	¼	cup chopped onion
2	cups shredded cabbage	1	teaspoon pepper
2	(8-ounce) cans no-salt chopped tomatoes	1	(10-ounce) package frozen whole corn kernels
2	cups chopped carrots		salt to taste

Wash and cut green beans into 1-inch pieces. Combine all ingredients except corn in a large Dutch oven. Bring to a boil. Cover, reduce heat and simmer about 1 hour. Add corn during the last 10 minutes.

Rochelle Mistretta

Grilled Vegetable Kabobs With Rice

4 servings

½	cup Italian dressing	8	small boiling onions
1	tablespoon minced fresh parsley *or* 1 teaspoon dried parsley flakes	8	cherry tomatoes
		8	medium fresh mushrooms
1	teaspoon dried basil	2	cups hot cooked long grain rice
2	medium yellow squash, cut into 1-inch slices		

Combine dressing, parsley and basil in a small bowl; cover and chill. Alternate squash, onions, tomatoes and mushrooms on 8 skewers. Coat grill with cooking spray. Place kabobs on rack and cook 15 minutes or until vegetables are tender, turning and basting frequently with dressing mixture. To serve, place ½ cup rice on each plate and top with 2 vegetable kabobs.

This quick and easy recipe is great for casual entertaining.

David LaPaglia

Lo Mein

4 servings

1	tablespoon dark sesame oil	3	tablespoons teriyaki sauce
1	large garlic clove minced	1	(8-ounce) package flat linguine
2	cups chicken broth	1	(16-ounce) package frozen stir-fry vegetables (partially thaw and chop much finer)
1	cup water		
1	teaspoon grated ginger root		
⅛	teaspoon crushed red pepper flakes	2	green onions, sliced

In large skillet, heat oil, garlic, chicken broth, water, ginger root, red pepper flakes and teriyaki sauce to boiling. Add linguine and simmer 8-10 minutes, stirring often. Add chopped vegetables and cook 4 minutes longer. Stir in green onions and serve immediately.

Delicious main dish or a perfect accompaniment to broiled steak or chicken.

Peg Kottke

Lowfat cooking tip:
Bake, roast, grill or broil meat, poultry and fish.

Stir-Fry With Linguine

8 servings

1 (12-ounce) package
   linguine
5 to 6 medium carrots,
   thinly sliced
1 bunch broccoli, cut in
   flowerets *or* 1
   (12-ounce) bag frozen
   broccoli
5 to 6 chicken breast halves,
   boned and skinned
3 to 4 garlic cloves, finely
   chopped
   olive oil
   sesame seed oil
   garlic powder

   soy sauce
2 to 3 small zucchini, thinly
   sliced
2 small yellow squash, thinly
   sliced
8 ounces fresh mushrooms,
   sliced (optional)
1 (10-ounce) package frozen
   pea pods, thawed
1 (8-ounce) bottle Dijon
   vinaigrette lite
   dressing
   about ¼ cup grated
   Parmesan cheese
   (more *or* less to taste)

Cook linguine according to package directions, rinse and drain well. Parboil carrots and broccoli separately and set aside. Cut chicken in small pieces and stir-fry half the chicken pieces and garlic in about 1 tablespoon each of olive and sesame seed oil. Remove chicken to a large glass bowl. Repeat with remaining chicken and garlic. Stir-fry carrots in a small amount of olive oil for 2-3 minutes, add to chicken in bowl and add a light sprinkle of garlic powder and soy sauce. Repeat with broccoli, zucchini, squash, mushrooms, and pea pods; each time adding a light sprinkle of soy sauce and an occasional sprinkle of garlic powder. Combine drained pasta with vegetables and blend about ¾ bottle Dijon vinaigrette dressing, adding more soy sauce and garlic powder to taste. Add Parmesan cheese and toss.

Team up crisp, colorful vegetables with linguine and chicken and you will have the right ingredients for a tasty meal. Make this dish once and your family will ask for it often.

Rita C. Leonard

Lowfat cooking tip:
Use a minimum amount of oil. Use aerosol
cooking spray or non-stick cookware.

Kidney Bean Casserole

4 servings

½	cup chopped onion	¼	cup water
¼	cup chopped green bell pepper	½	teaspoon chili powder
¼	cup chopped celery	¼	teaspoon pepper
2	large garlic cloves, minced	3	dashes hot sauce
1	(15½-ounce) can kidney beans, drained and rinsed	2	cups cooked rice (no salt *or* fat added)
1	cup peeled and chopped tomato	¼	cup shredded, reduced-fat sharp Cheddar cheese

Coat a large non-stick skillet with cooking spray. Place over medium heat until hot. Add onion, green pepper, celery and garlic; sauté until tender. Stir in beans and next 5 ingredients. Cover and cook 8-10 minutes, stirring often. Place hot rice in a 1 quart casserole, spoon bean mixture over rice. Sprinkle with cheese; cover and let stand 5 minutes.

Tasty, hearty and totally satisfying. A great diet dish.

Betty Curp

Scallop Provençale

4 servings

1¼	pounds bay scallops	2	medium tomatoes, cut into wedges
3	tablespoons all-purpose flour	1½	tablespoons dry vermouth
¼	teaspoon salt	2	teaspoons chopped fresh basil *or* ½ teaspoon dried basil
¼	teaspoon pepper		
1½	teaspoons vegetable oil		cooked rice
2	teaspoons olive oil		
2	garlic cloves, minced		

Rinse scallops in cold water, pat dry with paper towels. On sheet of wax paper, combine flour, salt and pepper. Dredge scallops in flour mixture, using up all of the flour. In a 12-inch nonstick skillet, combine oils and heat over medium-high heat; add scallops and garlic. Sauté until scallops are cooked through, about 5-7 minutes. Reduce heat, add remaining ingredients and cook until thoroughly heated. Serve with rice on the side.

Great flavor and low calorie!

Rita C. Leonard

Onion Halibut Bake

4 servings

1 tablespoon olive oil	1 tablespoon dried dill weed
2 cups sliced onions	4 halibut steaks

Preheat oven to 400°. Combine oil, onions and dill weed in a 9-inch square baking dish. Bake for 10-15 minutes or until onions begin to brown. Remove from baking dish and add halibut steaks. Place onion mixture on top. Bake for 15-20 minutes or until fish flakes.

Joyce Hirschman

Charcoal Grilled Swordfish

4 servings

½ cup soy sauce	1 teaspoon oregano
2 garlic cloves, chopped	½ cup orange juice
4 tablespoons tomato sauce	1 teaspoon freshly ground
2 tablespoons lemon juice	pepper
½ cup chopped fresh parsley	1½ pounds swordfish steaks

Combine all ingredients except swordfish. Pour over steaks and marinate for at least 2 hours. Have charcoal or gas grill well heated. Grill steaks, turning once and basting frequently during grilling. Grill 20 minutes or until fish flakes easily.

Good served with rice pilaf and fresh steamed broccoli.

Sarah W. D'Addabbo

Baked Whole Salmon

6 servings

1 whole salmon, (6-8 pounds), cleaned and scaled	2 tablespoons chopped fresh parsley
2 large lemons, thinly sliced	½ teaspoon freshly ground pepper
1 large onion, thinly sliced	½ teaspoon salt
½ cup dry white wine *or* dry vermouth	lemon wedges

Preheat oven to 350°. Place salmon on heavy duty foil. Layer fish with lemon and onion slices; add wine. Sprinkle with parsley, pepper and salt. Seal very tightly. Bake for 50-60 minutes or until fish is flaky and tender. Remove from oven, open foil and arrange salmon on a platter. Garnish with lemon wedges and serve.

Great way to retain all the flavor and juices.

Nancy Barnwell

235

Oven Fried Fish

4-6 servings

2 egg whites, slightly beaten	1 teaspoon parsley flakes
2 tablespoons vinegar	¼ teaspoon salt
1 cup corn flake crumbs	⅛ teaspoon pepper
¼ cup grated Parmesan cheese	6 fish fillets, cut in half

Preheat oven to 400°. In shallow dish, combine egg whites and vinegar, blend well. In another dish, combine corn flake crumbs, Parmesan cheese, parsley, salt and pepper. Dip fish fillet pieces in egg mixture and coat with crumb mixture. Place fillets on broiler pan that has been coated with vegetable cooking spray. Bake for 15 minutes or until fish flakes easily when tested with fork.

Enjoy the crispy, crunchy taste without the extra fat and calories.

Nancy R. Willingham

Baked Fish On A Bed Of Garden Vegetables

2 servings

2 (8-ounce) fish fillets	1 tablespoon chopped fresh parsley *or* ¾ teaspoon dried parsley
2 medium carrots, thinly sliced	
1 small onion *or* 3 scallions, chopped	
2 celery stalks, thinly sliced	1 tablespoon margarine
1 medium potato, thinly sliced	dash of pepper
	dash of paprika
	sprinkle of lemon juice

Preheat oven to 400°. Rinse fish, pat dry with paper towel and set aside. Arrange vegetables and parsley in a shallow baking dish. Dot with margarine and cover. Bake for 10 minutes. Add fish to baking dish, sprinkle with pepper, paprika and lemon juice. Bake for an additional 8-10 minutes or until fish is flaky.

Quick and colorful.

Pat O'Brien

Quick And Easy Stir-Fry

4 servings

1 tablespoon vegetable oil	1 (24-ounce) package
1 pound package chicken	frozen Oriental-style
breast nuggets,	vegetables
uncooked and	3 tablespoons lite soy sauce
unbreaded	½ cup water
	cooked rice

Preheat large skillet over medium heat. Add oil and stir-fry chicken nuggets about 3 minutes. Add frozen vegetables and stir until vegetables are separated. Add soy sauce and ½ cup water and stir. Cover and cook until vegetables are crisp tender. Serve over rice.

Temple Hughes

Tee's Mexican Chicken

4 servings

4 chicken breast halves,	½ cup grated low-fat Cheddar
boned and skinned	cheese
1 medium jar chunky salsa	tortilla chips, crumbled
(mild, medium *or* hot)	

Preheat oven to 350°. Place chicken in a covered casserole dish. Bake for 1 hour. Pour salsa over chicken and top with cheese. Bake uncovered until cheese is melted and salsa is bubbly, about 5-10 minutes. Sprinkle with tortilla chips and serve.

Great with Mexican rice.

Theresa Ellison

Lowfat cooking tip:
Baste meats and poultry with broth or stocks
and reduce amount of butter or margarine.

Mexican Chicken Kiev

8 servings

8	chicken breast halves, skinned and boned	¼	cup grated Parmesan cheese
1	(7-ounce) can diced green chilies	1	tablespoon chili powder
		½	teaspoon salt
4	ounces Monterey Jack cheese, cut in 8 strips	¼	teaspoon ground cumin
		¼	teaspoon black pepper
½	cup dry bread crumbs	4	tablespoons butter, melted

Pound chicken pieces to about ¼-inch thickness. Put about 1 tablespoon chilies and 1 Jack cheese strip in center of each chicken piece. Roll up and tuck ends under. Combine bread crumbs, Parmesan cheese, chili powder, salt, cumin and pepper. Dip each stuffed chicken in shallow bowl containing 4 tablespoons melted butter and roll in crumb mixture. Place chicken rolls, seam side down, in oblong baking dish and drizzle with a little melted butter. Cover and chill 4 hours or overnight. Bake uncovered at 400° for 20 minutes or until done. Serve with **Tomato Sauce**.

Tomato Sauce: 2 cups

1	(16-ounce) can tomato sauce	⅓	cup sliced green onions
			salt and pepper
½	teaspoon ground cumin		hot pepper sauce

Combine tomato sauce, cumin, and green onions in small saucepan. Season to taste with salt, pepper, and hot pepper sauce. Heat well.

Makes a marvelous party dish.

Nancy Barnwell

Lowfat cooking tip:
Use marinades of lemon juice, different types of vinegars or fruit juices mixed with herbs when grilling or broiling and also to tenderize leaner cuts of meat.

Chicken Cordon Bleu With White Wine Sauce

8 servings

8	chicken breast halves, boned and skinned	4	thin slices boiled ham, cut in half
8	teaspoons chopped fresh parsley	1	tablespoon warm water
8	thin slices mozzarella cheese	1	tablespoon reduced calorie mayonnaise
		¼	cup seasoned dry bread crumbs

Preheat oven to 425°. Pound chicken breasts until flat. Sprinkle with parsley. Top each breast with slice of cheese and ½ slice of ham. Roll up tightly. Stir together water and mayonnaise in shallow dish. Roll each piece of chicken in mayonnaise mixture and then in bread crumbs. Spray baking dish with cooking spray. Arrange chicken rolls, seam side down in a single layer. Bake for 15-20 minutes or until browned and cheese is melted.

Wine Sauce:

1	cup low sodium chicken broth, fat skimmed	onion powder and white pepper to taste
3	tablespoons dry white wine	pinch ground nutmeg (optional)
3	tablespoons instant blend flour	1 tablespoon minced fresh parsley
¾	cup skim milk	

Combine broth and wine in a non-stick saucepan. Bring to a boil, reduce heat and simmer. In a cup, mix together flour and milk until smooth. Stir into simmering broth. Cook and stir until mixture is thick and bubbling. Sprinkle with onion powder, pepper and nutmeg. Pour over chicken and add parsley for garnish.

Great slim and healthy recipe.

Susan Brillaud

Baked Lemon Chicken

4 servings

4	chicken breast halves, skinned	1	teaspoon grated lemon rind
1	small onion, chopped	¼	teaspoon ground nutmeg
2	tablespoons chopped fresh dill	3	tablespoons fresh lemon juice
		⅔	cup water

Place chicken breasts in an 8-inch square baking dish. Sprinkle with onion, dill, lemon rind and nutmeg. Combine lemon juice with ⅔ cup cold water. Pour over chicken. Cover and marinate at least 2 hours or overnight in refrigerator. Preheat oven to 375°. Bake chicken uncovered 45 minutes, basting frequently with pan juices.

Georgeanne Hofer

Lemon Chicken With Thyme

4 servings

3	tablespoons all-purpose flour	1	large onion, chopped
½	teaspoon salt	1	cup chicken broth
¼	teaspoon pepper	3	tablespoons lemon juice
4	chicken breast halves, boned and skinned	¼	teaspoon thyme
2	tablespoons olive oil		lemon wedges
1	tablespoon margarine	2	tablespoons chopped fresh parsley

In plastic bag, combine flour, salt and pepper; shake to mix. Add chicken and shake to coat. Remove chicken and reserve excess flour. In large skillet, warm 1 tablespoon olive oil over medium heat. Add chicken and brown on one side, about 5 minutes. Add remaining oil, turn chicken and brown well on other side, 5 minutes or more. Transfer chicken to plate and set aside. Add margarine and onion to skillet; sauté until softened, about 3 minutes. Stir in reserved flour and cook about 1 minute. Add broth, 2 tablespoons lemon juice and thyme; bring mixture to a boil, stirring constantly. Return chicken to skillet, reduce heat and cover. Cook until chicken is tender and opaque throughout, about 5 minutes. Remove chicken to serving plate and stir remaining lemon juice into sauce in skillet. Pour sauce over chicken. Garnish chicken with lemon wedges and a sprinkling of parsley.

Serve this luscious dish with steamed broccoli and if you are not counting calories, serve over a nest of lightly buttered angel hair pasta.

Dorothy B. Watkins

Sesame-Ginger Chicken

4 servings

1	tablespoon sesame seeds, toasted	2	tablespoons lite soy sauce
2	teaspoons grated fresh ginger	4	chicken breast halves, skinned and boned
2	tablespoons honey		vegetable cooking spray
			green onion strips

Combine first 4 ingredients in a small bowl; stir and set aside. Pound chicken pieces to about ¼-inch thickness. Coat grill rack with cooking spray. Grill chicken on rack for 4 minutes on each side, basting frequently with soy sauce mixture. Transfer cooked chicken to serving platter and garnish with green onions.

David LaPaglia

Chicken Dijon

6 servings

6	chicken breast halves, skinned	¼	cup Dijon mustard
	salt and pepper	⅓	cup plain lowfat yogurt
		1	cup Italian bread crumbs

Preheat oven to 350°. Lightly grease or spray baking sheet with vegetable spray. Sprinkle chicken lightly with salt and pepper. Mix mustard into yogurt. Spread each piece of chicken with mustard mixture, then roll in bread crumbs. Place chicken in single layer on baking sheet. Bake for 45-50 minutes for bone-in chicken, 30-35 minutes for boneless or until golden brown.

Good served with boiled new potatoes, steamed broccoli and soft bread sticks.

Lela A. Wiseman

Lowfat cooking tip:
Use extra lean ground beef or ground turkey for spaghetti sauce, chili and casseroles.

Chicken Caruso And Rice

6 servings

6	chicken breasts, boned and skinned	1 teaspoon oregano
	garlic salt to taste	½ cup chopped green bell pepper
	pepper to taste	½ cup chopped celery
1	tablespoon margarine	½ cup chopped carrots
1	(15½-ounce) can tomato sauce	cooked rice

Cut chicken breasts into strips. Season with garlic salt and pepper. Melt margarine in skillet and sauté chicken strips for 2 minutes. Stir in tomato sauce and oregano; cover and simmer 10 minutes. Add vegetables and simmer until crisp tender. Serve over rice.

Variation: Other vegetables can be substituted in this dish. If you add extra vegetables, you may want to add more tomato sauce and oregano.

Carol Panasuk

Grilled Mustard Chicken Breasts

4 servings

4	boneless chicken breast halves, boned and skinned	¼ cup lemon juice
		1 teaspoon Worcestershire sauce
¼	cup Dijon mustard	salt and pepper to taste

Paint chicken breasts on both sides with mustard. Combine lemon juice and Worcestershire sauce and pour over chicken. Let marinate at room temperature for 15 minutes. Preheat broiler or outdoor grill. Grill chicken 4 minutes on each side or until just tender. Season to taste with salt and pepper and serve hot.

Delicious and incredibly low-calorie.

Nancy Barnwell

Grilled Oriental Turkey Tenderloins

4 servings

¼	cup soy sauce	1	teaspoon minced fresh
¼	cup vegetable oil		ginger *or* ¼ teaspoon
¼	cup sherry *or* dry wine		ground ginger
¼	cup thinly sliced green	1	garlic clove, minced
	onions	1	pound turkey tenderloins
2	tablespoons lemon juice		

Combine all ingredients, except turkey, in shallow dish or large sealed plastic bag. Add turkey and marinate for at least 4 hours or overnight in refrigerator. Grill tenderloins, reserving marinade for basting, 8-10 minutes per side, baste frequently while grilling.

Add some flair to this entrée by serving it with rice and stir-fried vegetables.

Diane O'Shea

Turkey Scaloppine With Sherried Cream

4 servings

3	tablespoons all-purpose flour	½	teaspoon cornstarch
¼	teaspoon dried rosemary, crumbled	¼	cup plain low-fat yogurt
		¼	cup low-fat sour cream
¼	teaspoon thyme	¼	cup dry sherry
⅛	teaspoon black pepper	⅓	cup low-sodium chicken broth
4	(¼-inch thick) turkey breast cutlets (about 1 pound)	1	teaspoon Dijon *or* spice brown mustard
1	tablespoon margarine	1	tablespoon minced fresh parsley

Combine first 4 ingredients together on a plate. Dredge cutlets into mixture, coating evenly and shake off excess. Spray skillet with cooking spray, add margarine and melt over moderately high heat. Brown cutlets, about 2 minutes on each side. Transfer cutlets to platter and keep warm. In a small bowl, combine together cornstarch, yogurt and sour cream; set aside. Discard any drippings from skillet, add sherry and boil, uncovered, for 30 seconds. Add chicken broth, cornstarch mixture and mustard and cook, stirring constantly for 2-3 minutes or until sauce is slightly thick. Spoon sauce over cutlets and sprinkle with parsley. Serve with baked potatoes or rice.

A light and luscious creation that is low in fat and sodium.

Rita C. Leonard

Turkey Meatloaf

6-8 servings

1	(10-ounce) package frozen chopped spinach, thawed and squeezed dry	1½	teaspoons dried basil
		2	teaspoons salt
		1	teaspoon pepper
		2	pounds ground turkey
5	slices firm white bread	2	teaspoons lemon juice
1	medium onion, chopped	½	cup ketchup
1	tablespoon vegetable oil	2	tablespoons butter or
2	eggs		margarine, melted
½	cup milk		

Preheat oven to 350°. Thaw spinach and squeeze dry. Process bread into fine crumbs, set aside. Sauté onion in oil until soft, about 2 minutes. Whisk eggs with milk, basil, salt and pepper. In a large bowl, combine together spinach, bread crumbs, onion, egg mixture, turkey and lemon juice. Mix well. Turn into a buttered loaf pan and brush top with ketchup. Bake for 40-50 minutes or until browned. Baste loaf twice with butter.

Dolores W. Mistretta
Fort Myers, Florida

Marinated Flank Steak

8 servings

½	cup vegetable oil	1	teaspoon freshly ground pepper
⅓	cup soy sauce		
¼	cup red wine vinegar	1	large onion, sliced
¼	cup lemon juice	1	clove garlic, minced
3	tablespoons Worcestershire sauce	2	pounds flank steak or London broil
2	tablespoons Dijon mustard		

Combine first 9 ingredients together in a bowl. Place steak in a shallow dish or bowl, pour marinade over it, cover and refrigerate. Marinate for 12-24 hours. When ready to cook, preheat broiler or outdoor grill. Remove meat from marinade and grill to desired doneness, basting occasionally. Cut meat on the bias into thin slices and serve hot.

Makes a tasty, tender and memorable main dish.

Nancy Barnwell

244

Pepper Steak

6 servings

1½ pounds lean round steak
vegetable cooking spray
½ cup chopped green onions
⅛ teaspoon garlic powder
2 (8-ounce) cans no-salt
added tomatoes,
chopped
1 tablespoon Kitchen
Bouquet

2 tablespoons
Worcestershire sauce
1 cup water
2 medium-sized green bell
peppers, sliced thin
1 tablespoon cornstarch
¼ cup water
cooked rice

Slice steak diagonally across grain into ¼-inch strips. Coat large skillet with cooking spray; place over medium-high heat until hot. Add steak strips, chopped onions and garlic; cook until steak is browned. Drain and transfer steak mixture onto paper towels. Wipe remaining pan drippings with paper towel. Return steak mixture to skillet. Add tomatoes and next 3 ingredients. Bring mixture to a boil; cover, reduce heat and simmer 1 hour, stirring occasionally. Add green peppers during last 5 minutes. Thicken sauce with mixture of cornstarch and water. Serve over cooked rice.

Your family or guests will never know this recipe is calorie wise.

Rochelle Mistretta

Braised Beef

4 servings

¼ cup Tamari *or* soy sauce
¼ cup Italian dressing
1 pound sirloin steak *or*
braised deer, cut in
thin slices
1 tablespoon olive oil
8 green onions, cut in 1-inch
lengths

½ pound fresh snow peas,
trim and remove
string
½ cup vegetable broth
¼ cup Tamari *or* soy sauce
2 tablespoons sherry
4 cups cooked brown rice

Combine Tamari and Italian dressing and marinate meat for 4 hours. Heat olive oil in wok or frying pan. Brown meat for 5 minutes or until cooked. Remove to a bowl. Add onions and peas to oil and stir-fry for 30 seconds over high heat. Add broth, cover and simmer for 30 seconds. Add Tamari, sherry and meat; stir until heated through. Serve over brown rice.

Joyce Hirschman

Beef Salad Stir-Fry

4-6 servings

2	tablespoons water	¼	teaspoon hot red pepper
1	tablespoon orange juice		flakes
1	tablespoon soy sauce	1	garlic clove, minced
¾	pound beef round steak,	4	ounces uncooked whole
	trimmed of fat, and		wheat spaghetti
	cut into thin strips	2	cups chopped fresh
2	tablespoons white vinegar		broccoli
1	tablespoon soy sauce	1	small red pepper, chopped
1	tablespoon orange juice	4	cups shredded Chinese
2	teaspoons sesame oil		cabbage
		⅓	cup sliced green onions

In small bowl, combine first 3 ingredients and marinate meat for 30 minutes, then drain. Meanwhile in small bowl, combine next 6 ingredients. Set aside. Cook spaghetti and drain. Heat large non-stick skillet over medium-high heat until hot. Stir-fry beef strips for 2 minutes. Add broccoli and pepper. Stir-fry 2 minutes more until beef is brown and vegetables are tender. In very large bowl, combine beef mixture, spaghetti, Chinese cabbage and green onions. Pour vinegar mixture over salad. Toss lightly. Serve immediately.

A delicious medley of vegetables and lean beef enhanced by a zesty sauce.

Mary Beth Harja

Spaghetti Sauce

4-6 servings

2	tablespoons olive oil	1	teaspoon onion powder
1	onion, chopped	1	teaspoon vege-sal (found
1	cup sliced fresh		at health food stores)
	mushrooms		*or* vegetable seasoning
1	teaspoon chopped garlic	½	cup water
1	green bell pepper,	2	cups tomato sauce
	chopped	2	cups cooked lentils
1	teaspoon basil	⅛	teaspoon vege-sal
1	teaspoon oregano	⅛	teaspoon cayenne pepper

Sauté first 9 ingredients for 10-15 minutes. Add water, tomato sauce, lentils and seasonings. Simmer for ½ hour, stirring frequently.

This sauce is good for any type of pasta.

Joyce Hirschman

246

Orange Poppy Seed Muffins

1 dozen

1¼	cups all-purpose flour	½	cup skim milk
½	cup sugar	⅓	cup oil
⅓	teaspoon salt	½	teaspoon orange extract
⅓	cup poppy seeds	¼	cup freshly squeezed
2	teaspoons baking powder		orange juice
1	egg	2	tablespoons orange zest

Preheat oven to 375°. Oil muffin cups generously. Combine flour, sugar, salt, poppy seeds and baking powder. Beat in egg. Combine milk, oil, orange extract and orange juice in another bowl. Add orange zest. Add wet ingredients to flour mixture and blend until smooth. Fill muffin cups ⅔ full. Bake for 20 minutes or until golden. Cool on a wire rack.

A mouth watering muffin that won't add inches to your waist.

Nancy Barnwell

Yum Yum Dessert

20 servings

1	angel food cake (already baked)	3	cups skim milk
1	(20-ounce) can crushed pineapple, drain well and reserve juice	2	bananas, sliced
		1	(8-ounce) container frozen whipped topping, thawed
1	(6-ounce) package sugar-free instant vanilla pudding		

Line bottom of a 9x13-inch glass baking pan with slices of angel food cake. Top slices with drained pineapple and spoon about ½ of reserved juice over cake. Mix vanilla pudding with cold milk and pour over cake mixture. Place slices of bananas over pudding. Spread whipped topping over top. Keep refrigerated until serving time. Best if used within 24 hours of preparation time.

This dessert was served at our 1989 Card Party / Luncheon / Fashion Show.

Women's Guild

Pineapple Ice

2 servings

1 (13-ounce) can crushed
   pineapple,
   unsweetened

2 tablespoons frozen
   pineapple juice
   concentrate, thawed
   or any frozen fruit
   concentrate, thawed
1 egg white
1 papaya *or* cantaloupe

Combine crushed pineapple, juice concentrate and egg white in food processor or blender. Process until blended. Place purée in a covered container in freezer until frozen, about 2-3 hours. To serve, cut papaya in half. Discard seeds, scoop out pulp and slice. Place pineapple ice in shell and surround with papaya slices. *Note:* Pineapple ice can be served without fruit, place in a parfait or sherbet glass and top with a cherry or fresh mint sprig.

A cool and refreshing treat.

Jill L. Gasperini

Lowfat cooking tip:
For cheese-based casseroles, use lowfat or reduced-fat cheese. Top with just a sprinkling of stronger cheeses such as sharp Cheddar or Romano. These cheeses provide more flavor, reducing the amount needed.

Celebrity Favorites

Braciole

6-8 servings

2 (1¼ pound) round steaks, all fat trimmed
   salt and pepper to taste
1 (16-ounce) can spinach, drain and reserve liquid
½ loaf day old crusty bread
¼ cup finely chopped onion
1 garlic clove, finely chopped
¼ cup egg substitute
2 tablespoons Romano or Parmesan cheese

Pound each piece of steak to flatten evenly. Salt and pepper steaks. Squeeze spinach as dry as possible. Dampen bread with liquid from spinach and squeeze dry. Mash spinach and bread together. Add remaining ingredients and blend well. Spread spinach mixture on steaks. Roll each piece jelly roll style and tie securely with string. Lightly brown steaks in skillet sprayed with cooking spray. Transfer steaks to a deep baking dish, add gravy and bake covered at 350° for 2½-3 hours.

Gravy For Braciole:

1 celery stalk, chopped
¼ cup finely chopped onion
1 teaspoon olive oil
½ teaspoon rosemary
¼ teaspoon thyme
2 (16-ounce) cans tomatoes, chopped
2 (8-ounce) cans tomato sauce
8 ounces fresh mushrooms, sliced
   parsley
   salt and pepper to taste

Sauté celery and onion in skillet sprayed with olive oil cooking spray and 1 teaspoon olive oil. Add remaining ingredients and simmer for 1½-2 hours.

Stuffed Eggplant *and linguine tossed with a warm olive oil, sweet basil and parsley mixture are tasty accompaniments to this entrée.*

Reverend Milton J. Guthrie, Pastor
Our Lady of Perpetual Help Church
Germantown, Tennessee

Stuffed Eggplant

4 servings

1	large eggplant	1	teaspoon diet margarine
1	cup water		butter flavored cooking
½	teaspoon salt		spray
1	cup chopped fresh		salt and pepper to taste
	mushrooms	½	cup evaporated skim milk
3	tablespoons chopped	2	tablespoons fine dry
	onion		bread crumbs
1	garlic clove, minced		imitation bacon bits

Wash eggplant, cut in half lengthwise and remove pulp; leaving ¼-inch shell. Chop pulp and combine with water and salt in saucepan. Bring to a boil, cover, reduce heat and simmer for 10 minutes. Drain well. Sauté mushrooms, onion and garlic in skillet sprayed with butter flavored cooking spray and margarine. Add eggplant, salt, pepper and evaporated milk. Stir well. Spoon into eggplant shell, sprinkle with bread crumbs. Bake at 350° for 40 minutes. Sprinkle bacon bits on top and bake 5 more minutes.

Reverend Milton J. Guthrie, Pastor
Our Lady of Perpetual Help Church
Germantown, Tennessee

Okra Gumbo

6 servings

6	slices bacon, chopped	1	(16-ounce) can water
1	large onion, chopped	1	(10-ounce) can Rotel
¼	teaspoon salt		tomatoes, diced
¼	teaspoon pepper	1	pound okra, sliced
½	teaspoon chili powder		cooked rice
1	(16-ounce) can tomatoes,		
	chopped		

Fry bacon in a Dutch oven until crisp; drain on paper towels, reserving 2 tablespoons drippings. Cook onion in drippings until tender. Add salt, pepper and chili powder. Stir in tomatoes, water and Rotel tomatoes. Add okra and bacon. Cover and simmer until okra is tender. Serve over rice.

Reverend Michael L. Stewart, Pastor, 1986-1992
Our Lady of Perpetual Help Church
Germantown, Tennessee

Almond-Orange Biscotti

20-24 slices

2¼ cups all-purpose flour
1⅛ cups sugar
¼   teaspoon baking powder
    pinch of salt
¾   cup egg substitute
1   tablespoon vegetable oil
¼   teaspoon almond extract
    finely grated zest of
    1 orange
½   cup coarsely chopped
    almonds

Preheat oven to 350°. Grease and flour a baking sheet. Shake off excess. In a large bowl, sift flour, sugar, baking powder and salt together. Make a well in center of mixture. To the well, add remaining ingredients. With hands, work dry mixture with liquids until a dough has been formed. Divide dough in half. On a lightly floured surface, shape dough into 2 flat-bottomed cylinders, 1-inch high, 2½-inches wide and 8-inches long. Transfer each to baking sheet. Bake for 30-35 minutes, until lightly colored on top. Remove from oven and cool slightly. Holding a long sharp knife by the handle and tip, cut cylinders diagonally into ¾-inch slices. Carefully place slices back on baking sheet, cut sides down; return them to oven for 15 more minutes or until sides are golden and biscotti have dried a bit. Remove from oven and cool on wire racks. The biscotti should be somewhat hard and crunchy.

Reverend Milton J. Guthrie, Pastor
Our Lady of Perpetual Help Church
Germantown, Tennessee

Eggs With A Crunch

feeds regiment

Take 12 pounds dried eggs; add 3 whole eggs, shell and all. Follow normal instructions for scrambling eggs. When first soldier bites egg shell, he will shout joyously, "We've got fresh eggs". The whole regiment's day will be made when they can "lord it over" the other soldiers because "we had fresh eggs for breakfast".

Reverend Ned Elliott, Pastor, 1969-1986
Our Lady of Perpetual Help Church
Germantown, Tennessee

Shrimp Diane

4 servings

1	(8-ounce) package regular and wild rice blend, cooked	⅛	teaspoon red pepper sauce
½	cup lightly salted butter	½	teaspoon ground cayenne pepper
¼	cup chopped green onions	½	teaspoon salt
1	garlic clove, minced	¼	teaspoon black pepper
¼	to ½ pound fresh mushrooms, sliced	¼	teaspoon basil
		¼	teaspoon thyme
3	tablespoons fresh parsley, minced	⅛	teaspoon oregano
			juice of ½ lemon
6	tablespoons *Fish Stock* or clam juice	1	pound raw medium shrimp, shelled and deveined
2	teaspoons Dijon mustard		
¼	teaspoon Worcestershire sauce		

Cook rice according to package directions. Meanwhile, melt butter in a large skillet. Sauté onions and garlic just short of browning, 3-5 minutes. Add mushrooms and parsley; sauté until mushrooms shrink, 5 minutes. Add stock or clam juice, mustard, Worcestershire and red pepper sauce, stirring to blend. Combine dry seasonings together and add to mixture, stirring well to blend. Squeeze juice of ½ lemon into skillet and simmer for about 5 minutes on low heat. When rice is ready, add shrimp to skillet, turn heat to medium and cook until shrimp turn pink, about 3-5 minutes. Serve over wild rice.

Fish Stock:

1	large white onion, quartered		shells and tails of 1 pound shrimp
3	large carrots, halved	3	quarts water
3	celery stalks, halved		

Simmer all ingredients in water for 3 hours or more. Strain broth and discard vegetables and shells. Stock can be frozen for later use.

Most Reverend Daniel M. Buechlein, O.S.B., D.D.
Bishop of the Catholic Diocese of Memphis

Cincinnati Chili

8-10 servings

2	to 3 pounds ground beef	5	bay leaves
4	cups cold water	2	teaspoons cinnamon
1	(6-ounce) can tomato paste	1	teaspoon allspice
2	large onions, chopped (about 1½ cups)	2	cayenne peppers (more to taste)
1½	tablespoons vinegar	1½	tablespoons unsweetened cocoa
1	teaspoon Worcestershire sauce		salt and pepper to taste
1	garlic clove, chopped fine	1½	pounds spaghetti, cooked al dente
2	tablespoons chili powder		

Condiments:

	chili pepper	1	(16-ounce) can kidney beans
1	pound grated Cheddar cheese	1	onion, chopped fine (optional)
1	box oyster crackers		

In a large saucepan, crumble ground beef into the water. Add all of the ingredients except spaghetti and bring to a boil. Stir well, breaking all the meat up before it cooks. Cover and simmer 2 or more hours, stirring occasionally. *Note:* The proper way to serve this chili is over spaghetti in an oval dish. There should be a piece of pepper for every serving for absolute authenticity. For a "3-Way," top it off with a pile of grated cheese and with a dish of crackers on the side. To make a "4-Way," add a spoonful of onions before the cheese is placed on top. For a "5-Way," add beans in addition to onions and cheese.

Brother Chris Englert, F.S.C.
Principal, Christian Brothers High School

A recipe not shared with others is soon forgotten, but when it is shared, it will be enjoyed by future generations.

Modern Mock Turtle Soup

8-10 servings

1	pound ground beef	1	tablespoon whole allspice
2	beef bouillon cubes		*or* pickling spice tied
2	quarts water		in a bag
1	cup wheat flour		salt and pepper to taste
1	large onion, chopped	2	hard-cooked eggs,
	juice of 1 lemon		chopped fine
1	(10-ounce) bottle ketchup		oyster crackers
1	(16-ounce) can beef gravy		lemon slices
1	tablespoon A.1. sauce		sherry wine (optional)
2	tablespoons vinegar		

In a Dutch oven, brown ground beef and drain. Add beef bouillon cubes and water, bring to a boil and stir to dissolve. Mix wheat flour with enough water to make a paste. Stir into beef mixture. Add chopped onion and juice of lemon. Add remaining ingredients except the eggs, crackers, lemon slices and sherry wine. Bring mixture to a boil, lower heat and simmer at least 2 hours. Add eggs during last 15 minutes of cooking time. Serve piping hot with oyster crackers, lemon slices and/or jigger of sherry wine.

Brother Chris Englert, F.S.C.
Principal, Christian Brothers High School

Yummy Green Beans

4 servings

1	pound young and small	2	tablespoons butter *or*
	green beans		margarine
4	quarts boiling water	1	large garlic clove,
2	tablespoons salt *or* other		crushed
	seasonings		salt and pepper to taste

String beans, wash well and boil rapidly in salted water, uncovered, until barely tender and still firm (taste them to make sure). Drain and run under cold water to stop the cooking. Pat dry. Melt butter and add garlic and cook gently until softened. DO NOT BROWN! Pour over beans and taste for seasoning. *Note:* Can be made ahead. To reheat, put in microwave for 2 minutes on high or heat in saucepan over low heat.

Barbara Bush
United States First Lady

255

Old Fashioned Bread Pudding

12 servings

8	slices raisin bread (lightly spread with butter *or* margarine)	4	cups milk (whole, 2 percent *or* skim)
½	to ¾ cup sugar	2	teaspoons vanilla
½	teaspoon cinnamon extra raisins *or* fruit to taste	4	eggs, beaten *or* equivalent egg substitute
		½	teaspoon salt

Preheat oven to 350°. Cut raisin bread into quarters. Put one layer of bread in a buttered 9x13-inch baking dish. Mix sugar and cinnamon together and sprinkle bread with sugar mixture and raisins. Continue alternating bread, sugar and raisin mixtures until dish is full. Combine together milk, vanilla, eggs and salt and pour over bread. Bake until puffed and lightly brown; about 30 minutes.

Barbara Bush
United States First Lady

Old Fashioned Rice Pudding

8 servings

4	cups milk	½	cup raisins, dried cherries *or* any favorite dried fruit
¼	cup long grain rice, uncooked		
½	cup sugar	¼	teaspoon cinnamon *or* nutmeg
½	teaspoon salt		
		1	teaspoon vanilla

Preheat oven to 300°. Butter a 6-cup mold or baking dish. Mix all ingredients, pour into prepared dish and bake 3½ hours, stirring every 30 minutes for the first 2 hours. Bake until rice is very tender.

Barbara Bush
United States First Lady

A personalized cookbook is a gift that is appreciated for all occasions.

Mrs. Lucillie's Pound Cake

1 loaf pan

2	cups all-purpose flour	1	cup butter, room
2	cups sugar		temperature
5	large eggs, room	2	teaspoons vanilla
	temperature		

Preheat oven to 300°. Blend dry ingredients together, then add eggs, one at a time. Beat for about 1 minute after each addition. Add butter and vanilla, blend well. Pour into a greased 5x9-inch loaf pan and bake for 1 hour. *Note:* It is important that the butter and eggs be at room temperature.

This is Governor Ned McWherter's favorite cake which his mother often made for him.

The Honorable Ned McWherter
Governor, State of Tennessee

Zucchini Con (with) Farfalle

4-6 servings

5	tablespoons olive oil	1	pound farfalle (small
5	small zucchini, cut into		bowtie shaped
	sticks about 1½		pasta), cooked al
	inches long		dente and drained
2	large onions, minced	½	cup freshly grated
1	garlic clove, minced		Parmesan cheese
⅔	cup whipping cream		salt and freshly ground
			pepper to taste
			freshly grated Parmesan
			cheese

Heat oil in large non-aluminum skillet over medium-high heat. Add zucchini and sauté quickly until golden. Remove with slotted spoon and set aside. Add onions and sauté until golden. Add garlic and cook 1 minute. Stir in cream, increase heat and boil until sauce is reduced by ⅓. Add pasta, zucchini, ½ cup Parmesan cheese, salt and pepper; toss thoroughly until heated through. Serve immediately with additional Parmesan cheese.

Very elegant and delicious pasta dish; easy, quick to prepare.

Laura and Paul Cardelli
Cardelli's Catering

Shells A La Thom

8-10 servings

1	tablespoon butter	2	tablespoons grated
1	pound ricotta cheese		Parmesan *or* Romano
1	pound medium *or* large		cheese
	macaroni shells,		salt and freshly ground
	cooked al dente and		pepper
	drained	2	to 2½ quarts of your
⅓	cup chopped fresh Italian		favorite Italian
	parsley		tomato sauce

Melt butter in large skillet over low heat. Add ricotta cheese and stir until melted. Add pasta, turning until well coated. Sprinkle parsley and Parmesan or Romano cheese over top and toss gently. Season with salt and pepper to taste. Transfer to platter. Ladle some sauce over top and serve immediately. Pass remaining sauce at table.

Multo bene!

Laura and Paul Cardelli
Cardelli's Catering

Deviled Crab

4-6 servings

1	cup finely chopped celery	1	teaspoon salt
1	large green bell pepper,	1½	teaspoons dry mustard
	finely chopped		dash Tabasco® sauce
1	cup finely sliced green	½	cup heavy cream
	onions	1	cup butter, melted
½	cup chopped fresh parsley	1	cup coarsely crushed
2	pounds lump crabmeat		cracker crumbs
1½	cups coarsely crushed		
	cracker crumbs		

Preheat oven to 350°. In a large bowl, combine all ingredients except 1 cup cracker crumbs and toss lightly. Spoon mixture into a buttered baking dish or crab shells. Top with cracker crumbs and bake for 25-30 minutes or until top is lightly browned.

Fred W. Smith, Chairman and C.E.O.
Federal Express

Chicken With Ripe Olives

6-8 servings

1½	to 2 cups all-purpose flour	½	teaspoon thyme
	salt and pepper	¾	teaspoon salt
1	large fryer, cut into	1	(16-ounce) can Italian
	serving pieces		plum tomatoes,
4	tablespoons olive oil		chopped
1	garlic clove, split	¼	to ½ cup white wine
⅓	cup cognac	1	tablespoon all-purpose
1	bay leaf, broken		flour
3	tablespoons chopped	1	cup pitted ripe black
	fresh parsley		olives
1	teaspoon sage		

Season flour with salt and pepper. Dredge chicken in flour, shake off excess. In a large skillet, heat oil and cook garlic until slightly golden. Discard garlic. Brown chicken, adding more oil as necessary. Arrange chicken in a casserole dish. Warm cognac in a ladle. Ignite cognac and pour over chicken. Add bay leaf, parsley, sage, thyme and salt. Add tomatoes and stir well to blend. Mix wine with 1 tablespoon flour and stir until smooth. Pour over chicken. Bake covered for 1 hour or until chicken is tender. After 30 minutes of cooking time, sprinkle olives over chicken and continue to bake. Serve with pasta.

Laura and Paul Cardelli
Cardelli's Catering

Chocolate Chip Pie

8-12 servings

1	(9-inch) deep dish pastry	1	cup butter *or* margarine,
	shell, unbaked		melted and cooled
2	eggs	1	(6-ounce) package
½	cup all-purpose flour		semi-sweet chocolate
½	cup sugar		chips
½	cup light brown sugar		whipped cream *or* ice
			cream

Preheat oven to 325°. In large bowl, beat eggs until foamy. Beat in flour and sugars until well blended. Blend in melted butter. Place chips in bottom of unbaked pie shell. Pour mixture over the chips. Bake for 1 hour. Serve warm topped with whipped cream or ice cream. *Note:* Do not double this recipe. Reheat leftovers in foil.

Rob Cadwallader, Tennis Pro
The Racquet Club

Brooklyn Bridge Lard Bread

8-10 servings

3	pounds bread dough *or* 3 loaves frozen dough	½	pound sliced Italian salami, cubed
½	teaspoon salt	½	pound Cheddar cheese, cubed
¼	teaspoon pepper all-purpose flour	½	pound provolone cheese, cubed
½	cup shortening, room temperature		

If you are using frozen dough, defrost thoroughly. Add salt and pepper to dough. Roll out all 3 loaves together on a floured board. Rub shortening over dough. Add salami, Cheddar and provolone cheese and knead these ingredients into dough. Grease a round tube pan with shortening. Shape dough around hole in center of pan. Cover pan with a dish towel and place in warm place to rise. When dough rises over pan, place in a preheated 350° oven and bake for 45 minutes. Serve warm.

When I make this bread, I have to make two, one for the family to pull apart in the kitchen and the other for the table. This is not hard to prepare and is a meal by itself.

Bridgette Analfitano Correale, Owner
Brooklyn Bridge Italian Restaurant and Catering

Breast Of Chicken Saltimbocco

6 servings

3	whole chicken breasts, split, skinned and boned	6	thin slices proscuitto
¼	teaspoon rubbed sage	¼	cup butter
¼	cup all-purpose flour	¼	cup dry Marsala wine
		1	(10½-ounce) can chicken broth

Place chicken breasts between wax paper and flatten with meat mallet. Rub with sage. Dredge each breast lightly in flour and shake off excess. Top each breast with sliced proscuitto and press into breast. Heat butter in skillet and sauté chicken breasts until lightly browned. Add Marsala wine and bring to a boil. Stir to loosen brown bits. Add chicken broth and bring to a boil. Reduce heat and simmer 5 minutes or until sauce has slightly thickened.

Frank A. Grisanti, C.E.C.
Chef/Owner
Frank Grisanti's Italian Restaurant

Orange Roughy With Basilica Sauce

4 servings

3	tablespoons olive oil	2	tablespoons chopped
3	tablespoons chopped onion		mushrooms
3	teaspoons chopped garlic		salt and pepper to taste
½	cup chopped peeled fresh	2	tablespoons chopped fresh
	tomatoes, with juice		basil
⅔	cup dry white wine	2	teaspoons chopped fresh
½	cup fish stock *or* clam		parsley
	juice	4	(8 to 10-ounce) orange
1	tablespoon capers		roughy fillets
1	teaspoon lemon juice		salt and pepper to taste
¼	teaspoon Worcestershire	½	cup water
	sauce	1	tablespoon olive oil

For **Basilica Sauce**, heat olive oil in a medium saucepan; sauté onion and garlic. Add tomatoes and wine; bring to a boil. Add fish stock or clam juice, capers, lemon juice and Worcestershire sauce. Return to a boil, reduce heat and simmer for 5 minutes. Remove from heat; add mushrooms, salt, pepper, basil and parsley. Stir well to blend, cover pan and set aside. Preheat oven to 425°. Place fish in a 9x9-inch baking dish and sprinkle with salt and pepper to taste. Add water and olive oil and bake uncovered for 10-12 minutes. Remove from oven and cover with heated **Basilica Sauce** and serve.

A suggested wine for this entrée is Livio Feluge Pinot Griegio.

Vince Correale, Owner
Brooklyn Bridge Italian Restaurant and Catering

Rice And Green Chili Casserole

10 servings

1	cup chopped onion		salt and pepper to taste
¼	cup margarine	3	(4-ounce) cans chopped
4	cups cooked rice		green chilies, mild
2	cups sour cream	2	cups grated Cheddar
1	cup cottage cheese		cheese

Preheat oven to 375°. Lightly grease a 7x12-inch baking dish. Sauté onion in margarine for about 5 minutes. Remove from heat. Stir in rice, sour cream and cottage cheese. Salt and pepper to taste. Layer ½ rice mixture in baking dish, then ½ chilies and ½ grated cheese. Repeat. Bake uncovered for 25 minutes or until bubbly. *Note:* Mozzarella or your favorite cheese can be substituted for the Cheddar cheese.

Chuck Stobart, Head Coach
Memphis State University Football

Uncle Jim's "Best In The Family" Pesto Sauce

4 servings

1 cup fresh basil	1 tablespoon grated
2 garlic cloves, minced	Parmesan cheese
1 tablespoon olive oil	1 pound linguine pasta
	Parmesan cheese

Combine basil, minced garlic, olive oil and Parmesan cheese in blender or food processor. Process to blend and set aside. Cook linguine according to package directions and drain. Add pesto sauce to linguine and garnish with desired amount of Parmesan cheese. *Note:* This meal can be prepared in 15 minutes.

If you have a green thumb, you can grow basil in your garden from May to November like Uncle Jim does. When the plants reach 15-18 inches high, clip the leaves almost to the root. (Leave plant to grow again.) Wash leaves only. Drain and dry in the sun. Place 1½ cups in a blender, add 1 teaspoon olive oil and chop. Place in a jar. Cover with oil and add a teaspoon of salt. Seal tightly and keep in refrigerator. Use basil when needed. If all this sounds like work...it is!

Bridgette Analfitano Correale, Owner
Brooklyn Bridge Italian Restaurant and Catering

Pappy's Lobster Shack Rolls

2 dozen rolls

1 package active dry yeast	1 teaspoon salt
⅓ cup warm water	3 cups all-purpose flour,
3 eggs	sifted
½ cup shortening, melted	½ cup margarine *or* butter,
⅓ cup warm milk	melted
1 tablespoon sugar	

Dissolve yeast in water. In a mixing bowl, beat eggs, shortening, milk, sugar, salt and dissolved yeast. Beat well. Add flour and work in well. Knead in bowl until dough is smooth. Cover and let rise in a warm place until doubled in size. Punch dough down. Pull off small pieces of dough, shape into a small ball and put into greased muffin tins. Cover and let rise. Bake at 400° for 10-12 minutes. Brush with melted butter.

Pappy Sammons' Original Recipe

Uncle Joe's Filetta Sauce And Pasta

6-8 servings

3	tablespoons olive oil	1	tablespoon pesto sauce
½	medium onion, sliced		(commercial *or* refer
½	pound small fresh		to UNCLE JIM'S
	mushrooms *or* 1		"BEST IN THE
	(8-ounce) jar		FAMILY" PESTO)
	mushrooms, drained		salt to taste
1	pound boiled ham, sliced	4	quarts water
	very thick and cut	2	pounds ziti pasta
	into strips	1	teaspoon salt
2	(28-ounce) cans Progresso		grated Parmesan cheese
	purée		

In a large skillet, heat olive oil and brown onion and mushrooms until golden. Add ham and toss for 5 minutes. Add purée, pesto and salt to taste; cook on medium heat for 5 minutes, stirring occasionally. Turn heat down to low and simmer for 20-30 minutes. Stir frequently. In a large pot, bring 4 quarts water to a boil, add ziti and salt. Cook al dente, about 9-10 minutes. Drain. Place in a large serving bowl and add sauce. Serve with grated Parmesan cheese.

This is a meal that can be prepared and served within 45 minutes. Add a tossed salad, loaf of bread and a bottle of wine.

Bridgette Analfitano Correale, Owner
Brooklyn Bridge Italian Restaurant and Catering

BBQ Beans

8 servings

32	ounces fancy pork and	4	ounces BBQ sauce
	beans	1	teaspoon prepared
2	teaspoons dark chili		mustard
	powder	½	cup chopped red onion
4	teaspoons dark brown	½	pound chopped BBQ
	sugar		shoulder
4	ounces Worcestershire		
	sauce		

Mix all ingredients well. Cover and bake at 250° for 1 hour.

Walker Taylor, Owner
The Germantown Commissary

Shrimp Fria Diavolo

4 servings

2	tablespoons minced fresh garlic	1	(16-ounce) can plum tomatoes, undrained
2	tablespoons diced onion	4	leaves fresh basil
2	tablespoons olive oil	1	tablespoon chopped fresh oregano
16	medium-size shrimp, shelled and deveined	¾	pound linguine pasta
1¾	ounces brandy		pinch salt and pepper
2	ounces white wine (preferably a Chablis)		

In large skillet, sauté garlic and onion in olive oil until onions are translucent, about 1 minute on high. Add shrimp and cook until shrimp are just pink. Deglaze pan with brandy, BE VERY CAREFUL BECAUSE MIXTURE WILL FLAME. After flames subside, add the white wine. Remove shrimp from pan and add tomatoes, basil and oregano. Cook on simmer for 8-10 minutes. Meanwhile, cook linguine in a large pot of salted (just a pinch) boiling water for 7-8 minutes or until al dente. Drain. When sauce is done, return shrimp to sauce to reheat. Add salt and pepper. *Note:* If shrimp are left in sauce during cooking, they will overcook.

George Correale, Head Chef
Brooklyn Bridge Italian Restaurant and Catering

Roasted Cornish Hens Al Barolo

6 servings

6	Rock Cornish hens (1½ pounds each)	1	garlic clove, split
¾	teaspoon salt	½	teaspoon rosemary leaves
6	green onions	1	cup Barolo red wine
1	lemon, cut in 6 wedges		watercress *or* Italian parsley
¼	cup butter		

Preheat oven to 400°. Sprinkle each hen inside and out with salt. Place 1 green onion and a wedge of lemon inside each hen. Tie legs together. Arrange hens in shallow roasting pan. Melt butter in small saucepan. Add garlic, rosemary and ½ cup red wine; reserve remaining wine. Brush over hens. Roast hens, uncovered, brushing often with remaining sauce until hens are brown, approximately 45-60 minutes. Transfer to heated platter. Remove strings, keep warm. Pour drippings into 1 cup measure and add reserved wine. Pour into small saucepan and bring to a boil. Serve sauce with hens and garnish with watercress or Italian parsley. Risotto is an excellent accompaniment.

Frank A. Grisanti, C.E.C.
Chef/Owner
Frank Grisanti's Italian Restaurant

Italian Style Roast Beef With Wine

15-20 servings

1	(5 to 6-pound) pike's peak *or* sirloin tip roast		Worcestershire sauce Kitchen Bouquet
8	to 10 garlic cloves, cut into pieces	½	to 1 cup dry red wine salt and pepper to taste
¼	pound Romano cheese, cut into pieces *or* ½ pound grated Parmesan cheese	2	cups water

Wash and dry roast thoroughly and place in a roasting pan. Cut ¼-inch deep slits over surface of roast. As you cut each slit, hold open and fill with Worcestershire sauce. Push in a piece of garlic and a piece of cheese. (If grated Parmesan cheese is used, use a pinch.) Continue until all slits are stuffed. Pour ½ to 1 cup wine over roast, including sides and bottom, letting some of the wine into the slits. Rub Kitchen Bouquet generously over entire roast. Salt and pepper to taste. Place on roasting rack in pan. Add 2 cups water to seasonings which have fallen into pan. Cover roast with aluminum foil, forming a tent and leaving ends open. Bake at 325° for 30-35 minutes <u>per</u> <u>pound</u> or use meat thermometer for desired doneness. Baste 4-5 times with drippings. Let stand 10 minutes before slicing. Thinly slice against the grain of the meat and serve with natural juices. *Note:* Prepare roast in pan you will use for roasting, allowing excess liquids and pieces to stay in pan. Better if refrigerated overnight after preparation and before roasting.

Leftovers make delicious French dip sandwiches.

Rose and Raoul Vanelli
Classic Catering by Vanelli's

A simple meal becomes a gourmet's delight with an elegant sauce enhancing meat, fish or fowl.

Cranberry Nut Cheesecake

16 servings

Crust:

1 cup sifted all-purpose flour	1 egg yolk, slightly beaten
1 teaspoon sugar	1 teaspoon vanilla
¼ teaspoon cinnamon	¼ cup finely ground walnuts
½ cup butter, room temperature	*or* pecans

Preheat oven to 400°. Butter sides of a 9-inch springform pan; set aside. In a medium-size bowl, combine flour, sugar and cinnamon; mix well. Cut in butter with pastry blender until mixture resembles coarse crumbs. Add egg yolk and vanilla, stir just until dough holds together. Set aside ⅔ of the dough. Mix nuts into remaining ⅓. Press nut dough evenly into bottom of prepared pan. Press remaining dough evenly over sides to a height of 2-inches. If crust becomes soft, refrigerate 10 minutes. Bake for 10 minutes or until lightly golden. (Crust may shrink on sides.) Cool on wire rack.

Cheese Filling:

5 (8-ounce) packages cream cheese, softened	2 egg yolks, room temperature
1¾ cups sugar	¼ cup sour cream
3 tablespoons all-purpose flour	1 teaspoon grated lime rind
⅛ teaspoon salt	½ teaspoon grated lemon rind
5 eggs, room temperature	2 teaspoons fresh lime juice
	1 teaspoon vanilla

Increase oven temperature to 475°. In a large bowl, beat cream cheese until smooth. In a separate bowl, combine sugar, flour and salt; stir to blend and gradually beat into cheese. Beat in eggs and yolks, one at a time, beating well after each addition. Combine sour cream, lime and lemon rinds, lime juice and vanilla in small bowl; blend into cheese mixture. Place springform pan on a foil-lined jelly roll pan. Pour cheese mixture over crust. Bake for 10 minutes. Lower heat to 200° and continue to bake for 1 hour or until cake is set. Turn oven off. Let cake sit in oven with door ajar for ½ hour. Transfer to wire rack to cool completely. Cover and refrigerate until thoroughly chilled. Remove sides of pan. Spread top of cheesecake with **Cranberry Topping.**

continued on page 267

Cranberry Nut Cheesecake continued from page 266

Cranberry Topping:

2	cups fresh *or* frozen cranberries	1	tablespoon fresh lime juice
¾	cup sugar		walnut *or* pecan halves (optional)
¼	teaspoon ground cinnamon		sugar frosted cranberries (optional)
⅛	teaspoon salt		
⅔	cup water		

In a medium saucepan, combine all ingredients except lime juice. Cook over medium heat, stirring occasionally, until berries begin to pop, about 7 minutes. Reduce heat to low; cook 6 minutes longer. Force mixture through a strainer. Stir in fresh lime juice and cool. Spoon over chilled cheesecake. Chill at least ½ hour before serving. Garnish with nut halves and frosted cranberries, if you wish.

Fred W. Smith, Chairman and C.E.O.
Federal Express

BBQ Nachos

1	(10-ounce) can Rotel tomatoes	½	pound chopped BBQ shoulder
1	pound pasteurized process cheese, cubed	¼	cup chopped jalapeño peppers
½	pound warm salted corn tortilla chips	4	ounces BBQ sauce (hot *or* mild)

In a microwave dish, mix Rotel with cheese. Microwave until smooth, stirring often. Dip can also be melted in a small saucepan over low heat. Set aside to cool. Using about half the Rotel dip or about 8 ounces, spoon dip over chips. Top with BBQ shoulder, peppers and BBQ sauce.

Walker Taylor, Owner
The Germantown Commissary

To conserve costly energy, use the smallest size pan possible for the quantity of food to be cooked.

Elvis's Fried Peanut Butter And Banana Sandwich

2 tablespoons smooth peanut butter	2 slices white bread
1 ripe banana, mashed	2 tablespoons margarine

Spread peanut butter and banana between slices of bread. Melt margarine in frying pan over medium heat. Brown sandwich on both sides in melted margarine. Serve immediately while still warm. Eat with knife and fork.

Elvis's most famous favorite snack.

Submitted by Elvis Presley Enterprises

Green Gumbo

8 servings

1 (2-pound) veal brisket	½ cup vegetable oil
1 large slice lean ham *or* ½ pound Polish sausage	⅔ cup all-purpose flour
about 3 pounds leaves of	1 cup chopped onion
collard, mustard,	2 quarts water
turnip, scallions,	⅛ teaspoon cayenne pepper
parsley, watercress,	1 teaspoon ground pepper
spinach, green	1 teaspoon salt
cabbage, chicory,	2 bay leaves
carrot tops *or* beet	½ teaspoon thyme
tops (choose at least	½ teaspoon marjoram
7 greens)	2 whole cloves
⅓ cup water	6 whole allspice
	cooked rice

Cut veal in bite-size pieces and set aside. Cut ham in small cubes and if sausage is used, cut into thin slices. Coat skillet with vegetable spray and brown sausage. Drain. Soak and wash all greens thoroughly. Trim off all hard, coarse stems. Place all greens in a 3 or 4-quart saucepan and add ⅓ cup water. When it begins to boil, reduce heat. Cover and cook 12-15 minutes. Drain and save liquid. Chop greens fine and reserve. Make a roux with oil and flour. Refer to **Roux** recipe for instructions. When roux is a nice brown, add the onion, veal, ham or sausage, reserved liquid and remaining ingredients except rice. Simmer 1 hour, 15 minutes. Serve over boiled rice.

Marguerite Piazza
Memphis Music Legend
Ardent Supporter of St. Jude Children's Research Hospital

Desserts

Fresh Apple Cake

16 servings

2	cups sugar	¼	teaspoon cloves
1½	cups oil	2	teaspoons vanilla
3	eggs	3	cups peeled, chopped
3	cups all-purpose flour		apples
1	teaspoon baking soda	1	cup chopped pecans *or*
1	teaspoon salt		walnuts
1	teaspoon cinnamon		whipped cream *or* ice
½	teaspoon nutmeg		cream (optional)

Preheat oven to 325°. In a mixing bowl, beat sugar, oil and eggs until smooth. Sift together flour, baking soda, salt, cinnamon, nutmeg and cloves. Gradually add to egg mixture and mix until smooth. Stir in vanilla, apples and nuts. Mix until smooth. Bake in a greased tube pan for 1 hour and 15 minutes. Remove cake from oven and immediately pour topping over cake. Let cake cool in pan.

Topping:

1	cup packed brown sugar	½	cup margarine
¼	cup milk		

Combine topping ingredients, bring to a boil and boil for 3 minutes.

Wonderful served with whipped cream or ice cream!

Nancy Quinn

Raw Apple Cake

12-16 servings

¾	cup margarine *or* butter	3	cups pared chopped apples
1½	cups white sugar	½	cup brown sugar
2	eggs, beaten	1	teaspoon cinnamon
2¼	cups all-purpose flour	½	cup chopped pecans
1½	teaspoons baking soda		whipped cream (optional)
½	teaspoon salt		quartered maraschino
¾	cup cold strong coffee		cherries (optional)
1	teaspoon vanilla		

Preheat oven to 350°. In mixing bowl, cream butter and white sugar; add eggs and mix well. Sift flour, soda and salt together; add to creamed mixture. Add coffee and vanilla, mix well. Fold in chopped apples. Pour into a greased 9x13-inch pan. Mix brown sugar, cinnamon and chopped nuts and sprinkle over batter. Bake for 45-55 minutes or until cake tests done. If desired, serve in squares with whipped cream and top with quartered maraschino cherries.

Moist and flavorful, a great snacking cake.

Terry Curp

Chocolate Kahlua Cake

10-12 servings

1	box chocolate cake mix	¾	cup Kahlua liqueur
½	cup vegetable oil	½	cup water
1	(6-ounce) package instant chocolate pudding	6	tablespoons Kahlua liqueur
4	eggs	1	cup sifted powdered sugar

Preheat oven to 350°. Combine the first 6 ingredients in a mixing bowl and beat well, about 2 minutes. Pour into a greased and lightly floured bundt pan. Bake 45-50 minutes or until cake springs back when lightly touched. Combine 6 tablespoons Kahlua and powdered sugar. While cake is still warm in pan, poke holes in cake; pour liqueur mixture over cake. Allow cake to cool in pan at least 2 hours before removing.

After cake is cooled and on serving platter, sprinkle with sifted powdered sugar for an extra special touch.

Jan Harvey

1-2-3-4 Cake

10-12 servings

½	cup butter, softened	1	teaspoon vanilla
½	cup margarine, softened	3	cups sifted cake flour
2	cups sugar	¼	teaspoon salt
2	eggs	3	teaspoons baking powder
2	egg yolks	1	cup milk

Preheat oven to 350°. Cream butter, margarine and sugar until light and fluffy. Add eggs, egg yolks and vanilla. Beat well. Sift flour 3 times, adding salt and baking powder. Add dry ingredients alternately with milk, ending with flour. Pour into a greased and floured 10-inch tube pan. Bake for 10 minutes. Lower temperature to 325° and bake for an additional 40 minutes or until cake tests done with cake tester. Let cool in pan 10 minutes before turning out onto plate.

A moist and fine textured-type cake, similar to a pound cake.

Temple Hughes

271

Italian Cream Cake

10-12 servings

½	cup margarine	1	cup buttermilk
½	cup vegetable shortening	1	(3.5-ounce) can flaked
2	cups sugar		coconut
5	eggs yolks	1	teaspoon vanilla
2	cups all-purpose flour	1	cup chopped pecans
1	teaspoon soda	5	egg whites, stiffly beaten

Preheat oven to 350°. Grease and flour three 8-inch cake pans and set aside. Cream margarine, shortening and sugar. Add egg yolks; beat well. Combine flour and soda; add to creamed mixture alternately with buttermilk. Stir in coconut, vanilla and nuts until well blended. Fold in egg whites. Pour batter into prepared cake pans and bake approximately 25-30 minutes or until cake tests done. Let cool about 10 minutes, remove from cake pans and cool completely on wire cake rack. Frost with **Cream Cheese Frosting.**

Cream Cheese Frosting:

1	(8-ounce) package cream cheese, softened	1	(1 pound) box powdered sugar
¼	cup margarine, softened	1	teaspoon vanilla
		½	cup chopped pecans

Cream margarine and cream cheese in a medium mixing bowl. Add powdered sugar and beat until well blended; blend in vanilla. Stir in nuts.

A heavenly finale to any meal!

Gretchen Mattingly

 Wrap fresh flowers in wet paper towel and then in foil. Place in center of cake cooked in a tube pan or use blossoms around any dessert or punch bowl.

Rum Almond Pound Cake

10-12 servings

3	cups sugar	1½	teaspoons vanilla
1	cup butter, softened	1½	teaspoons almond extract
6	eggs	¾	cup sliced almonds,
3	cups cake flour		toasted
1	cup whipping cream		

In a mixing bowl, cream sugar and butter thoroughly. Add eggs, one at a time, beating well after each addition. Add flour alternately with cream and beat until blended. Add flavorings. Pour into a well greased and floured tube or bundt pan. Put cake in cold oven, turn temperature to 350° and bake for 1 hour or until a light brown crust forms on top. Do not overbake. Cool on rake about 30 minutes before removing from pan. Pierce cake with long fork and sprinkle toasted almonds on top. Spoon Rum Sauce over cake. This cake is also delicious by itself without the sauce. *Note:* To make cake flour, remove 2 tablespoons of all-purpose flour from each cup and add 1 tablespoon of cornstarch to each cup.

Rum Sauce:

½	cup butter	¼	cup water
1	cup sugar	2	ounces rum

For sauce, heat all ingredients to a boil, stirring constantly. Boil and stir 1 minute or until sugar is completely melted.

A cake for all seasons!

Sharon Amos

Cockeyed Cake

9-12 servings

1½	cups sifted all-purpose flour	1	cup sugar
3	tablespoons unsweetened cocoa powder	5	tablespoons oil
		1	tablespoon vinegar
1	teaspoon baking soda	1	teaspoon vanilla
½	teaspoon salt	1	cup cold water

Preheat oven to 350°. Sift flour, cocoa, soda, salt and sugar together. Put mixture back in sifter and sift right into a greased 9x9-inch pan. Make three grooves in the dry mixture. Pour oil in one groove, vinegar in the second and vanilla in the third. Pour cold water over all. Beat with spoon until nearly smooth and flour is completely moistened. Bake for 30 minutes. This recipe can be doubled and baked in a 9x13-inch pan.

Makes a delicious moist cake even without the eggs.

Jane Reynolds

Swiss Chocolate Pound Cake

10-12 servings

1	box Swiss chocolate cake mix	1	(12-ounce) package semi-sweet chocolate chips
1	(3½-ounce) package instant chocolate pudding	2	eggs
		1¾	cups milk

Preheat oven to 350°. Stir all ingredients together. (It is not necessary to beat.) Pour into a generously greased and floured bundt pan. Bake for 45-55 minutes. Cool cake in pan for 25 minutes before removing. Good 'as is' *or* with **Chocolate Glaze.**

Chocolate Glaze:

2	tablespoons unsweetened cocoa	1	tablespoon vegetable oil
1	tablespoon plus 2 teaspoons water	1	tablespoon light corn syrup
		1	cup powdered sugar

Combine first 4 ingredients in a small saucepan. Cook and stir over low heat until mixture is smooth. Remove from heat and beat in powdered sugar. Drizzle over cake.

A very rich and luscious chocolate cake.

Lela Wiseman

White Coconut Cake

12 servings

1	box white cake mix	1	(8-ounce) container frozen whipped topping, thawed
1	(15-ounce) can cream of coconut	1	cup flaked coconut, toasted

Prepare cake mix according to package directions. Pour into a greased and floured 9x13-inch pan. Stir cream of coconut until well blended. As soon as cake is out of oven, poke holes with a fork and slowly pour cream of coconut over cake. Cool cake completely and spread with whipped topping. Sprinkle toasted coconut on top. Store covered in refrigerator.

Easy and elegant!

Rae P. Podgorski

Copper Mountain Caramel Cake

20 servings

1	box German chocolate cake mix	1	(14-ounce) can sweetened condensed milk
1	(12.25-ounce) jar butterscotch topping *or* caramel topping		

Make cake according to package directions. Pour into a greased 9x13-inch pan. While cake is still warm, pierce cake multiple times with a fork. Mix butterscotch topping and condensed milk together and pour over warm cake. Refrigerate. Frost when cool.

Frosting:

4	chocolate covered toffee candy bars	1	(12-ounce) container frozen whipped topping, thawed

To make frosting, pulverize candy bars by hand or in a food processor. Fold into whipped topping and frost cake. Refrigerate.

Lynne Grunthaner

Texas Sheet Cake

24-30 servings

2	cups all-purpose flour	4	tablespoons unsweetened cocoa powder
2	cups sugar	1	cup water
½	teaspoon salt	2	eggs, beaten
½	cup sour cream	1	teaspoon baking soda
1	teaspoon vanilla		
1	cup margarine		

Preheat oven to 350°. In a large bowl, combine flour, sugar and salt; set aside. In a medium saucepan, combine sour cream, vanilla, margarine, cocoa and water. Bring mixture to a boil, remove from heat and blend with flour mixture using a mixer on low speed or stir by hand. Stir in eggs and soda. Pour batter into a greased and floured 11x17-inch sheet pan. Bake for 20 minutes. Cool before spreading with frosting.

Frosting:

½	cup margarine	1	(16-ounce) box powdered sugar
⅓	cup milk		
4	tablespoons unsweetened cocoa powder	1	teaspoon vanilla

In a saucepan, bring margarine, milk and cocoa to a boil. Remove from heat and stir in powdered sugar. Add vanilla and blend well. Frost cooled cake.

A great dessert for children and adults.

Nancy A. Ehrman

275

Cranberry-Banana Nut Cake

12-16 servings

1½	cups sugar	2	cups mashed bananas
⅔	cup shortening		(4 medium)
3	eggs	1	(16-ounce) can whole
3½	cups sifted self-rising flour		berry cranberry
1	cup chopped walnuts		sauce
¼	teaspoon baking soda		

Preheat oven to 325°. Cream sugar and shortening until light and fluffy. Add eggs, blend well. Add flour, walnuts, baking soda and mashed bananas, blend well. Stir in cranberry sauce. Pour into a greased and floured bundt pan. Bake 1 hour 10 minutes to 1 hour 15 minutes, or until toothpick inserted in center comes out clean. Cool in pan 10 minutes. Turn out on wire rack to cool. Drizzle with **Hot Milk Icing**. *Note:* To compensate if using "all-purpose" flour, add 4 teaspoons baking powder, plus ¾ teaspoon salt and increase baking soda to ½ teaspoon.

Hot Milk Icing:

2	cups powdered sugar, sifted	2	tablespoons butter *or* margarine, melted
¼	cup hot milk	½	teaspoon vanilla

Combine all ingredients and beat until smooth enough to drizzle on cake. *Note:* If freezing cake, frost only after it has been thawed. Cake is also good sliced and spread with soft cream cheese instead of frosting.

A cake that is not too sweet and lusciously different.

Gloria Arnold

 One cup of cake flour equals 1 cup all-purpose flour minus 2 tablespoons.

Almond Cheesecake With Raspberry Sauce

12 servings

1½	cups finely crushed chocolate sandwich cookies (about 15 cookies)	1	(8-ounce) can almond paste, crumbled
3	tablespoons margarine *or* butter, melted	1	cup sugar
		4	eggs
3	(8-ounce) packages cream cheese, softened	1	(8-ounce) carton sour cream
			fresh raspberries (optional)

Preheat oven to 325°. In a small bowl, combine cookie crumbs and margarine. Press into bottom of a greased 9-inch springform pan. In a large mixing bowl, beat cream cheese and almond paste on medium-high speed until combined. Beat in sugar until fluffy. Add eggs and sour cream all at once, beating on low just until combined. Pour into crust. Bake for 1 hour or until center is nearly set when gently shaken. Cool for 15 minutes, loosen crust from sides of pan. Cool for 30 minutes more, remove sides of pan. Cool completely. Chill 4-6 hours. Serve cheesecake with **Raspberry Sauce** and fresh raspberries.

Raspberry Sauce:

2	(10-ounce) packages frozen red raspberries in lite syrup, thawed	¾	cup sugar
		1½	teaspoons lemon juice

In a blender, blend berries until smooth. Press through a sieve to remove seeds. In a saucepan, combine puréed raspberries, sugar and lemon juice. Heat just until sugar dissolves, cool. Pour into small container, cover and chill. Serve cheesecake with sauce and fresh raspberries.

A sensational finale to a special dinner.

Rita C. Leonard

Banana Cheesecake

10-12 servings

Crust:

1½ cups quick-cooking oats	½ cup firmly packed brown sugar
½ cup finely chopped pecans	⅓ cup butter, melted

Preheat oven to 350°. Stir together oats, pecans and brown sugar. Add butter and stir until all ingredients are moistened. Press mixture into bottom and about 1¾-inches up the sides of a 9-inch springform pan. Bake for 18-20 minutes or until golden. Cool.

Filling:

2 (8-ounce) packages cream cheese, softened	¾ cup sugar
	2 teaspoons lemon juice
1 cup mashed ripe banana	4 eggs

Beat together cream cheese, banana, sugar and lemon juice until mixture is smooth. Add eggs, one at a time, beating well after each addition. Turn into partially baked crust. Continue baking for 40-45 minutes or until center is almost set. Remove from oven and immediately spread with topping.

Topping:

1 cup sour cream	1 tablespoon vanilla
2 tablespoons sugar	whipped cream (optional)

Stir together sour cream, sugar and vanilla. Spread over baked cheesecake. Continue baking for 10 minutes. Remove from oven; loosen cake from sides of pan and cool completely on wire rack before removing sides. Chill several hours or overnight before serving. Garnish with whipped cream if desired.

Banana and cheesecake lovers rejoice! This is a winning combination you won't want to miss.

Diane O'Shea

A fine meal is never complete without a special dessert.

Fabulous Cheesecake

12-14 servings

Crust:

1¼ cups graham cracker crumbs	⅓ cup butter, melted
	¼ cup sugar

Combine crust ingredients and mix thoroughly. Grease bottom and halfway up sides of a 9-inch springform pan. Cover sides of pan with 1 cup of mixture; cover bottom of pan with remaining mixture. Refrigerate to harden.

Filling:

2 (8-ounce) packages cream cheese, softened	½ cup sugar
	3 medium eggs
	¾ teaspoon vanilla

Topping:

1 pint sour cream	1 (16-ounce) can frozen strawberries, thawed (optional)
¼ cup sugar	
1 teaspoon vanilla	amaretto (optional)

Preheat oven to 375°. Combine the 4 filling ingredients in mixing bowl; beat until smooth, about 3 minutes. Pour into pan spreading evenly. Bake for 20 minutes. Remove from oven and place on cake rack to cool for 15 minutes. Meanwhile, combine first 3 topping ingredients and spread very gently over cooled, baked cheesecake. Increase oven temperature to 475° exactly 2 minutes prior to returning cake to oven. Return cake to oven and bake for about 10 minutes. Remove from oven and let cool on cake rack for 6 hours. Cover with plastic wrap and refrigerate. Do not cut for at least 12 hours. Before serving, go around springform pan with a knife and remove pan carefully. To serve, purée strawberries and add amaretto to taste. Spoon purée on individual serving plates and top with a slice of cheesecake.

Elegant! The recipe title says it all!

Gretchen Mattingly

Lemon Fluff Cheesecake

20-24 servings

Graham Cracker Crust:

½	cup margarine, melted	2½	cups crushed graham crackers
½	cup sugar		

Filling:

2	(3-ounce) packages lemon flavored gelatin	2	cups powdered sugar
2	cups boiling water	2	teaspoons vanilla
3	(8-ounce) packages cream cheese, softened	2	(8-ounce) containers frozen whipped topping, thawed

Mix crust ingredients together. Press ½ mixture into 9x13-inch pan. Reserve remaining half for topping. For filling, dissolve gelatin in boiling water, stirring well; set aside to cool. Blend cream cheese, powdered sugar and vanilla with electric mixer, beating until smooth. Add cooled gelatin, beat well. (This mixture may tend to be on the watery side.) Fold in whipped topping. Pour into graham cracker crust. Sprinkle reserved crust mixture over filling. Chill and slice.

An incredibly light and luscious cheesecake!

D. J. Kopriva

New York Style Cheesecake

12-16 servings

Crust:

1½	cups graham cracker crumbs	6	tablespoons butter, melted
		¼	cup sugar

Combine crust ingredients and mix thoroughly. Press mixture into a greased 8-inch springform pan. Chill in freezer for 10 minutes.

Filling:

5	(8-ounce) packages cream cheese, softened	⅛	cup lemon juice
¾	cup sugar	1	(14-ounce) can sweetened condensed milk
2	eggs	1	(21-ounce) can cherry pie filling (optional)
1	teaspoon vanilla		
2	tablespoons cornstarch		

Preheat oven to 375°. Mix all ingredients, except pie filling, with a mixer until smooth and creamy. Pour into crust and bake 45 minutes. Cool in oven with door opened and oven off for 3 hours. This can be topped with a can of cherry pie filling.

A must for the cheesecake lover.

Linda Wolowicz

Best Ever Pastry Shell

4 (9-inch) deep dish pastry shells

4	cups all-purpose flour, lightly spooned into cup	1¾	cups shortening
		½	cup water
1	teaspoon sugar	1	teaspoon white vinegar *or* cider vinegar
2	teaspoons salt	1	large egg

Mix first 3 ingredients well with fork. Add shortening and cut in with pastry cutter until mixture resembles cornmeal. In a small bowl, beat the water, vinegar and egg together with a fork. Combine the 2 mixtures, stirring with a fork until all is moistened. Divide dough in 4 equal portions and with hands, shape into a slightly round patty. Wrap each patty in plastic wrap and chill ½ hour. When ready to roll, lightly flour both sides of patty, roll, and turn into a 9-inch deep dish pie plate. Trim and flute edges. To bake shell without filling, prick all over with fork. Bake at 450° for approximately 10 minutes or until light golden brown. *Note:* Wrapped pastry freezes well and can be stored up to 2 weeks in the refrigerator.

A light and flaky pie crust that is truly the best.

Cookbook Committee

Fresh Blueberry Pie

8 servings

1	(9-inch) pastry shell, baked	2	tablespoons butter
¾	cup sugar	1½	tablespoons lemon juice
2½	tablespoons cornstarch	½	cup heavy *or* whipping cream
¼	teaspoon salt	1	tablespoon powdered sugar
⅔	cup water		
3	cups <u>fresh</u> blueberries	¼	teaspoon vanilla

Combine sugar, cornstarch and salt in saucepan. Blend in water and 1 cup blueberries. Bring to a boil, stirring constantly, until very thick. Stir in butter and lemon juice. Cool slightly. Fold in remaining berries. Chill about 1 hour. Beat heavy cream until thick, add powdered sugar and vanilla. Spread whipped cream over bottom of baked pie shell. Top with blueberry filling. Chill 1-2 hours before serving.

Whipped cream mixture is always doubled at my house.

Barbara Martin

Sour Cream Apple Pie

8-10 servings

1	(9-inch) *or* (10-inch) deep dish pastry shell	¼	teaspoon nutmeg
3	tablespoons all-purpose flour	1	egg, slightly beaten
		1	cup sour cream
¾	cup sugar	¼	teaspoon vanilla
¼	teaspoon salt	3	cups thinly sliced cooking apples, peeled

Crumb Topping:

½	cup sugar	½	cup chopped walnuts
⅓	cup all-purpose flour	¼	cup margarine *or* butter, melted
1	teaspoon cinnamon		

Prepare pastry shell with a high fluted edge. In a large bowl, sift together flour, sugar, salt and nutmeg. Stir in next 3 ingredients. Fold in apples. Spoon into pastry shell. Bake in a 400° oven for 15 minutes. Lower heat to 350° and continue to bake for 30 minutes longer. Meanwhile, prepare crumb topping by mixing the sugar, flour, cinnamon and walnuts together. Stir in margarine and mix until crumbly. Remove pie from oven, reset oven temperature to 400°. Sprinkle pie with topping and bake for an additional 10 minutes or until topping is nicely browned. Cool slightly on wire rack and serve barely warm.

Variation: Use 2 tablespoons flour, 1 teaspoon vanilla, 1 (21-ounce) can apple pie filling, omit nutmeg and bake at 425° for 25 minutes. For topping, omit cinnamon and walnuts and bake for 20 minutes more.

Old-fashioned goodness in every bite!

Carlene Pelletier
Maggie Poston

When rolling cookie dough, sprinkle board with powdered sugar instead of flour. This makes the dough less heavy.

Apple Walnut Upside Down Pie

1 (10-inch) pie

4	tablespoons butter, melted	⅞	cup sugar
⅓	cup brown sugar	3	tablespoons all-purpose
⅓	cup chopped walnuts		flour
	pastry for 10-inch double	¾	teaspoon ground cinnamon
	crust pie	⅛	teaspoon ground nutmeg
4	cups peeled and cored	¼	teaspoon salt
	apples (cut in ¾-inch		whipped cream
	cubes)		

Preheat oven to 375°. Melt butter and add brown sugar, stir to mix. Spread butter mixture in bottom of a 10-inch pie pan. Sprinkle chopped walnuts over butter mixture. Divide pie pastry in half, roll each half to ⅛-inch thickness. Gently line 1 crust <u>on top</u> of nuts, being careful not to make holes in dough from nuts. Trim pastry even with edge of pan. Gently fill crust with cubed apples. Combine sugar, flour, cinnamon, nutmeg and salt. Blend thoroughly. Sprinkle evenly over apples. Place remaining crust on top of pie and trim even with edge of pie pan. Prick top with tines of fork, do not slash with a knife. Seal crust edges and roll edges toward center of pie. There should be no crust touching the trim of the pan. (Remember, this pie will be inverted.)

Bake for 50-55 minutes. Remove from oven, carefully run a knife around the edge of pan to loosen pie; invert onto plate, let stand 2 minutes. Remove pan. Serve warm with whipped cream.

Easy! Easy! Easy to make and so good!

Mary Limbacher

Chocolate Chess Pie

6-8 servings

1	(9-inch) pastry shell,	2	eggs
	unbaked	1	(5-ounce) can evaporated
1½	cups sugar		milk
3	tablespoons unsweetened	1	teaspoon vanilla extract
	cocoa powder	1	(8-ounce) container frozen
¼	cup butter *or* margarine,		whipped topping,
	melted		thawed

Preheat oven to 350°. In mixing bowl, combine sugar and cocoa together. Add butter and stir well to blend. Add eggs, beat well with electric mixer, about 5 minutes. Add evaporated milk and vanilla. Pour into pie shell. Bake for 35-45 minutes. Top with whipped topping.

Guaranteed to satisfy your chocolate passion.

Rhonda Green

283

Strawberry Ribbon Pie

6-8 servings

1	(9-inch) graham cracker pie shell	1	(3-ounce) package cream cheese, softened
1	(3-ounce) package red flavored gelatin	1/3	cup sifted powdered sugar
1/4	cup sugar	1	teaspoon vanilla
1 1/4	cups boiling water		dash salt
1	(10-ounce) package frozen strawberries	1	cup heavy cream, whipped
1	tablespoon lemon juice		

Dissolve gelatin and sugar in boiling water. Add frozen strawberries and lemon juice; stir until strawberries thaw. Chill until partially set. Blend cream cheese, powdered sugar, vanilla and salt. Fold in small amount of whipped cream, then fold in remaining whipped cream. Spread half white cheese mixture over bottom of pie shell, cover with half of gelatin mixture. Repeat layers, chill overnight. *Note:* Heavy cream will whip faster if bowl and mixer beaters are chilled before using.

A delicious cool dessert for a summer day!

Michal Farrar

Pumpkin Chiffon Pie

8 servings

1	(9-inch) pastry shell, baked	1/2	teaspoon ginger
1	tablespoon unflavored gelatin	1/2	teaspoon allspice
		1/2	teaspoon salt
1/4	cup cold water	2	tablespoons butter
1 1/2	cups cooked pumpkin	1/2	cup milk
1	cup brown sugar	3	eggs (separated)
2	teaspoons cinnamon	2	tablespoons sugar
			whipped cream

Soften gelatin in cold water for 5 minutes. Combine the next 8 ingredients with slightly beaten egg yolks in top of a double boiler. Cook over boiling water until thickened. Add gelatin and stir until dissolved. Cool until mixture begins to congeal. Beat egg whites, add sugar and beat until stiff. Fold into pumpkin mixture. Pour into baked pie shell and chill until firm. Top with whipped cream.

Ann Marie Gully

After Dinner Mint Pie

6-8 servings

2 cups (24) crushed chocolate cream-filled cookies
¼ cup margarine, melted
¼ cup milk
1 (7-ounce) jar marshmallow creme

few drops peppermint extract
few drops green food coloring
2 cups whipping cream, whipped

Combine crumbs and margarine; reserve ½ cup for topping. Press remaining crumb mixture into bottom and sides of a 9-inch pie pan. Chill for 1 hour. Gradually add milk to marshmallow creme, mixing until well blended. Add extract and food coloring. Fold in whipped cream. Turn into pie pan. Freeze for at least 3 hours. Sprinkle with remaining crumbs. Thaw slightly before serving. Slice with warm knife for easier cutting.

Dessert fit for a king and so easy to prepare.

Sarah W. D'Addabbo

Nutty Fudge Pie

8 servings

1 (9-inch) pastry shell, unbaked
1 cup sugar
½ cup all-purpose flour
2 eggs, well beaten
½ cup margarine, melted

1 teaspoon vanilla
1 (6-ounce) package semi-sweet chocolate chips
1 cup chopped pecans

Preheat oven to 350°. Blend sugar, flour, eggs, margarine and vanilla until smooth. Stir in chocolate chips and nuts. Pour into pie shell and bake 30-40 minutes or until firm and pie crust is browned. Cool before slicing. Store in refrigerator.

A real hit! And so easy!

Nicki Knight

If raisins are heated in the oven before being added to cakes or muffins, they will be more evenly distributed.

Chocolate Pecan Pie With Rum

6-8 servings

1	(9-inch) deep dish pastry shell, unbaked	2	tablespoons margarine *or* butter, melted
¾	cup semi-sweet chocolate chips	1	cup light corn syrup
		1	cup sugar
1½	cups pecan halves	3	eggs, slightly beaten
2	tablespoons rum (more to taste)		

Preheat oven to 350°. Sprinkle chocolate chips, then pecans in bottom of pie shell; set aside. Combine remaining ingredients in mixing bowl and stir until very well blended. Pour mixture into pie shell and bake for 50-55 minutes. Cool before serving. Avoid using frozen pie shell if possible.

An irresistible and truly decadent dessert laced with rum. Pure indulgence in every bite.

Diana Wade

Chocolate Peanut Drops

3½ dozen

5	cups frosted flakes cereal	1	(12-ounce) package semi-sweet chocolate chips
1	cup salted peanuts (optional)		
1	(12-ounce) package peanut butter chips		

In large bowl, stir cereal and peanuts. Place peanut butter chips and chocolate chips in a small microwavable bowl. Heat on high for 2 minutes, stirring halfway through cooking. After cooking, stir chips again until smooth. Pour melted chips over cereal and peanuts, stirring until well coated. Drop by rounded tablespoons onto cookie sheet lined with wax paper. Chill until set, about 15 minutes. Store at room temperature.

Kids love these easy, no-bake cookies!!

Jean M. Morton

Burried Cherry Cookies

3-4 dozen cookies

½	cup margarine, softened	¼	teaspoon salt
1	cup sugar	1	(10-ounce) jar maraschino
1	egg		cherries, drain and
1½	teaspoons vanilla		reserve juice
1½	cups all-purpose flour	1	(6-ounce) package
½	cup unsweetened cocoa		semi-sweet chocolate
	powder		chips
¼	teaspoon baking soda	½	cup sweetened condensed
¼	teaspoon baking powder		milk

Preheat oven to 350°. Beat margarine and sugar until fluffy. Add egg and vanilla and beat well. In a separate bowl, stir together flour, cocoa, soda, baking powder and salt. Add flour mixture to margarine mixture, beating until well mixed. Shape dough into 1-inch balls. Place about 2 inches apart on ungreased cookie sheet. Press down center of each ball with your thumb. Place a cherry in the center. In a small saucepan, combine chocolate chips and condensed milk. Cook and stir over low heat until melted. Stir in 4 teaspoons cherry juice. Spoon 1 teaspoon frosting over each unbaked cherry cookie, spreading to cover cherry. Thin frosting with cherry juice if necessary. Bake 10 minutes or until edges are firm.

Our tasting ladies loved these cookies!

Paula Hlobik

Ginger Cookies

2-3 dozen cookies

1	cup sugar	1	teaspoon baking soda
¾	cup shortening, melt and	½	teaspoon cinnamon
	cool	½	teaspoon ginger
1	egg	¼	teaspoon salt
¼	cup Brer Rabbit molasses		additional sugar
2	cups all-purpose flour		

With electric mixer, cream sugar and shortening. Add egg and blend well. Add molasses and mix. Combine dry ingredients together and add to batter. Chill batter 2 hours. Roll batter into 1-inch balls and roll balls in sugar. Bake at 350° for 10 minutes. Cool a few minutes before removing from cookie sheet.

Jimmie Cusack

Fruitcake Cookies

3-4 dozen

⅔ cup packed brown sugar
½ cup butter *or* margarine, softened
1 egg
1 teaspoon vanilla
1 cup all-purpose flour
½ teaspoon baking soda
⅛ teaspoon salt
1 (8-ounce) package pitted whole dates, snipped
1 (4-ounce) container candied cherries, chopped (⅔ cup)
2 candied pineapple slices, chopped
¾ cup coarsely chopped pecans
¾ cup coarsely chopped walnuts

Preheat oven to 325°. In a large mixing bowl, cream together sugar and butter until light and fluffy. Add egg and vanilla, beat well. Stir together flour, soda and salt. Add to creamed mixture, beating until combined. Add dates, mix well. Stir in remaining fruits and nuts. Chill batter. Drop by slightly rounded tablespoons onto greased cookie sheet. Bake for 12 minutes. Store baked cookies overnight in airtight container to soften.

Moist, chewy, and absolutely divine! Sure to become a holiday favorite.

Rita C. Leonard

Lace Cookies

2-3 dozen

¼ cup butter
2¼ teaspoons all-purpose flour
½ cup plus 1 tablespoon brown sugar
½ cup plus 1 tablespoon quick-cooking oats
¼ teaspoon salt
1 teaspoon corn syrup
¼ teaspoon vanilla

Preheat oven to 375°. Melt butter. In a medium bowl, combine flour, sugar, oats and salt. Pour butter over ingredients. Stir well to blend. Stir in corn syrup and vanilla. Drop by ½ teaspoon on a non-stick cookie sheet and bake for 3-4 minutes. Remove cookies from sheet before completely cooled. *Note:* Cookies can also be rolled around finger (but don't wait until they have completely cooled) and filled with whipped cream when ready to serve.

Kids of all ages will love these delicate cookies.

Joan Foote

Brown Edged Cookies

4-5 dozen

1	cup butter *or* margarine	1¾	cups all-purpose flour
1	cup sugar	½	teaspoon salt
1	egg	½	teaspoon vanilla

Preheat oven to 350°. Cream butter and sugar well. Add egg, beat 3 minutes. Add flour and salt gradually; blend well. Add vanilla. Drop by teaspoonful 2-inches apart on a slightly greased cookie sheet. Bake for 10-12 minutes. Let harden before removing from pan.

This is a delicious cookie passed down from my grandmother.

Margie Brennan

German Vanilla Cookies

3-4 dozen cookies

1	cup butter	1	teaspoon vanilla
¾	cup powdered sugar	2¼	cups all-purpose flour
1	egg yolk		raspberry jelly

Preheat oven to 325°. Beat butter until creamy. Add sugar and beat until light and fluffy. Add yolk and vanilla. Beat well. Gradually add flour to butter mixture and mix until smooth. Roll dough into small balls, about ¾-inch in diameter. Place balls 2-inches apart on ungreased cookie sheet. Flatten slightly with fingers and make a depression in each with thumb. Bake 15 minutes. Cool and fill with raspberry jelly or chocolate glaze. *Note:* Before rolling dough into small balls, let batter sit to swell for several minutes. It will be less sticky for rolling.

Chocolate Glaze:

3	squares semi-sweet chocolate	2	tablespoons butter
		1	tablespoon corn syrup

Combine all ingredients in a small saucepan and melt over low heat, stirring constantly.

A light cookie that will literally melt in your mouth.

Rita C. Leonard

289

Cookies

Lunch Box I Love U's

2 dozen cookies

½	cup butter flavored shortening	1	teaspoon vanilla
1½	cups sugar	2	cups chunky peanut butter
1½	cups firmly packed brown sugar	6	cups quick-cooking oats
4	eggs	2½	teaspoons baking soda
		1	cup semi-sweet chocolate chips

Preheat oven to 350°. In a large mixing bowl, cream shortening and both sugars. On low speed of mixer, add eggs and beat until mixture is fluffy. Add vanilla and peanut butter. Mix well. Combine oats and baking soda in separate bowl, then add to mixture stirring by hand. Pour in chocolate chips and mix. Drop by ¼ cup scoop, 4-inches apart onto ungreased, non-stick cookie sheet. Bake 12-15 minutes. Cool on wire rack. Cookies will be very large.

These cookies are a great treat for a lunchbox or afternoon "pick me up" with coffee.

Karla K. Doyle

Best Ever Chocolate Chip Cookies

10 dozen

2	cups margarine, softened	2	teaspoons baking powder
2	cups sugar	3	cups chopped nuts (optional)
2	cups packed brown sugar	2	(12-ounce) bags semi-sweet chocolate chips
4	eggs		
2	teaspoons vanilla	1	(8-ounce) chocolate Hershey bar, finely grated
5	cups quick-cooking oats		
4	cups all-purpose flour		
1	teaspoon salt		
2	teaspoons baking soda		

Preheat oven to 350°. Cream butter and sugars together. Add eggs and vanilla. Set aside. Put rolled oats in blender and process until it turns to powder; 1 to 2 cups at a time works better. Add powderized oats and other dry ingredients to mixture. Stir in nuts, chips, and Hershey bar. Roll dough into 1 to 1½-inch balls and bake on ungreased cookie sheet 2 inches apart. Bake for 8-10 minutes. Do not overbake. Cookies will be soft coming out of oven.

Sure to win "Brownie Points" with this cookie!

Meg Smerbeck

Sensational Peach Cobbler

15-16 servings

2	tablespoons unsalted butter, melted	1	tablespoon fresh lemon juice
5	pounds peaches, skinned, halved, pitted and cut into ½ inch slices	½	teaspoon ground cinnamon
1½	cups sugar	¼	teaspoon ground nutmeg
¼	cup instant tapioca		pinch of salt

To peel peaches, dip completely into boiling water for about 20-30 seconds. Remove and with the tip of a paring knife, remove skin, working from top to bottom. Generously grease a 10x14-inch baking dish with 2 tablespoons butter. Place peaches in a large bowl, add all other ingredients and toss gently. Let stand 10 minutes. (Can be prepared 2 hours ahead. Let stand at room temperature.)

Biscuits:

2	cups all-purpose flour	¼	cup unsalted butter, chilled and cut into pieces
¼	cup sugar		
1	tablespoon baking powder		
1	teaspoon baking soda	1	cup sour cream
1	teaspoon salt		vanilla ice cream

Preheat oven to 425°. Combine flour, sugar, baking powder, baking soda and salt in processor. Add butter and cut in, using on/off turns until mixture resembles coarse crumbs. (A bowl can be used and cut in butter with a pastry cutter; can also be prepared 2 hours ahead, cover and refrigerate.) Add sour cream and blend just until soft dough forms. Turn dough out onto lightly floured surface and knead just until no longer sticky, about 30 turns. Roll dough out to ½-inch thickness Cut with a floured 3-inch round cutter. Gather scraps, reroll and cut out additional circles. Transfer fruit mixture to prepared dish. Top mixture with biscuits, spacing evenly. Bake until juices bubble and thicken and biscuits are deep golden brown, about 35 minutes. Cool cobbler slightly and serve warm with vanilla ice cream.

A sensational finale to your barbecue or block party.

Rita C. Leonard

"Outer Banks" Fruit Cobbler

6-8 servings

½	cup butter *or* margarine, melted	¼	cup water
1	quart fresh fruit (blackberries, peaches, blueberries, straw-berries, *or* raspberries)	1	cup all-purpose flour
		1	cup sugar
		2	teaspoons baking powder
		½	teaspoon salt
½	cup sugar	1	cup milk

Preheat oven to 350°. Spread butter in an 8x8-inch glass dish. Heat fruit with sugar and water, stir gently until sugar is dissolved; set aside. Mix together the flour, sugar, baking powder, salt and milk; blend well. Pour thin dough in pan over melted butter. Top with hot fruit. Bake for 30-35 minutes. Serve with **Lemon Sauce.** *Note:* Well drained canned fruit can be used.

Lemon Sauce:

¼	to ½ cup sugar	1	teaspoon grated lemon rind
1	tablespoon cornstarch		
1	cup water	2	tablespoons lemon juice
2	to 3 tablespoons butter		

Combine sugar, cornstarch and water; cook over low heat until thick. Remove from heat, add remaining ingredients. To serve, pour over baked cobbler.

Pat Ingram

Fruit Pizza

10-12 servings

1	package slice and bake sugar cookies	fresh fruit, sliced (straw-berries, kiwi, peaches, blueberries, raspberries, apples or bananas)
1	(8-ounce) package cream cheese, softened	
¼	cup powdered sugar	
1	tablespoon vanilla	

Glaze:

½	cup apricot preserves	2	tablespoons Amaretto

Preheat oven to 350°. Spray pizza pan with cooking spray. Slice cookies ⅛-inch thick and place on pizza pan. Oil fingers and press cookies to form a crust covering the pan. Bake for 12 minutes. Let cool completely. Combine cream cheese, powdered sugar and vanilla. Spread on cooled cookie crust. Arrange fresh fruit slices on top in a circular pattern, using 4 to 5 different fruits. Cook glaze ingredients in saucepan until clear and runny. Cool slightly and drizzle over fruit.

A beautiful dessert.

Patti Trethaway

Ya Ya Bread Pudding

12 servings

1	loaf French bread (about 18-inches)	2	tablespoons vanilla
4	cups milk	1	teaspoon cinnamon
3	eggs, beaten	1	cup chopped pecans
2	cups sugar	3	tablespoons butter

Break bread into bite-size pieces. Place into a large bowl and let harden overnight or several days. When ready to prepare, cover with milk and soak 1 hour. Mix well. Add eggs and sugar, blend well. Stir in vanilla, cinnamon and nuts. Melt butter in a 9x13-inch baking dish, coating all sides by tilting. Pour pudding in dish and bake at 375° for 1 hour. *Note: It is important to use crusty French bread and having it dried out. Bread pudding and sauce can be reheated.*

Bourbon Sauce:

½	cup butter	1	egg, beaten
1	cup sugar	¼	cup bourbon

In top of double boiler, melt butter and sugar. Gradually whisk in egg. Heat until hot and thick. Cool slightly and add bourbon. Serve warm sauce over pudding. *Note: This recipe can be simplified by using a saucepan and eliminating the egg.*

Your kitchen will smell heavenly when making this wonderful bread pudding.

Ann Cobb

Chocolate Fantasy

6-8 servings

1	(12-ounce) package semi-sweet chocolate chips	2	teaspoons vanilla
		1½	dozen ladyfingers, split
6	tablespoons water	1	(8-ounce) container
6	eggs, separated		frozen whipped
4	tablespoons sugar		topping, thawed *or*
			whipped cream

Melt chocolate chips with water in top of double boiler. Beat egg yolks with sugar. Add to chocolate and when mixture thickens, remove from heat. Beat egg whites until stiff and gently fold into slightly cooled chocolate. Add vanilla. Line the bottom and sides of medium glass bowl with ladyfingers, cover with chocolate. Repeat layering. Refrigerate for at least 3 hours. Top with whipped topping.

Easy and addictive!

Rosalie A. Johnson

293

Bavarian Tart

24 squares

Bottom Crust:

1	cup butter, softened	1½	cups all-purpose flour
⅔	cup sugar	1½	cups chopped pecans
½	teaspoon vanilla		

Filling:

2	(8-ounce) packages cream cheese, softened	2	eggs
½	cup sugar	1	teaspoon vanilla

Topping:

2	(29-ounce) cans Bartlett pears, drained	2	teaspoons cinnamon
		2	teaspoons sugar

Cream all ingredients for the bottom crust. Press creamed mixture into ungreased 9x13-inch pan. Bake at 375° for 10 minutes. Remove and allow to cool. For filling, blend cream cheese and sugar together, add eggs and vanilla, mix well. Smooth filling over cooled crust. Drain 2 cans of pears and cut in wedges. Cover filling with pear wedges. Mix cinnamon and sugar together and sprinkle over top. Bake for 30 minutes in a 350° oven.

Different and absolutely divine!

Marcy Holladay

Chocolate easily absorbs odors from other foods. Wrap tightly and store in a cool, dry place.

Holiday Meringues

10 servings

3	egg whites, room temperature	1	teaspoon vanilla extract
¼	teaspoon cream of tartar	1	cup sugar
		1	quart lime sherbet

In a small mixing bowl, beat egg whites at high speed until foamy. Add cream of tartar and vanilla, beating until soft peaks form. Gradually add sugar, 1 tablespoon at a time, beating until stiff peaks form. Spoon meringue into 10 mounds on a baking sheet lined with heavy brown paper. Shape meringues into circles, using the back of a spoon to mound the sides at least ½-inch higher than the centers. Bake at 225° for 1 hour. Turn oven off and let meringues cool completely before opening the oven door. Transfer meringues to serving plates. Scoop sherbet into shells; top with **Cranberry Sauce** and serve immediately.

Cranberry Sauce:

½	cup sugar	2	cups cranberry juice cocktail
2	tablespoons cornstarch		
⅛	teaspoon salt	1	tablespoon lemon juice

Combine all ingredients in a heavy saucepan; stir well. Place over medium heat, stirring constantly, until mixture comes to a boil. Boil 1 minute; remove from heat. Cover and chill thoroughly.

A light and colorful dessert for the Christmas holidays.

Barbara Davock

For best results in angel food cake, use 3-day old eggs and separate whites just before using.

Pecan Puffs

2-3 dozen

½	cup margarine *or* butter	2	tablespoons sugar
1	cup all-purpose flour, sifted	¾	cup finely chopped pecans

Preheat oven to 325°. In mixing bowl, cream margarine. Add flour and sugar, mix well. Stir in chopped nuts. Line a cookie sheet with foil. Form dough into ¾-inch balls. Dip finger in flour and make a dent in the middle of each ball. Bake for 20 minutes. When they are slightly brown on the edges, they are done. Fill indented cookie with **Fondant Filling**.

Fondant Filling:

½	cup powdered sugar	2	tablespoons butter *or* margarine, softened
2	tablespoons unsweetened cocoa powder	1	tablespoon heavy cream
			few drops vanilla

In small mixing bowl, sift sugar and cocoa together. Add butter and blend well. Add enough cream to make the consistency of a thick fondant. A decorating tube can be used to fill cookies.

Marie S. Rivalto

Potted Dessert

1	(20-ounce) package chocolate cream filled cookies	¾	cup sugar
¼	cup butter, softened	2	(3¾-ounce) boxes instant vanilla pudding
1	(8-ounce) package cream cheese, softened	1	(16-ounce) container frozen whipped topping, thawed

Crush bag of cookies and set aside. With electric mixer, beat butter, cream cheese and sugar until creamy. Set aside. Prepare pudding as directed and fold in whipped topping. In 6-inch clay pot, layer ½ cookie crumbs, spread cream cheese mixture over crumbs, then pudding mixture over cream cheese. Top with remaining cookie crumbs. Decorate with silk stemmed flowers and gummy worms. Decorate pot with bow.

Looks just like a potted plant. Great done in blue or pink flowers for a newborn!

Linda D. Domer

Chocolate-Cream Cheese Delights

36-40 bars

Chocolate Crust:

1 cup all-purpose flour	¾ cup semi-sweet chocolate chips, melted
¼ cup brown sugar	
½ cup margarine, softened	

Filling:

½ cup sugar	1 cup all-purpose flour
½ cup brown sugar	½ teaspoon baking powder
⅓ cup margarine, softened	¼ teaspoon salt
1 (8-ounce) package cream cheese, softened	1 tablespoon vanilla

Preheat oven to 325°. Mix crust ingredients with a fork and press on bottom and sides of an ungreased 8x8-inch pyrex pan. Beat filling ingredients until smooth. Spread over chocolate crust. Bake for 38-40 minutes. Cool 30 minutes.

Glaze:

¼ cup semi-sweet chocolate chips, melted	2 teaspoons water

Blend melted chocolate chips with water and drizzle over top of cooled bars. Chill at least one hour. Cut into small bars.

A rich and delightful cookie bar!

Dorothy Shelton

To make a bundt dish, place an empty juice glass in the center of mixture in a 2 quart casserole. Twist glass to remove after cooking.

Luscious Ladyfinger Dessert

8-10 servings

2	(3-ounce) packages ladyfingers	½	cup sugar
¼	cup brandy *or* dark rum	2	cups whipping cream
1	(8-ounce) package cream cheese, softened	1	teaspoon vanilla
		1	(21-ounce) can cherry pie filling

Lightly grease bottom of a 9-inch springform. Brush all ladyfingers lightly with brandy. Line sides of pan with half of the ladyfingers, stand pieces on end with round sides out. Using an electric mixer, beat cream cheese in bowl for 1 minute or until creamy. Gradually add sugar and continue beating for 1 minute. Combine whipping cream and vanilla in another bowl. Beat until stiff but not dry. Fold whipped cream mixture into cream cheese mixture. Spread half of cheese filling in bottom of pan. Arrange remaining ladyfingers rounded sides up over the filling. Top with remaining cheese filling. Spread evenly. Cover and refrigerate overnight. Next day, spread cherry pie filling on top and refrigerate at least 2 hours. Serve chilled.

Variation: Eliminate brandy, use 11 ounces cream cheese, ¾ cup sugar and 1 quart sliced fresh strawberries instead of cherry filling. Line ladyfingers on bottom and sides and layer cheese filling then strawberries. Repeat, ending with strawberries. Garnish with reserved whole strawberries and a dollop of whipped cream under each berry if desired.

This beautiful make-ahead dessert is the perfect finale to your finest meal.

Nancy Dick
Liz Gano

Aunt Wanda's Cheesecake Dessert

12-16 servings

½ cup butter, softened	1 cup plus 1 tablespoon
8 tablespoons sugar	sugar
2 eggs	4 eggs, separated
2 cups all-purpose flour	4 tablespoons all-purpose
1 teaspoon baking powder	flour
pinch of salt	1 teaspoon vanilla
2 (8-ounce) packages cream	3 cups milk
cheese, softened	cinnamon

Preheat oven to 350°. For crust, combine the first 6 ingredients together and beat with electric mixer until well blended. Spread in bottom and up the sides of an ungreased 9x13-inch pan. In a mixing bowl, beat together cream cheese, sugar, egg yolks and flour until well blended. Add vanilla and milk; blend well. In a separate bowl, beat egg whites until peaks form, but not too stiff. Fold into cheese mixture. Pour over crust and bake 45-60 minutes. Sprinkle cinnamon on top. Cool and refrigerate.

A light custard-type cheesecake. Different and delicious.

Pauline Cychowski

Strawberries With Toffee Sauce

4-6 servings

¾ cup sugar	1 quart fresh strawberries,
½ cup whipping cream	hulled and sliced
¼ cup light corn syrup	sour cream (optional)
2 tablespoons butter	ice cream (optional)
½ cup chopped Heath bars	
(2-3 bars)	

In a small saucepan, combine sugar, whipping cream, corn syrup and butter. Bring to a boil and boil for 1 minute. Remove from heat and add chopped bars. Let bars melt; stir. Serve over strawberries or if you prefer, top strawberries with sour cream or ice cream first and then top with toffee sauce. *Note:* Heath bars are easily chopped if frozen first.

A simple and scrumptious dessert.

Maureen Kolb

Strawberry Squares

12 servings

Crust:

1 cup all-purpose flour	1 cup chopped pecans
¼ cup packed brown sugar	½ cup butter, melted

Preheat oven to 350°. Combine all ingredients together and spread mixture on cookie sheet. Bake for 20 minutes. Cool. Break crust up with fork to recrumble and sprinkle ⅔ mixture in a 9x13-inch glass pan. Reserve remaining crumbs.

Filling:

2 egg whites	⅔ cup sugar
1 (10-ounce) package frozen strawberries, partially thawed	2 tablespoons lemon juice
	1 cup heavy cream

In a mixing bowl, beat egg whites until soft peaks form. Add remaining ingredients except cream and beat on high until mixture is thick, about 8-10 minutes. In a separate bowl, whip cream and fold into strawberry mixture. Pour mixture over crust and sprinkle remaining crumbs on top. Freeze until serving time. Cut into squares.

Variation: For filling, use 4 egg whites, ¾ to 1 cup sugar, 2 teaspoons lemon juice and 1 (8-ounce) carton frozen whipped topping, thawed, instead of heavy cream.

Easy and great for a crowd.

Lois Poper
Terry Curp

You can cut a meringue pie cleanly by coating both sides of the knife lightly with butter.

Lemon Squares

20-24 squares

Crust:

2 cups all-purpose flour	½ cup powdered sugar
1 cup margarine	

Preheat oven to 300°. Combine all ingredients and mix thoroughly. Press dough in bottom of a greased 9x13-inch pan. Bake for 30 minutes or until lightly browned.

Filling:

4 eggs, beaten	¼ cup all-purpose flour
2 cups sugar	1 teaspoon baking powder
½ cup fresh lemon juice	powdered sugar

In mixing bowl, combine eggs, sugar and lemon juice. Add dry ingredients and beat until fluffy. Spread evenly over baked crust. Bake at 300° for 30-40 minutes. Cut into squares while still warm and dust with powdered sugar.

Variation: Use ½ each of crust ingredients, spread in 8x8-inch pan and bake at 325° for 20 minutes. For filling use 2 eggs, 1 cup sugar, 2 tablespoons flour, 2 tablespoons lemon juice and ½ teaspoon salt, omit baking powder, bake at 325° for 30 minutes.

Mary Fehse
Susan Weiland

Caramel Brownies

15-18 servings

¾ cup chopped nuts	50 caramels
1 box German chocolate cake mix	⅓ cup evaporated milk
⅓ cup evaporated milk	1 cup semi-sweet chocolate chips
¾ cup butter, melted	

Preheat oven to 350°. Mix first four ingredients; pat half of the cake mixture into a 9x13-inch pan. Bake 6 minutes. While cake is baking, melt caramels and milk in microwave, stirring frequently. Immediately after removing cake pan from oven, sprinkle chocolate chips over cake. Spread melted chocolate chips evenly with the back of a spoon. Pour melted caramels over the chocolate chips. Spoon remaining cake batter over top of the caramels. Bake for an additional 10 minutes. Cool and cut into squares. *Note:* It is much easier to cut if refrigerated first.

Pure delight in every bite.

Peg Gould

301

Chocolate Peppermint Bars

about 52 bars

4 eggs	½ teaspoon peppermint
2 cups sugar	extract
1 cup unsweetened cocoa	1 teaspoon vanilla
powder	1 cup margarine, melted
1 cup all-purpose flour	

Preheat oven to 350°. Beat eggs and sugar by hand until thick. Add cocoa and flour, mixing well. Add peppermint extract, vanilla and margarine. Spread mixture on a greased 11x17-inch jelly roll pan. Bake for 15 minutes. Do not overbake.

Frosting and Glaze:

2¾ cups powdered sugar	2 (1-ounce) squares
½ cup <u>butter</u>, softened	unsweetened
½ teaspoon peppermint extract	chocolate
green food coloring	2 tablespoons butter
milk	

Beat sugar and butter until creamy. Add peppermint extract, a few drops of food coloring and enough milk to make consistency for icing. Frost cake. Let set before adding chocolate glaze. For glaze, melt together chocolate and butter; spread on top of frosting with a pastry brush. Chill before cutting. Cut into 1x4-inch bars.

Absolutely divine!

Mary Fehse

 To keep icings moist and to prevent cracking, add a little baking soda to the icing.

Chocolate Revel Bars

approximately 75 bars

Crust:

1	cup margarine, softened	2½	cups all-purpose flour
2	cups brown sugar	1	teaspoon baking soda
2	eggs	1	teaspoon salt
2	teaspoons vanilla	3	cups quick-cooking oats

Filling:

1	(15-ounce) can sweetened condensed milk	2	tablespoons margarine
		½	teaspoon salt
1	(12-ounce) package semi-sweet chocolate chips	1	cup chopped walnuts
		2	teaspoons vanilla

Preheat oven to 350°. Cream margarine and sugar together until light, add eggs, beating well. Add vanilla. Sift flour, soda and salt together and add to creamed mixture, blending well. Stir in oats. Pat ⅔ of oat mixture into bottom of greased 10x15-inch pan. In heavy saucepan, over low heat, melt together condensed milk, chocolate chips, margarine and salt; stirring constantly. Add walnuts and vanilla; stir until smooth. Spread chocolate mixture over crust. Sprinkle top with remaining oat mixture. Bake for 25-30 minutes.

Guaranteed to disappear quickly!

Carlene Pelletier
Madawaska, Maine

Salted Nut Bars

48 bars

3	cups all-purpose flour	2	cups mixed nuts
1½	cups firmly packed brown sugar	½	cup light corn syrup
		2	tablespoons butter
½	teaspoon salt	1	teaspoon water
1	cup butter *or* margarine, softened	6	ounces butterscotch chips

Preheat oven to 350°. In a large bowl, mix together flour, brown sugar, salt and butter. Blend well and press into an ungreased 11x17-inch jelly roll pan. Bake for 10-12 minutes. Sprinkle nuts over crust. In a saucepan, combine corn syrup, butter, water and butterscotch chips. Bring to a boil and boil for 2 minutes, stirring constantly. Pour over nuts. Bake for an additional 10-12 minutes. Cool completely and cut into bars.

Deliciously different.

Rhonda Green

Cracker Toffee Bars

20-24 servings

36	(2x2-inch) saltine crackers (1 stack)	8	ounces semi-sweet chocolate chips
1	cup unsalted butter	1	to 2 cups coarsely
1	cup dark brown sugar		chopped nuts

Preheat oven to 350°. Grease a 10x15-inch jelly roll pan. Cover bottom of pan with a single layer of crackers. Melt butter with sugar. Boil for 3 minutes, stirring constantly. Pour over crackers, spreading evenly. Bake for 15 minutes. Sprinkle chocolate chips over top. Cool for 5 minutes then spread melted chocolate. Sprinkle with nuts. Refrigerate until cool. Break into pieces like peanut brittle and store in a tightly closed container.

These keep well in a closed container, if you can keep your family away from them.

Catherine E. Motta
Washington, D. C.

Incredible Edibles

approximately 100 pieces

2	cups graham cracker crumbs	¾	cup butter *or* margarine, melted
2	cups powdered sugar	1	(12-ounce) package semi-sweet chocolate chips
1	(12-ounce) jar peanut butter		

Mix first 4 ingredients with electric mixer and pat evenly in an ungreased 9x13-inch pan. Melt chocolate chips in top of double boiler and spread over mixture. Cool in refrigerator and cut into small pieces. *Note:* Before cutting into pieces, let stand at room temperature for a few minutes to prevent chocolate from cracking.

Variation: Use 1½ cups crumbs, 1 cup crunchy peanut butter and 1 cup margarine. Melt chocolate chips with ½ cup butter or margarine.

This easy, no-fuss fudge is truly a treat!

Rose Kull
Sue Musacchio

Cajun Fudge

50 pieces

4	cups sugar	1	(12-ounce) can evaporated
1	heaping tablespoon		milk
	unsweetened cocoa	1	cup lightly salted butter
	powder	1½	cups chopped pecans
		1	tablespoon vanilla

In a large 4-quart saucepan, mix sugar and cocoa until all lumps are gone. Add evaporated milk and butter and bring to a boil over medium heat. Boil for 15 minutes, stirring constantly. Add pecans and return to boil, boil 5 more minutes. Add vanilla and boil 5 more minutes or until you can drag your spoon across the bottom of the pan and see the bottom. Spoon very quickly on foil sheets like pralines. Cool and store in candy jar. These can be individually wrapped and frozen or put into a ziploc bag and frozen. *Note:* Do not use a cast iron skillet or copper bottom pot. Use a stainless steel saucepan and spoon.

This candy makes a nice hostess gift.

S. Kay Clifton

Marshmallow Chocolate Chip Fudge

5 pounds

5	cups sugar	18	ounces semi-sweet
1	(14-ounce) can sweetened		chocolate chips
	condensed milk	2	teaspoons vanilla
1	cup butter *or* margarine	1	cup chopped nuts
1	(7-ounce) jar		(optional)
	marshmallow creme		

Combine sugar, milk and butter in a heavy medium-sized pan. Over medium-low heat, bring mixture to a boil, stirring constantly, and boil for 13 minutes or until soft-ball stage on a candy thermometer. Remove from heat. Quickly add remaining ingredients before mixture cools and stir until smooth. Pour into a buttered 9x13-inch pan. Cool and cut into squares.

Sure to satisfy your sweet tooth and a cinch to make.

Jane Reynolds

Peanut Butter Fudge

7-8 dozen pieces

2 cups sugar	1 cup marshmallow creme
½ (12-ounce) can evaporated milk	1 teaspoon vanilla
	½ cup chopped walnuts
1 cup chunky peanut butter	

In a heavy medium-sized pan, mix the sugar and evaporated milk. Over medium-low heat, bring to a boil, stirring constantly. Boil for exactly 5 minutes. Remove from heat and quickly stir in peanut butter, marshmallow, vanilla and walnuts. Turn into a buttered 9x9-inch pan. Let cool and cut into squares.

Roberta Guerrette
St. Agatha, Maine

Caramels

about 90-100 caramels

1 cup butter	1 cup light corn syrup
1 (16-ounce) package light brown sugar	1 (14-ounce) can sweetened condensed milk
dash of salt	1 teaspoon vanilla

Butter a 9x9-inch pan, set aside. Melt butter in a heavy 3-quart saucepan. Add sugar and salt, stir thoroughly. Stir in the corn syrup. Add condensed milk and stir. Clip candy thermometer to side of pan; cook, stirring constantly over medium heat to 245° (firm ball stage). This will take 12-15 minutes. Remove from heat, stir in vanilla. Pour into pan. When cool, cut into squares and wrap pieces individually in plastic wrap.

Chocolate Caramels:

Prepare as above except add 2 (1-ounce) squares unsweetened chocolate, cut up, when adding the condensed milk.

Easy and oh, so good! A holiday treat your family and friends will always love. For gift giving, rewrap in colored foil.

Rita C. Leonard

 When icing a cake, try dusting a little cornstarch on the surface of the cake to keep icing from running off.

Oven Caramel Corn

20-24 cups

20	to 24 cups popped corn	½	teaspoon salt
2	cups light brown sugar	½	teaspoon baking soda
½	cup butter	½	teaspoon vanilla
½	cup light corn syrup		

Spray a large pan or oven roaster with non-stick cooking spray. Pan should be big enough to stir popcorn. Mix together brown sugar, butter, corn syrup and salt in a large saucepan. Boil for 6 minutes, stirring constantly. Remove from heat, add baking soda and vanilla; stir well. Pour over popped corn, stirring well. Bake in a 200 to 225° oven for 1 hour, stirring every 15 minutes. Remove from oven and pour on waxed paper; cool. When cool, break apart and store in plastic containers.

Variation: Use 1 cup margarine, 1 teaspoon baking soda and pinch cream of tartar. Omit salt and vanilla. Boil ingredients 5 minutes instead of 6; after mixing corn with syrup, spread corn thinly over 3 buttered cookie sheets and bake for 1 hour at 200°.

Peg Kottke
Linda D. Domer

Scandia (Candied Pecans)

2 cups candied pecans

1	egg white	2	cups pecans
½	cup sugar	¼	cup margarine
	dash salt		

Preheat oven to 350°. Mix egg white, sugar and salt together. Stir in pecans. In a small pan, melt butter and add nut mixture. Spread mixture in a lightly buttered 9x13-inch pan and bake for 20-30 minutes, stirring occasionally. Immediately pour on wax paper and separate.

What a snack!

Florence Powell

Spiced Pecans

2 cups

2	tablespoons cold water	1½	teaspoons ground cloves
1	egg white, slightly beaten	1½	teaspoons ground allspice
¼	cup sugar	2	cups whole pecans
1½	teaspoons cinnamon		

Preheat oven to 250°. Beat water with egg white until combined. Add sugar, cinnamon, cloves and allspice; beat. Allow to stand for 15 minutes for sugar to dissolve. Toss egg mixture with pecans, coating well. Spread nuts on an oiled baking sheet and bake for 1 hour. Allow to cool in pan. Break up nuts and store in an airtight container.

Nancy Barnwell

Mamow's Carmel Icing

frosts 1 (2-layer) cake

1	cup buttermilk	1	cup butter
1	teaspoon baking soda	2	cups sugar

Combine buttermilk and soda. In a black iron skillet, combine all ingredients and slowly cook until mixture comes to a soft boil. Let cool and frost a two layer yellow cake. *Note:* Only use a black iron skillet.

Delicious!

Catherine Brannon

The layers of a cake will come out of their pans without sticking if you will set the hot pans on a damp cloth when they come out of the oven.

Index

Asterisk indicates a
Light and Luscious Recipe . . . . *
ACCOMPANIMENTS
Creole Rice Dressing 226
Herb Butter 27
Leniwe Pierogi 183
Noodle Pudding Soufflé 194
Sausage And Spinach Bread Stuffing . 227
APPETIZERS: Cold
Addictive Avocado Dip 60
Canapé Pie 39
Caramel Apple Dip 187
Caviar Pie 40
Cheese Ball 56
Cheese Ring 57
Chutney Cheese Spread 57
Crabmeat Appetizer 60
Crustacean Dip 62
Dried Beef Cheese Ball 56
Easy But Elegant Liver Pâté 41
Ecuadorian Shrimp Cebiché 75
Fat Free Mexican Dip 230*
Fruit Dip 187
Guacamole 16
Italian Cheese Ball 56
Kahlua-Cinnamon Fruit Dip 186
Marinated Artichokes And
    Mushrooms 212
Pizza Dip 65
Ripe Olive Spread 64
Salsa Fresca 16
Scandia (Candied Pecans) 307
Seafood Cocktail Sauce 68
Sharp Dip For Veggies 64
Shrimp Diablo 43
Smoked Salmon Spread 63
Spiced Pecans 308
Strawberries Extraordinaire 187
Surprise Sandwiches 54
Susie's Onions 50
Taco Dip 67
Tea Sandwiches 51
Terry's Tortilla Pinwheels 51
Tuna Pâté 42
Vegetable Dip 65
Vegetable Pizza 50
APPETIZERS: Hot
Artichoke Dip 58
Bacon Crisps 45
Baked Brie 33
BBQ Nachos 267
Blue-Crab Stuffed Mushrooms 10
Bread Roll 55
Brie En Croute 38
Burgundy Mushrooms 48
California Artichoke Spread 59

Camille's Clam And Swiss Spread . . . 61
Cheese Crispies 46
Cheese Soufflé Spread 59
Christine's Coquille St. Jacques 44
Crab Dip 62
Crab Sandwich 54
Daddy's Tasty Chicken 45
Fiery Bean Dip 67
Holiday Appetizer Quiche 53
Hot Cheese Dip 58
Hot Clam Dip 61
Hot Crab Dip 61
Kahlua-Pecan Brie 38
Madeira Mushrooms 48
Mini Blintzes 199
Mock Oysters Rockefeller 63
Mushroom Turnovers 47
Pesto And Cheese In Phyllo 29
Reuben Dip 66
Sausage Roll 198
Sensational Spinach Dip 22
Sesame Seed Chicken 43
Spicy Beef Dip 66
Spicy Crab Bites 42
Stuffed Bread 55
Stuffed Mushrooms 49
Stuffed Mushrooms Parmigiana 49
Swiss And Rye Appetizers 52
Three Pepper Quesadillas 52
Water Chestnuts 46
APPLES
Apple Oat Muffins 119
Apple Walnut Upside Down Pie 283
Caramel Apple Dip 187
Cheese Apple Omelet 196
Fresh Apple Cake 270
Jewish Apple Cake 112
Raw Apple Cake 270
Sausage Apple Ring 197
Sour Cream Apple Pie 282
Supremes De Volaille A L'orange
    En Pommes 150
Tossed Salad With Apples And Cheese . 29
ARTICHOKES
Artichoke And Chicken Casserole . . . 159
Artichoke Dip 58
California Artichoke Spread 59
Eileen's Italian Artichokes And
    Chicken With Pasta 181
Marinated Artichokes And
    Mushrooms 212
ASPARAGUS
Asparagus Soup 76
Asparagus Supreme 204
Asparagus With Pasta 180
Asparagus With Vinaigrette 91

Index

AVOCADOS
Addictive Avocado Dip 60
Guacamole 16
BANANAS
Banana Bread 114
Banana Cheesecake 278
Banana-Berry Compote 188
Cranberry-Banana Nut Cake 276
Elvis's Fried Peanut Butter And
  Banana Sandwich 268
**BAR COOKIES AND SQUARES (See
  COOKIES and DESSERTS)**
BEANS
Baked Beans 204
BBQ Beans 263
Bean And Bacon Soup 77
Fiery Bean Dip 67
Kidney Bean Casserole 234*
Quick Tamale Pie 136
Red Beans And Rice Cajun Style 225
Refried Beans 15
3 Bean 2 Cheese Casserole 205
BEEF
Barbecue Brisket 128
Beef And Vegetable Soup 80
Beef Burgundy 132
Beef Noodle Bake 177
Beef Rolls Italian Style 132
Beef Salad Stir-Fry 246*
Beef-Caraway Stew 136
Braciole 250
Braised Beef Tips 131
Braised Beef 245*
Brisket For Eight 129
Burritos 133
Cavatini 174
Cincinnati Chili 254
Easy But Elegant Liver Pâté 41
Easy Tortilla Soup 82
Eggplant And Ground Beef Casserole . 134
Five Hour Stew 137
Flank Steak Marinade 142
Grillades (Gree yods) 18
Hamburg-Vegetable Soup 86
Individual Beef Wellingtons 130
Irish Stew 138
Italian Stuffed Shells 20
Italian Style Roast Beef With Wine . . 265
K. C. Steak Soup 81
Lemon-Herb Marinade 228
Lena's Meatballs And Sausage In
  Sauce 178
Mama Lucy's Spaghetti And
  Meatballs 179
Marie's Rolled Meatloaf 134
Marinated Flank Steak 244*
Modern Mock Turtle Soup 255

Oven Barbecue — Texas Style 128
Pepper Steak 245*
Poor Man's Stroganoff 135
Reuben Casserole 129
Roast Beef Tenderloin 131
Saralynn's Chili 133
Simple Beef Stew 137
Spaghetti Sauce 246*
Spicy Beef Dip 66
Stir-Fry Sauce 141
Stuffed Pumpkin 218
Sweet Lasagna 176
Tamale Pie 135
BEVERAGES
Amaretto Liqueur 72
Champagne Punch 70
Coffee Cordial 68
Eva's Cranberry Tea 69
Fireside Coffee Mix 69
Irish Creme Liqueur 72
Raspberry Champagne Punch 70
Red Robbins 70
Sangria 71
Slush 71
BLUEBERRIES
Blueberry Buttermilk Muffins 120
Blueberry Salad 88
Fresh Blueberry Pie 281
BREADS (Also see MUFFINS)
BREADS: Coffee Cake
Coffee Cake 110
Pecan Coffee Cake 110
Polish Placek (Polish Coffee Cake) . . . 111
Raisin Coffee Cake 112
Raspberry Cream Cheese Coffee Cake . 113
BREADS: Fruit
Banana Bread 114
Jewish Apple Cake 112
Rhubarb Bread 115
BREADS: Miscellaneous
Beat-The-Clock Buttermilk Biscuits . . 122
Beer Bread 123
Bishop Bread 116
Breakfast Pull Apart Rolls 119
Brooklyn Bridge Lard Bread 260
Herb Butter 27
Herb Butter Sticks 126
Monkey Bread 117
Nanny Gilchrist's Irish Soda Bread . . 124
Old Fashioned Bread Pudding 256
Orange Biscuit Ring 117
Orange Poppy Bread 115
Parmesan Pull Aparts 126
Pumpkin Bread 114
Stuffed Bread 55
Ya Ya Bread Pudding 293
Zucchini Bread 116

Index

BREADS: Yeast
Anadama Bread 123
Cinnamon Rolls 118
Daddy's Raisin Bread 122
Easy Yeast Rolls 124
Kay's Refrigerator-Freezer
  Homemade Rolls 125
Maggie's Dinner Rolls 125
Pappy's Lobster Shack Rolls 262
BROCCOLI
Broccoli & Rice Casserole 207
Broccoli And Cauliflower Salad 92
Broccoli Casserole 207
Broccoli Cheese Soup 77
Broccoli Salad 92
Broccoli Tortellini Salad 106
Chicken and Broccoli Casserole 159
Crumb-Topped Broccoli 31
Mock Oysters Rockefeller 63
BRUNCH
Apple Oat Muffins 119
Banana Bread 114
Banana-Berry Compote 188
Basic Crêpes 199
Bavarian Tart 294
Beat-The-Clock Buttermilk Biscuits . 122
Bishop Bread 116
Blueberry Buttermilk Muffins 120
Breakfast Pull Apart Rolls 119
Canapé Pie 39
Caramel Apple Dip 187
Cheese 'n Chicken Quiche 193
Cheese Apple Omelet 196
Chili Huevos 197
Cinnamon Rolls 118
Classic Quiche 192
Coffee Cake 110
Cranberry Compote 189
Cranberry-Banana Nut Cake 276
Creamy Strawberry Crêpes 200
Daddy's Raisin Bread 122
Diane's Breakfast 231*
Favorite Fruit Salad 90
Favorite Pancakes 198
Florentine Crêpe Cups 201
Fresh Apple Cake 270
Fruit Dip 187
Fruit Pizza 292
Green Chile Quiche 193
Hash Brown Potato Casserole 219
Holiday Appetizer Quiche 53
Italian Zucchini Pie 190
Jewish Apple Cake 112
Kahlua-Cinnamon Fruit Dip 186
Loretta's Pear Salad 89
Mini Blintzes 199
Monkey Bread 117
Noodle Pudding Soufflé 194

Oatmeal Date Muffins 120
Orange Biscuit Ring 117
Orange Poppy Bread 115
Orange Poppy Seed Muffins 247*
Peach Melba Crêpes 200
Pecan Coffee Cake 110
Pineapple-Cheese Surprise 188
Pizza Quiche 194
Polish Placek (Polish Coffee Cake) . . 111
Pumpkin Bread 114
Pumpkin Pecan Muffins 121
Raisin Coffee Cake 112
Raspberry Cream Cheese Coffee Cake . 113
Raw Apple Cake 270
Rhubarb Bread 115
Salmon Quiche 195
Sausage And Rice Casserole 196
Sausage Apple Ring 197
Sausage Deep Dish Pie 190
Sausage Roll 198
Sausage-Filled Crêpes 202
Scalloped Pineapple 188
Spinach Pie (Spanakopeta) 191
Spinach Quiche 192
Strawberries Extraordinaire 187
Strawberry Microwave Jam 189
Zucchini Bread 116
CABBAGE
Braised Red Cabbage With
  Cranberries 26
Coleslaw 103
Italian Coleslaw 103
CAKES
Almond Cheesecake With Raspberry
  Sauce 277
Aunt Wanda's Cheesecake Dessert . . 299
Autumn Harvest Cheesecake 27
Banana Cheesecake 278
Chocolate Kahlua Cake 271
Cockeyed Cake 273
Copper Mountain Caramel Cake . . . 275
Cranberry Nut Cheesecake 266
Cranberry-Banana Nut Cake 276
Date-Nut Cake Roll 36
Fabulous Cheesecake 279
Fresh Apple Cake 270
Italian Cream Cake 272
Lemon Fluff Cheesecake 280
Mamow's Carmel Icing 308
Mocha Nut Torte 21
Mrs. Lucillie's Pound Cake 257
New York Style Cheesecake 280
1-2-3-4 Cake 271
Raw Apple Cake 270
Rum Almond Pound Cake 273
Swiss Chocolate Pound Cake 274
Texas Sheet Cake 275
White Coconut Cake 274

Index

CANDY
Cajun Fudge 305
Caramels 306
Cracker Toffee Bars 304
Incredible Edibles 304
Marshmallow Chocolate Chip Fudge . . 305
Oven Caramel Corn 307
Peanut Butter Fudge 306
Scandia (Candied Pecans) 307
Spiced Pecans 308

CARROTS
Carrots With Tarragon 31
Marinated Carrots 209
North African Carrot Salad 93
Shredded Carrots 209
Zesty Carrots 208

CHEESE
Almond Cheesecake With Raspberry
  Sauce 277
Aunt Wanda's Cheesecake Dessert . . . 299
Autumn Harvest Cheesecake 27
Baked Brie 33
Banana Cheesecake 278
Blue Cheese Rice 224
Blue Cheese Sauce With Pasta 180
Brie En Croute 38
Broccoli Cheese Soup 77
Camille's Clam And Swiss Spread . . . 61
Cheese 'n Chicken Quiche 193
Cheese Apple Omelet 196
Cheese Ball 56
Cheese Crispies 46
Cheese Ring 57
Cheese Soufflé Spread 59
Cheesy Baked Chicken Breasts 154
Chocolate-Cream Cheese Delights . . . 297
Chutney Cheese Spread 57
Cranberry Nut Cheesecake 266
Dieter's Delight 231*
Dried Beef Cheese Ball 56
Fabulous Cheesecake 279
Gratineed Ziti And Spinach Parmesan . 182
Hot Cheese Dip 58
Italian Cheese Ball 56
Janey's Cheese Soup 78
Jo's Spinach & Ricotta Dumplings . . . 215
Kahlua-Pecan Brie 38
Lemon Fluff Cheesecake 280
New York Style Cheesecake 280
Pesto And Cheese In Phyllo 29
Pineapple-Cheese Surprise 188
Sausage-Filled Crêpes 202
Sensational Stuffed Eggplant 211
Sharp Dip For Veggies 64
Shells A La Thom 258
Stuffed Pasta Shells 185
Swiss And Rye Appetizers 52
Swiss Beans 206

3 Bean 2 Cheese Casserole 205
Tossed Salad With Apples And Cheese . 29

CHICKEN
Artichoke And Chicken Casserole . . . 159
Baked Lemon Chicken 240*
Breast Of Chicken Saltimbocco 260
Celestial Chicken 149
Cheese 'n Chicken Quiche 193
Cheesy Baked Chicken Breasts 154
Chicken and Broccoli Casserole 159
Chicken and Pasta Salad 105
Chicken Caruso And Rice 242*
Chicken Chimichangas 163
Chicken Cordon Bleu With White
  Wine Sauce 239*
Chicken Cordon Bleu 153
Chicken Curry 146
Chicken Dee-Licious 145
Chicken Dijon 241*
Chicken Enchiladas 161
Chicken Fajitas 14
Chicken Fricassée With Mushrooms . . 148
Chicken Marsala 30
Chicken Monterey 153
Chicken Puffs 157
Chicken Scampi 157
Chicken Squares 158
Chicken Taco Salad 104
Chicken Tikka 147
Chicken With Lemon Butter 144
Chicken With Mushroom Sauce 148
Chicken With Ripe Olives 259
Chicken With Walnuts 156
Cornish Hens Mont Ventoux 23
Cornish Hens 160
Crab-Stuffed Chicken Breasts 155
Daddy's Tasty Chicken 45
Donna's Tasty Chicken Casserole . . . 160
Easy Chicken Dinner 158
Easy Mustard-Honey Chicken 143
Eileen's Italian Artichokes And
  Chicken With Pasta 181
Elegant Chicken Dijon 143
Enchilada Casserole 162
Gene And Ina Mae's Chicken 149
Grilled Mustard Chicken Breasts . . . 242*
Italian Style Chicken Kiev 156
Lemon Chicken With Thyme 240*
Luscious Chicken Salad 105
Marie's Chicken Sherry 152
Mexican Chicken Kiev 238*
Pecan Chicken With Dijon Cream
  Sauce 144
Pollo Ala Tino 152
Quick And Easy Stir-Fry 237*
Roasted Cornish Hens Al Barolo . . . 264
Sesame Seed Chicken 43
Sesame-Ginger Chicken 241*

Sour Cream Chicken Enchiladas ... 162
Stir-Fry With Linguine 233*
Stuffed Chicken 154
Supremes De Volaille A L'orange En
    Pommes 150
Tee's Mexican Chicken 237*
Thousand Dollar Chicken 151
Tortilla Casserole 163
Wonton Soup 82
Zesty Lemon Chicken 145

CHOCOLATE
After Dinner Mint Pie 285
Best Ever Chocolate Chip Cookies ... 290
Burried Cherry Cookies 287
Caramel Brownies 301
Chocolate Chess Pie 283
Chocolate Chip Pie 259
Chocolate Fantasy 293
Chocolate Kahlua Cake 271
Chocolate Peanut Drops 286
Chocolate Pecan Pie With Rum 286
Chocolate Peppermint Bars 302
Chocolate Revel Bars 303
Chocolate-Cream Cheese Delights ... 297
Copper Mountain Caramel Cake ... 275
Marshmallow Chocolate Chip Fudge . 305
Nutty Fudge Pie 285
Raspberry Chocolate Truffle Pie 32
Swiss Chocolate Pound Cake 274
Texas Sheet Cake 275

CLAM
Easy Clam Chowder 84
Camille's Clam And Swiss Spread 61
Hot Clam Dip 61

**COOKIES (Includes BARS and
    SQUARES)**
Almond-Orange Biscotti 252
Best Ever Chocolate Chip Cookies ... 290
Brown Edged Cookies 289
Burried Cherry Cookies 287
Caramel Brownies 301
Chocolate Peanut Drops 286
Chocolate Peppermint Bars 302
Chocolate Revel Bars 303
Chocolate-Cream Cheese Delights ... 297
Cracker Toffee Bars 304
Fruitcake Cookies 288
German Vanilla Cookies 289
Ginger Cookies 287
Incredible Edibles 304
Lace Cookies 288
Lemon Squares 301
Lunch Box I Love U's 290
Pecan Puffs 296
Salted Nut Bars 303
Strawberry Squares 300

CORN
Corn And Crabmeat Soup 78
Corn Salad 93
Easy Corn Casserole 210

CRABMEAT
Blue-Crab Stuffed Mushrooms 10
Corn And Crabmeat Soup 78
Crab Dip 62
Crab Noodle Casserole 171
Crab Sandwich 54
Crab Stuffed Fillet Of Sole 167
Crab Stuffed Potatoes 221
Crab-Stuffed Chicken Breasts 155
Crabmeat Appetizer 60
Crabmeat Delight 166
Crabmeat Salad 104
Deviled Crab 258
Hot Crab Dip 61
Jane's Crab Cakes 167
Spicy Crab Bites 42

CRANBERRIES
Braised Red Cabbage With
    Cranberries 26
Cranberry Compote 189
Cranberry Nut Cheesecake 266
Cranberry Salad Mold 89
Cranberry-Banana Nut Cake 276
Frozen Cranberry Salad 88

DATES
Date-Nut Cake Roll 36
Oatmeal Date Muffins 120

**DESSERTS (Also see CAKES, CANDY,
    COOKIES, PIES and PUDDINGS
    listings)**
Aunt Wanda's Cheesecake Dessert .. 299
Bavarian Tart 294
Caramel Brownies 301
Chocolate-Cream Cheese Delights .. 297
Chocolate Fantasy 293
Chocolate Peppermint Bars 302
Chocolate Revel Bars 303
Churros 16
Fruit Pizza 292
Holiday Meringues 295
Lemon Squares 301
Luscious Ladyfinger Dessert 298
Mamow's Carmel Icing 308
Old Fashioned Bread Pudding 256
Old Fashioned Rice Pudding 256
"Outer Banks" Fruit Cobbler 292
Pecan Puffs 296
Pineapple Ice 248*
Pop Rouge (Strawberry Ice Cream) ... 18
Potted Dessert 296
Salted Nut Bars 303
Sensational Peach Cobbler 291
Strawberries With Toffee Sauce 299
Strawberry Squares 300

Index

Ya Ya Bread Pudding 293
Yum Yum Dessert 247*
EGGPLANT
Eggplant And Ground Beef Casserole . 134
Sensational Stuffed Eggplant 211
Stuffed Eggplant 251
EGGS (Also see QUICHE)
Cheese Apple Omelet 196
Chili Huevos 197
Diane's Breakfast 231*
Eggs With A Crunch 252
FISH
Baked Fish On A Bed Of Garden
Vegetables 236*
Baked Whole Salmon 235*
Cajun Blackened Fish 165
Charcoal Grilled Swordfish 235*
Company Scrod-Baby Cod 166
Crab Stuffed Fillet Of Sole 167
Fish For Guests 166
Onion Halibut Bake 235*
Orange Roughy With Basilica Sauce . . 261
Oven Fried Fish 236*
Rotini With Anchovy Paste 183
Salmon Quiche 195
Smoked Salmon Spread 63
Tuna Casserole 171
Tuna Pâté 42
Tuna Stuffed Shells 186
FRUITS
Bavarian Tart 294
Burried Cherry Cookies 287
Cherry Almond Glazed Pork Loin . . . 138
Favorite Fruit Salad 90
Fruit Dip 187
Fruit Pizza 292
Fruitcake Cookies 288
Kahlua-Cinnamon Fruit Dip 186
Loretta's Pear Salad 89
"Outer Banks" Fruit Cobbler 292
Sensational Peach Cobbler 291
Rhubarb Bread 115
GREEN BEANS
Elegant Green Bean Casserole 206
Green Beans In Mustard Marinade . . 35
Green Beans With Almonds 27
Green Beans With Mushrooms 205
Swiss Beans 206
Yummy Green Beans 255
**MEATS (See BEEF, PORK, and VEAL
listings)**
MEXICAN
BBQ Nachos 267
Burritos 133
Chicken Chimichangas 163
Chicken Enchiladas 161
Chicken Fajitas 14
Chicken Taco Salad 104

Chili Huevos 197
Churros 16
Cincinnati Chili 254
Easy Tortilla Soup 82
Enchilada Casserole 162
Fat Free Mexican Dip 230*
Fiery Bean Dip 67
Green Chile Quiche 193
Guacamole 16
Mexican Chicken Kiev 238*
Mexican Muffins 121
Mexican Rice 15
Quick Tamale Pie 136
Refried Beans 15
Rice And Green Chili Casserole 261
Salsa Fresca 16
Saralynn's Chili 133
Sour Cream Chicken Enchiladas 162
Southwest Turkey Pie 164
Taco Dip 67
Tamale Pie 135
Tee's Mexican Chicken 237*
Terry's Tortilla Pinwheels 51
Three Pepper Quesadillas 52
Tortilla Casserole 163
MUFFINS
Apple Oat Muffins 119
Blueberry Buttermilk Muffins 120
Mexican Muffins 121
Oatmeal Date Muffins 120
Orange Poppy Seed Muffins 247*
Pumpkin Pecan Muffins 121
MUSHROOMS
Blue-Crab Stuffed Mushrooms 10
Burgundy Mushrooms 48
Chicken Fricassée With Mushrooms . . 148
Chicken With Mushroom Sauce 148
Fresh Mushroom Salad 98
Green Beans With Mushrooms 205
Madeira Mushrooms 48
Marinated Artichokes And
Mushrooms 212
Mushroom Casserole 210
Mushroom Cream Soup 79
Mushroom Turnovers 47
Mushroom Wild Rice 30
Stuffed Mushrooms 49
Stuffed Mushrooms Parmigiana 49
Wild Rice and Mushroom Soup 86
ONIONS
Cream Of Potato Leek Soup 81
Exquisite French Onion Soup 79
Onion Halibut Bake 235*
Susie's Onions 50
Vidalia Fried Onion Rings 211
Vidalia Onion Pie 212
ORANGES
Mandarin Salad 97

Orange Biscuit Ring 117
Orange Mustard Glaze 142
Orange Poppy Bread 115
Wild Rice and Orange Salad 101
PÂTÉ
Easy But Elegant Liver Pâté 41
Tuna Pâté 42
PASTA
Asparagus With Pasta 180
Beef Noodle Bake 177
Blue Cheese Sauce With Pasta 180
Broccoli Tortellini Salad 106
Cavatini 174
Chicken And Pasta Salad 105
Crab Noodle Casserole 171
Eileen's Italian Artichokes And
  Chicken With Pasta 181
Fettuccine Alfredo With Peas,
  Shrimp And Prosciutto 172
Fettuccine Pie 173
Gratineed Ziti And Spinach Parmesan . 182
Italian Stuffed Shells 20
Japanese Fried Spaghetti 174
Lena's Meatballs And Sausage In
  Sauce 178
Leniwe Pierogi 183
Linguine Case 184
Linguine With Spicy Tomato-Cream
  Sauce 185
Lo Mein 232*
Mama Lucy's Spaghetti And
  Meatballs 179
Marie's Pasta With Vodka Sauce . . . 182
Noodle Pudding Soufflé 194
Pasta With Sun-Dried Tomato Sauce . . 181
Pork Primavera 173
Rotini With Anchovy Paste 183
Scallops Fettuccine Regatta 172
Seafood Lasagna 175
Shells A La Thom 258
Shrimp Fria Diavolo 264
Spaghetti Vinaigrette 23
Spatoni Pasta Salad 106
Stir-Fry With Linguine 233*
Stuffed Pasta Shells 185
Sweet Lasagna 176
Tomato, Basil and Pasta Salad 107
Tuna Casserole 171
Tuna Stuffed Shells 186
Uncle Jim's "Best In The Family"
  Pesto Sauce 262
Uncle Joe's Filetta Sauce And Pasta . 263
Zucchini Con (with) Farfalle 257
PEACHES
Peach Melba Crêpes 200
Peaches And Cream Pie 24
PEAS
English Pea Casserole 213

Fettuccine Alfredo With Peas, Shrimp
  And Prosciutto 172
PIES
After Dinner Mint Pie 285
Apple Walnut Upside Down Pie 283
Best Ever Pastry Shell 281
Chocolate Chess Pie 283
Chocolate Chip Pie 259
Chocolate Pecan Pie With Rum 286
Fresh Blueberry Pie 281
Nutty Fudge Pie 285
Peaches And Cream Pie 24
Pumpkin Chiffon Pie 284
Raspberry Chocolate Truffle Pie 32
Sour Cream Apple Pie 282
Strawberry Ribbon Pie 284
Sweet Potato-Pecan Pie 12
PINEAPPLE
Pineapple Ice 248*
Pineapple-Cheese Surprise 188
Scalloped Pineapple 188
PORK
Bacon Crisps 45
Cherry Almond Glazed Pork Loin . . . 138
Crispy Pork Medallions 140
Diane's Breakfast 231*
Fettuccine Pie 173
Ham Basting Sauce 142
Iowa Pork Platter With Horseradish
  Sauce 139
Italian Sausage Soup With Tortellini . . 83
Italian Sausage With Potatoes 141
Italian Stuffed Shells 20
Lena's Meatballs And Sausage
  In Sauce 178
Orange Mustard Glaze 142
Pizza Quiche 194
Pork Primavera 173
Pork Tenderloin With Mustard Sauce . . 26
Sausage And Rice Casserole 196
Sausage And Spinach Bread Stuffing . 227
Sausage Apple Ring 197
Sausage Deep Dish Pie 190
Sausage Roll 198
Sausage-Filled Crêpes 202
Stir-Fry Sauce 141
Sweet Lasagna 176
Uncle Joe's Filetta Sauce And Pasta . 263
POTATOES
Better Than Ever Potato Salad 102
Crab Stuffed Potatoes 221
Cream Of Potato Leek Soup 81
Hash Brown Potato Casserole 219
Italian Sausage With Potatoes 141
New Potatoes Florentine 220
Potatoes Romanoff 220
Stuffed New Potatoes 217
Tasty Potato Casserole 219

Index

POULTRY (See CHICKEN and
  TURKEY listings)
PUDDINGS
  Chocolate Fantasy 293
  Old Fashioned Bread Pudding 256
  Old Fashioned Rice Pudding 256
  Ya Ya Bread Pudding 293
PUMPKIN
  Pumpkin Bread 114
  Pumpkin Chiffon Pie 284
  Pumpkin Pecan Muffins 121
  Pumpkin Soup 25
  Stuffed Pumpkin 218
QUICHE
  Cheese 'n Chicken Quiche 193
  Classic Quiche 192
  Green Chile Quiche 193
  Holiday Appetizer Quiche 53
  Italian Zucchini Pie 190
  Pizza Quiche 194
  Salmon Quiche 195
  Sausage Deep Dish Pie 190
  Spinach Pie (Spanakopeta) 191
  Spinach Quiche 192
  Vidalia Onion Pie 212
RAISINS
  Daddy's Raisin Bread 122
  Raisin Coffee Cake 112
RASPBERRIES
  Raspberry Chocolate Truffle Pie 32
  Raspberry Cream Cheese Coffee Cake . 113
  Splendid Raspberry Spinach 34
RICE
  Blue Cheese Rice 224
  Broccoli & Rice Casserole 207
  Chicken Caruso And Rice 242*
  Creole Rice Dressing 226
  Grilled Vegetable Kabobs With Rice . 232*
  Hearty Wild Rice Chowder 84
  Mexican Rice 15
  Mushroom Wild Rice 30
  Old Fashioned Rice Pudding 256
  Red Beans And Rice Cajun Style 225
  Ricardo's Rice 224
  Rice And Green Chili Casserole 261
  Rice Pulao 223
  Rice Salad 102
  Saffron Rice 35
  Sausage And Rice Casserole 196
  Shrimp Rice 170
  Spiced Rice 222
  Wild Rice and Mushroom Soup 86
  Wild Rice and Orange Salad 101
  Wild Rice Soup 83
SALAD DRESSINGS
  Dijon-Honey Dressing 107
  Dressing For Taco Salad 108
  Sweet And Sour Salad Dressing 108

SALADS: Fruit
  Blueberry Salad 88
  Cranberry Salad Mold 89
  Favorite Fruit Salad 90
  Frozen Cranberry Salad 88
  Lemon-Lime Salad 91
  Loretta's Pear Salad 89
  Strawberry Gelatin Salad 90
SALADS: Green Salad
  Alice B's Strawberry Salad 94
  Mandarin Salad 97
  Overnight Layered Green Salad 98
  Red & Green Christmas Salad With
    Warm Champagne Vinegar
    Dressing 94
  Secret Caesar Salad 19
  Spinach Salad With White Wine
    Vinegar Dressing 95
  Spinach Strawberry Salad With Nuts
    And Mushrooms 96
  Splendid Raspberry Spinach 34
  Strawberry-Spinach Salad 97
  Tossed Salad With Apples And Cheese . 29
  Warm Spinach Salad 95
SALADS: Meat/Seafood
  Beef Salad Stir-Fry 246*
  Chicken And Pasta Salad 105
  Chicken Taco Salad 104
  Crabmeat Salad 104
  Luscious Chicken Salad 105
SALADS: Pasta
  Broccoli Tortellini Salad 106
  Spatoni Pasta Salad 106
  Tomato, Basil and Pasta Salad 107
SALADS: Vegetable
  Asparagus With Vinaigrette 91
  Better Than Ever Potato Salad 102
  Braised Red Cabbage With
    Cranberries 26
  Broccoli And Cauliflower Salad 92
  Broccoli Salad 92
  Coleslaw 103
  Corn Salad 93
  Creamy Vegetable Salad 99
  Fire And Ice Tomatoes 100
  Fresh Mushroom Salad 98
  Italian Coleslaw 103
  Marinated Vegetable Salad 99
  North African Carrot Salad 93
  Olive Salad 11
  Pea Pod Salad 96
  Rice Salad 102
  Tomato Aspic 100
  Wild Rice and Orange Salad 101
SANDWICHES
  Bread Roll 55
  Brooklyn Bridge Lard Bread 260
  Crab Sandwich 54

Elvis's Fried Peanut Butter And
Banana Sandwich 268
Stuffed Bread 55
Surprise Sandwiches 54
Tea Sandwiches 51
SAUCES
Lemon-Herb Marinade 228
Orange Roughy With Basilica Sauce . 261
Roux 85
Stir-Fry Sauce 141
Turkey Scaloppine With Sherried
Cream 243*
SAUCES: Beef
Flank Steak Marinade 142
SAUCES: Chicken
Chicken Cordon Bleu With White
Wine Sauce 239*
Chicken With Mushroom Sauce 148
Pecan Chicken With Dijon Cream
Sauce 144
Supremes De Volaille A L'orange
En Pommes 150
SAUCES: Dessert
Almond Cheesecake With Raspberry
Sauce 277
Holiday Meringues 295
Rum Almond Pound Cake 273
Strawberries With Toffee Sauce 299
SAUCES: Pasta
Blue Cheese Sauce With Pasta 180
Lena's Meatballs And Sausage In
Sauce 178
Linguine With Spicy Tomato-Cream
Sauce 185
Marie's Pasta With Vodka Sauce . . . 182
Pasta With Sun-Dried Tomato Sauce . 181
Spaghetti Sauce 246*
Uncle Jim's "Best In The Family"
Pesto Sauce 262
Uncle Joe's Filetta Sauce And Pasta . 263
SAUCES: Pork
Ham Basting Sauce 142
Iowa Pork Platter With Horseradish
Sauce 139
Orange Mustard Glaze 142
Pork Tenderloin With Mustard Sauce . . 26
SAUCES: Seafood
Mustard Horseradish Sauce 142
Seafood Cocktail Sauce 68
SAUCES: Vegetables
Vegetable Marinade 227
Green Beans In Mustard Marinade . . . 35
SCALLOPS
Christine's Coquille St. Jacques 44
Scallops Fettuccine Regatta 172
Scallop Provençale 234*

SEAFOOD (Also see CRABMEAT,
SCALLOPS, and SHRIMP listings)
Crawfish Etouffée 165
Crustacean Dip 62
Mobile Bay Gumbo 85
Seafood Cocktail Sauce 68
Seafood Gumbo 17
Seafood Lasagna 175
SHRIMP
Baked Stuffed Shrimp 169
Boiled Shrimp (Peel-Em And Eat-Em) . 168
Creamy Shrimp Dish 170
Ecuadorian Shrimp Cebiché 75
Fettuccine Alfredo With Peas,
Shrimp And Prosciutto 172
Linguine Case 184
Mustard Horseradish Sauce 142
Peppered Shrimp 11
Shrimp Diablo 43
Shrimp Diane 253
Shrimp Fria Diavolo 264
Shrimp Rice 170
Shrimp Scampi 168
Tarragon-Rum Shrimp 34
Tequila Lime Prawns 169
SOUPS
Asparagus Soup 76
Bean And Bacon Soup 77
Beef And Vegetable Soup 80
Beef-Caraway Stew 136
Broccoli Cheese Soup 77
Corn And Crabmeat Soup 78
Cream Of Potato Leek Soup 81
Easy Clam Chowder 84
Easy Tortilla Soup 82
Easy Vegetable Soup 80
Ecuadorian Shrimp Cebiché 75
Elegant Pimiento Soup 75
Exquisite French Onion Soup 79
Five Hour Stew 137
Gazpacho 74
Green Gumbo 268
Hamburg-Vegetable Soup 86
Hearty Wild Rice Chowder 84
Irish Stew 138
Italian Sausage Soup With Tortellini . . 83
Janey's Cheese Soup 78
K. C. Steak Soup 81
Light Vegetable Soup 231*
Modern Mock Turtle Soup 255
Mushroom Cream Soup 79
Mobile Bay Gumbo 85
Okra Gumbo 251
Paul's Gazpacho 74
Pumpkin Soup 25
Seafood Gumbo 17
Simple Beef Stew 137
Wild Rice and Mushroom Soup 86

Index

Wild Rice Soup 83
Wonton Soup 82
SPINACH
Florentine Crêpe Cups 201
Gratineed Ziti And Spinach Parmesan . 182
Jo's Spinach & Ricotta Dumplings . . . 215
New Potatoes Florentine 220
Red & Green Christmas Salad With
Warm Champagne Vinegar
Dressing 94
Sausage And Spinach Bread Stuffing . . 227
Sensational Spinach Dip 22
Spinach Casserole 215
Spinach Madeline 216
Spinach Pie (Spanakopeta) 191
Spinach Quiche 192
Spinach Salad With White Wine
Vinegar Dressing 95
Spinach Soufflé 20
Spinach Strawberry Salad With Nuts
And Mushrooms 96
Spinach Stuffed Squash 214
Splendid Raspberry Spinach 34
Strawberry-Spinach Salad 97
Stuffed Pasta Shells 185
Warm Spinach Salad 95
SQUASH
Gloria's Squash Casserole 214
Italian Zucchini Pie 190
Spinach Stuffed Squash 214
Zucchini Bread 116
Zucchini Con (with) Farfalle 257
STRAWBERRIES
Alice B's Strawberry Salad 94
Banana-Berry Compote 188
Creamy Strawberry Crepes 200
Spinach Strawberry Salad With Nuts
And Mushrooms 96
Strawberries Extraordinaire 187
Strawberries With Toffee Sauce 299
Strawberry Gelatin Salad 90
Strawberry Microwave Jam 189
Strawberry Ribbon Pie 284
Strawberry Squares 300
Strawberry-Spinach Salad 97
SWEET POTATOES
Aunt Dess' Sweet Potato Casserole . . . 221
Stella's Sweet Potato Soufflé 222
Sweet Potato Croquettes 18
Sweet Potato-Pecan Pie 12

TOMATOES
Fire And Ice Tomatoes 100
Linguine With Spicy Tomato-Cream
Sauce 185
Pasta With Sun-Dried Tomato Sauce . 181
Spaghetti Vinaigrette 23
Tomato Aspic 100
Tomato, Basil and Pasta Salad 107
TURKEY
Grilled Oriental Turkey Tenderloins . 243*
Southwest Turkey Pie 164
Turkey Meatloaf 244*
Turkey Scaloppine With Sherried
Cream 243*
VEAL
Veal Parmesan 139
Wiener Schnitzel 140
VEGETABLES (Also see individual
Vegetable listings)
Baked Fish On A Bed Of Garden
Vegetables 236*
Beef And Vegetable Soup 80
Broccoli And Cauliflower Salad 92
Cascades Ratatouille 217
Creamy Vegetable Salad 99
Dieter's Delight 231*
Dominic's Peppers 213
Easy Vegetable Soup 80
Gazpacho 74
Green Gumbo 268
Grilled Vegetable Kabobs With Rice . 232*
Grilled Vegetables 24
Hamburg-Vegetable Soup 86
Lemon-Herb Marinade 228
Light Vegetable Soup 231*
Lo Mein 232*
Marinated Vegetable Salad 99
Okra Gumbo 251
Paul's Gazpacho 74
Pea Pod Salad 96
Quick And Easy Stir-Fry 237*
Sharp Dip For Veggies 64
Stir-Fry Sauce 141
Stir-Fry With Linguine 233*
Sweet & Sour Brussels Sprouts 208
Vegetable Dip 65
Vegetable Marinade 227
Vegetable Pizza 50
Water Chestnuts 46
Ways To Reduce Dietary Fat 230*

Our Lady of Perpetual Help Women's Guild
8151 Poplar Avenue
Germantown, Tennessee 38138

Please send ___ copy(ies) of Simple Elegance   @ $16.95 each _____
Postage and handling   @ $ 2.50 each _____
Gift Wrap   @ $ 1.00 each _____
                                                                   Total Enclosed _____
Name _____

Address _____

City_____State_____Zip _____

Make checks payable to *Simple Elegance*

All proceeds will be used for ongoing parish projects and community charities.

— —

Our Lady of Perpetual Help Women's Guild
8151 Poplar Avenue
Germantown, Tennessee 38138

Please send ___ copy(ies) of Simple Elegance   @ $16.95 each _____
Postage and handling   @ $ 2.50 each _____
Gift Wrap   @ $ 1.00 each _____
                                                                   Total Enclosed _____
Name _____

Address _____

City_____State_____Zip _____

Make checks payable to *Simple Elegance*

All proceeds will be used for ongoing parish projects and community charities.

— —

Our Lady of Perpetual Help Women's Guild
8151 Poplar Avenue
Germantown, Tennessee 38138

Please send ___ copy(ies) of Simple Elegance   @ $16.95 each _____
Postage and handling   @ $ 2.50 each _____
Gift Wrap   @ $ 1.00 each _____
                                                                   Total Enclosed _____
Name _____

Address _____

City_____State_____Zip _____

Make checks payable to *Simple Elegance*

All proceeds will be used for ongoing parish projects and community charities.